Literary Hasidism

Judaic Traditions in Literature, Music, and Art
Harold Bloom and Ken Frieden, *Series Editors*

Other titles in Judaic Traditions in Literature, Music, and Art

Bridging the Divide: The Selected Poems of Hava Pinhas-Cohen
Sharon Hart-Green, ed. and trans.

Early Yiddish Epic
Jerold C. Frakes, ed. and trans.

Letters to America: Selected Poems of Reuven Ben-Yosef
Michael Weingrad, ed. and trans.

Lingering Bilingualism: Modern Hebrew and Yiddish Literatures in Contact
Naomi Brenner

My Blue Piano
Else Lasker-Schüler; Brooks Haxton, trans.

Social Concern and Left Politics in Jewish American Art: 1880–1940
Matthew Baigell

The Travels of Benjamin Zuskin
Ala Zuskin Perelman

Vilna My Vilna: Stories by Abraham Karpinowitz
Helen Mintz, trans.

Literary Hasidism

The Life and Works of Michael Levi Rodkinson

JONATAN MEIR

Translated from the Hebrew by Jeffrey G. Amshalem

Syracuse University Press

First Edition 2016

16 17 18 19 20 21   6 5 4 3 2 1

Originally published in Hebrew as *Shivhei Rodkinson: Michael Levi Rodkinson and Hasidism* (Tel Aviv: Hakibbutz Hameuchad, 2012).

∞ The paper used in this publication meets the minimum requirements of the American National Standard for Information Sciences—Permanence of Paper for Printed Library Materials, ANSI Z39.48-1992.

For a listing of books published and distributed by Syracuse University Press, visit www.SyracuseUniversityPress.syr.edu.

ISBN: 978-0-8156-3459-1 (cloth)
978-0-8156-3447-8 (paperback)
978-0-8156-5371-4 (e-book)

Library of Congress Cataloging-in-Publication Data

Names: Meir, Jonatan, author. | Container of (expression): Meir, Jonatan. Shivhe Rodkinson. English.

Title: Literary Hasidism : the life and works of Michael Levi Rodkinson / Jonatan Meir ; translated from the Hebrew by Jeffrey G. Amshalem.

Other titles: Shivhe Rodkinson. English

Description: First edition. | Syracuse, New York : Syracuse University Press, [2016] | Series: Judaic traditions in literature, music, and art | Includes bibliographical references and index.

Identifiers: LCCN 2016016050 (print) | LCCN 2016016635 (ebook) | ISBN 9780815634591 (cloth : alk. paper) | ISBN 9780815634478 (pbk. : alk. paper) | ISBN 9780815653714 (e-book)

Subjects: LCSH: Hasidism—Controversial literature. | Rodkinson, Michael Levi, 1845–1904.

Classification: LCC BM198.2 .M4513 2016 (print) | LCC BM198.2 (ebook) | DDC 296.8/332–dc23

LC record available at https://lccn.loc.gov/2016016050

Manufactured in the United States of America

Contents

Preface

Literary Hasidism is a new exploration of the complex interactions between Hasidism and the Haskalah in the nineteenth century, as well as the entry of Jewish life into modernity in Europe and the United States through the early twentieth century, as embodied by one man: Michael Levi (Frumkin) Rodkinson (1845–1904). As journalist, author, and publisher, Rodkinson's literary projects spanned numerous countries and continents. His intellectual biography will be traced in this book, informed by dozens of unpublished manuscripts and rare volumes. Hero to some and scoundrel to others, Rodkinson's life was a complex and consequential pilgrimage from Hasidism to combative Haskalah, eventually anticipating and inspiring the neo-Romantic trends of the early twentieth century. Rodkinson is not merely a marker or a case study: his writings stand between and challenge familiar genres of the literature of Hasidism and the Haskalah. Moreover, his works not only reflected but also, more importantly, invented religious realities that shaped the self-awareness of his readers and catalyzed the formulation of spiritual and community life among Jews, who took his ideas to heart in surprising ways.

In current scholarship, Rodkinson is frequently mentioned in passing as a Hasidic author or an untiring if marginal publisher, but such notions are usually based on the criticism of his opponents and not Rodkinson's own writings, which for decades lay scattered and lost to the public eye. Yet there was no intellectual trend in which Rodkinson did not take part, even if he never stayed with any one of them for long. An examination of his lifelong role as a catalyzing agent of varied cultural phenomena, a survey of his diverse publishing activities in a number of countries, and an examination of his books themselves at respective stages will reward the reader with a new, thought-provoking, and frequently entertaining vantage point on pivotal events from the margins of the Jewish world.

Starting out as a prolific author who was among the first to publish Hasidic hagiography in the 1860s (the second stage of printing Hasidic hagiography after *Shivhei ha-Besht* [In Praise of the Ba'al Shem Tov]), Rodkinson quickly became a partisan of the Haskalah, lending his literary strength to religious reform, posing solutions to political antisemitism, and writing popular and widely read studies of Hasidism. His witty journalistic style, along with his founding of a newspaper with no clear ideological bent, place him among the pioneers of the nascent modern Jewish journalism. Not satisfied with his accomplishments, at the end of his days he attempted to present an English translation of the Babylonian Talmud as the basis for his envisioned reform of Judaism in America. He became an American reformer who was not part of the official Reform movement—clearing an alternative trail for Reform Judaism, a path not taken.

The changes Rodkinson underwent in his life, as well as his innovative approaches to Hebrew journalism and to the problem of modern political antisemitism (which in his eyes led necessarily to particular religious reforms), aroused fierce controversy in his own day. Some tried to describe him as an amoral and corrupt hypocrite, a man who changed his skin to match his surroundings. Due to a complete misunderstanding of the nature of Rodkinson's publishing and journalistic endeavors, which made room for a variety of literatures and gave voice to every intellectual stream of his day, his opponents painted him as a mercenary or even a modern-day Satan. This understanding has persisted even to the present day, and an arresting historical figure and the cultural trends he represented have been lost in the process.

Literary Hasidism aims to present a completely different picture of this colorful and prolific innovator who, if not always original or profound in his ideas, was creative and even groundbreaking in the ways he tried to disseminate those ideas and attempted to renew Jewish society through creating new literary and journalistic forms. At the center of the book stands Rodkinson's unusual and evolving relationship with Hasidism over the course of his life, a relationship that reflected the variety within the Jewish world of his century and even presaged new trends in our own time.

Literary Hasidism consists of an introduction and three chapters. It opens by telling the story of Rodkinson's most notable opponents (among them Ephraim Deinard), whose stories are so much a part of Rodkinson's, and whose perspectives on him and his work have shaped his portrayal by scholars until today. The first chapter includes the first substantial biography of Rodkinson to be written, describing his work as a publisher along with the varied responses to that work. The next two chapters, turning from the chronological to the thematic, complement the biography with a systematic examination of Rodkinson's relationship to Hasidic hagiography and to Hasidism in general over the course of his life. The resulting picture is meant to provide a different perspective on one of the central phenomena in Hasidic printing in those years: the appearance of hagiography as an established genre. The second chapter focuses on Rodkinson's publication in his early years, in which he published collections of Hasidic hagiographies, and recounts the reception of these "little booklets" in various communities. In the third chapter, I describe his writings on Hasidism from the mid-1870s, when his shift toward the Haskalah led him to cast Hasidism in a different light (in a positivist historical mode), until his final days in America, when he was already far from both of those ideological worlds. The book closes with observations on Rodkinson's influence on the writers of the neo-Hasidic movement who sprang up in the late nineteenth and early twentieth centuries.

A Hebrew version of this work appeared in 2012, as *Shivhei Rodkinson: Michael Levi Rodkinson and Hasidism* (Tel Aviv: Hakibbutz Hameuchad, 248 pages). In this English translation, new materials are presented, particularly from the Archives of the Jewish Theological Seminary, and the last chapter has been expanded.

Literary Hasidism

Introduction

Polemics and Perspectives

Michael Levi Frumkin-Rodkinson (1845–1904) underwent many metamorphoses in his life, moving from country to country and taking up a variety of literary and publishing activities.[1] He grew up in a Habad family and was among the pioneers of Hasidic hagiography. Later he turned to the Haskalah, forging relationships with religious reformers, publishing a number of controversial books, and translating portions of the Talmud into English as part of a program aimed at reforming religion and combating modern antisemitism. Rodkinson began his career in his birthplace of Dubrovno (1845–1862), moving on from there to a series of locales, including Chernobil (1863), Lvov (1864–1875), Zhitomir (1875–1880), Berlin (1881–1882), Hamburg (1882), London (1883), Berlin (1884), and Vienna (1885–1888), then finally to New York, Chicago, and Boston (1889–1904). Over those years Rodkinson composed several pamphlets, books, and essays, at first in the style of traditional Hasidic hagiography and homiletics and later in keeping with trends in Haskalah and religious reform. He also established newspapers and other periodicals in Hebrew, Yiddish, German, and English everywhere he went. At the center of his journalistic activity stood two newspapers, the Hebrew *Ha-Kol* (The Voice) and the Yiddish *Ha-Kol La-Am* (The People's Voice), published in Koenigsberg in the mid-1870s, newspapers that he tried until his death to restart in various places across Europe and America.

Throughout his life Rodkinson earned many critics, but none so fierce as the author, traveler, merchant, and bibliographer Ephraim

Deinard (1846–1930).[2] Deinard wrote regularly about Rodkinson, and even when the two left Europe for America the dispute moved with them. Deinard, who was among the last and most diehard opponents of Kabbalah and Hasidism, saw Rodkinson as entering dangerous waters by charting "a new course" for "the New False Haskalah" and "the literature of the new apostasy," which, as he saw it, was full of lewdness. His criticism of Rodkinson was part of his broader campaign against apologists for Hasidism, such as Eliezer Tsvi Hacohen Zweifel, and later against those neo-Romantic revivers of Hasidism such as Samuel Abba Horodecky, Avraham Kahana, and Hillel Zeitlin. He saw their writings as "Hasidic hagiography in Maskilic clothing" and a product of "the age of wanton Hasidism," the founder of which was in his eyes none other than Rodkinson, a man who "carried his Haskalah in his right hand and his Hasidism in his left," who lived "a life of promiscuity on the tab of the Haskalah," and whom Deinard dubbed "first among the priests of the Besht."[3]

Deinard presented the Hasidim as members of a wayward sect of Judaism, as Christians and Sabbatians had been in their time,[4] writing, "Such as these have already arisen, and without a doubt there will arise more half-Maskilim and half-Jesuits to cover the nakedness of Hasidism in the cloak of the Haskalah, who will blind the eyes of the people, leading them to believe in the new path of Israel Baal Shem Tov like the followers of Jesus."[5] Nor did Deinard spare those who wrote positively of Jesus of Nazareth. He called Joseph Klausner and Stephen Weiss "Servants of Baal," "converted without baptism," and "two calves of the House of Aven [Hosea 10:5] in Jerusalem and New York, who bow to the cross," and described their writings as born of the degenerate world of the Kabbalah, new Hasidism, and evangelical Christianity.[6] He similarly described the revivers of the Hebrew secular language, first among them Eliezer ben Yehudah, as "springing from the loins of the Hasidim"; in their creation of a "new jargon," a "Hebrew without religion," they had profaned the holy tongue and thereby resembled missionaries and Sabbatians, whose sole aim was to destroy Judaism.[7] So Deinard saw his struggles against the various forms of Jewish mysticism, "fraudulent" Zionism, and missionizing Christianity as one battle with many fronts.

In Deinard's eyes, Rodkinson was the spiritual father of this entire phenomenon, embracing not only the Christians, the Kabbalists, and the Hasidim but also socialists, anarchists, reformers, and the common rabble alike. He condemned every book Rodkinson printed and every deed he did, calling him a liar, charlatan, apostate, missionary, whoremonger, and more. He even described his own book *Mashgei Ivrim* (Errors of the Blind) as containing a study of "the genesis of the Hasidic Haskalah in Russia by Michael Levi Rodkinson, which has now become a plague, manufacturing their apostate books and a new form of lewdness," a phenomenon Deinard compared to "literary Bolshevism."[8] Deinard expressed his opinions in every forum available to him: the daily press, memoirs, travel journals (which he published throughout his life and which earned him the moniker "the Traveler"), special editions of chapbooks self-published at the printing house he set up upon his arrival in America in the 1890s, introductions to anti-Hasidic writings that he published from manuscript, various books penned against the Kabbalah and its emissaries (in which he described the Kabbalah as born of Christianity and called for the symbolic burial of its books on Mt. Meron),[9] and anti-Reform and anti-Christian writings (especially early anti-Christian manuscripts that he reissued).[10] These publications reflect only a portion of the debates in which Deinard was involved throughout his life, in which he used similarly fierce language as in the examples mentioned above. That being said, it seems that Rodkinson was a key figure in Deinard's polemics. Decades after Rodkinson's death, when Deinard had already lost his sight and had to rely on others to assist him in his work, he yet wrote about Rodkinson:

> I am aware that many people wonder why I have gone to such lengths to recount the abominations of this particular scoundrel [Rodkinson], when my people do not lack for scoundrels who are not worth the ink it takes to write of them; but my goal was not

> only to make it known who this son of Rodke was, but to alert the next generation, lest they be left unwitting and confused.[11]

Deinard justified his work further by saying that "the times demand that we reveal these villains in order to silence them forever," so that his readers would "keep away from their books as from a menstruant woman."[12]

Deinard's accusations were eventually quite influential, especially among scholars, as we will soon see, but in his own time he saw Rodkinson only prosper. So we hear Deinard crying out at Rodkinson's success in spreading "the new Hasidism" and its favored medium, the wonder tale:

> Rodkinson has paved the way with his wonder tales of these rabbis, and imitators have grown up like wild grass around him, so that now there is not a single rag [Yiddish journal] in all of America that does not print "the deeds of the holy ones" almost daily, and every lying good-for-nothing has found a way to make his living off of them, and the bigger the lie, the bigger his name and his paycheck. . . . We should not be surprised if his students some day compile a book telling "The Praises of Rodkinson," such as the tale that "the *tsadik* [The Holy Man]" himself sat seventeen times in jail, and every time the God of John the Baptist saved him in the merit of his holy fathers, along with the help of his quick feet and a little money passed under the table. Such a book would be the crown jewel in the literature of this new apostasy, and earn great wealth for its author.[13]

In his book on the "apostates of Israel," Deinard lashed out at the lot of them:

> Horodecky, Avraham Kahana, and Hillel Zeitlin—these writers cast about in the darkness to find holy men in heaven or on earth, even in the waters under the earth, but I will give them roast leviathan to feast on: a Hasid and grandson of a Hasid, and at the same time a Maskil like them; in him are gathered together all the virtues

> they sought in their holy men, especially Horodecky, who strives to raise the Besht to the level of Jesus of Nazareth, and [Yosef] Klausner, who brings Jesus down a bit to the level of the Besht, and makes of him a Hasidic rebbe, the Galilee Rav, going from Capernaum to Tiberias and Nazareth, blessing the women and collecting redemption money. I hope these men bless me for all the kindness I have done them with my book, the story of one of their brethren [Rodkinson], who has merited both tables, that of the Besht and that of Jesus, and became an example to the new-old world.[14]

Deinard similarly attacked those writers who defended the Besht and Hasidism, as in this letter to Avraham Kahana, who had published a book on the Besht in 1900:

> Upon my recent return from North Africa I found your book *The New Praises of the Baal Shem Tov* in the possession of Rabbi I. Yare and, to tell you the truth, sir, you have done little more than the first *Praises of the Baal Shem Tov* or from the second Rodkinson—except perhaps that you have written in a slightly more precise jargon than the former, who did not have recourse to the modern Hebrew jargon as you do. Indeed, however, it seems to me that your book is like Rosen's biography of that well-known man [Jesus of Nazareth] . . . you have made a reformer of one who never meant to introduce a single innovation. . . . As I said in my work *Sects of Israel*, the actual founder of the Hasidic sect was the Baal Shem Tov's grandson Rebbe Nahman. Indeed, I have proven that the founders of all such sects were in fact always and only the students.[15]

The remainder of his letter was full of curses against those behind the new batch of hagiographies, Rodkinson first among them.

While Deinard was indeed the fiercest, he was not the only critic of Rodkinson. The sword was taken up after him by Yosef Kohen-Tsedek (1827–1903), a Maskil from Lvov and notable publisher of several journals known for their conservative tendencies, among them *Meged Yerachim*, *Otzar ha-Chochmah* (The Storehouse of

Wisdom), *Ha-Mevaser* (The Harbinger), and *Or Torah* (Light of Torah) (all printed in Galicia).[16] Kohen-Tsedek published these periodicals in response to the journal *He-Halutz* (The Pioneer) put out by Yehoshua Heshel Schorr, whom he attacked throughout his books, along with his followers, as a "priest in Jewish clothing."

Kohen-Tsedek first encountered Rodkinson through the writings of Ephraim Deinard and others who were Rodkinson's opponents, meeting him only later in London. Rodkinson did not make a positive impression on Kohen-Tsedek, and the encounter led him to publish the polemical pamphlet *Mikha'el ha-Nehepach Le-Sama'el* (Michael Who Has Turned into Samael, 1879), which was meant "to uncover" Rodkinson's "true face" as a "Hasid-turned-Maskil" who vacillated between the two camps and had swindled the whole world. Forty-two copies of the pamphlet were printed and, at the advice of his friends and fellows, it was reprinted a year later under the name *Sfat Emet* (Language of Truth) (1880),[17] the extended title of which reveals the essence of his charges against Rodkinson:

> A conclusive response to the anonymous criticism in the journal *Ha-Kol* of my book *Mussar Haskel* [Fool's Reproof, a book of sermons by Kohen-Tsedek, published in London in 1878], criticism which is founded neither ethics nor on the intellect. A reliable critique of the books and articles of that duplicitous man, the fraud and impostor Michael [Rodkinson], owner of *Ha-Kol*, whose sly words praise the Hasidim and deceive the Maskilim. To make it known that the publisher of *Ha-Kol* has six wings, two heads and two faces. And also the chronicles of his life, the works wrought by the *tsadik*, and his singularity.[18]

Kohen-Tsedek not only accused Rodkinson of being two-faced; he also derided his relations with socialists and reformers, a derision that extended to accusations of collaborating with missionaries. It seems that one accusation brought more in its wake, so that any and all deviations from the creed, as defined by the Orthodox Maskilim, were marked with the same brand of heresy.

It is possible to name a number of other figures who looked askance at Rodkinson's activities, such as Aleksander Zederbaum and Perets Smolenskin, his competitors in publishing, and Joseph S. Bloch, who accused Rodkinson of collaborating with missionaries and antisemites (especially August Rohling). Others, such as Nehemiah Shmuel Leibowitz (1862–1939), criticized both Deinard and Rodkinson.[19] Leibowitz's opposition was not based on ideological claims so much as on personal impressions from his close acquaintance with both men. So, for example, he wrote in his book *Ha-Mavet be-Panim Sohakim* (Laughing in the Face of Death):

> It is well known that Rodkinson and Deinard quarreled their whole lives. Once I mentioned their names in a letter to the great man Meir Ish Shalom, of blessed memory, and he answered me: "My dear brother! You have mentioned in your letter two names that deserve to be blotted out, though their fates be different—for Deinard deserves the lowest ring of Hell, while Rodkinson only the first ring."[20]

As we see here, Leibowitz attacked Deinard much more fiercely than he did Rodkinson, a fact we can attribute to personal friction between the two. He published a number of pamphlets, some of them anonymously, accusing Deinard of plagiarism and fraud. So he wrote, for example:

> Many are considered dead even in life. . . . Regarding the inciter Deinard and his lies, see Rabbi E. Z. Zweifel's introduction to his book *Sanegor* [Apologetics]; everything he has written there is factual and accurate and stamped with the seal of truth. . . . With each book Deinard publishes, he spreads his impurity and divisiveness. . . . It seems that this man was created only to glory in lies, to stir up arguments, to hurl accusations and to print his dirty books. . . . Alas for such a writer, who wastes both paper and ink.[21]

In time he came to regret printing these words against Deinard. He wrote in 1918, "I, in my youth and my ignorance, commented on

Deinard's books. . . . Now I see my foolishness, and I have burned my own books, *Tene Bikurim* [First Fruits], *Eikhah Rabati* [The Great Lamentation], *Teshuvah Shniyah* [Second Response], and last but not least, *Ephraim Deinard and His Books in America*, and thanks be to God that few of them have circulated."[22] And yet Leibowitz continued his fierce criticism of Deinard and his "lies." Immediately after printing these expressions of regret, Leibowitz wrote to Israel Davidson:

> I have been plagued by this ugliness more than twenty-five years. At every chance they fall upon me to devour me. No man can endure always being pursued, as I am; at times, even without reason, the pursued becomes the pursuer, and throws a rock to chase away the dog. Of course, victory over Deinard would be considered no great honor. . . . Nevertheless, it was a good thing that I did, spreading the word about Deinard. You, I, and everyone who knows him realizes what this scoundrel is made of, but with the passing of time everything will be forgotten, and his lies, having been printed, will not be erased unless I leave a record of this damnable goat.[23]

Deinard, for his part, called Leibowitz "a cheat" and "a man with the mind of a woman," and spread a rumor that he had escaped from a sanitarium. He was even concerned enough to warn "the children of Europe" of the danger of the duplicity of this "second Rodkinson."[24] As we can see, every man had his foes as well as his supporters.

By the same token, not everyone thought so negatively of Rodkinson. Take the example of Nahum Sokolow, who carried on a correspondence with Rodkinson and had even written in the latter's newspaper *Ha-Kol* early in his career. In a feuilleton dedicated to Rodkinson and Kohen-Tsedek,[25] who had passed away during that same year of 1904, Sokolow wrote:

> I did not know Mr. Michael Rodkinson personally, but we all had our differences with him since the days of *Ha-Kol*. Perhaps there was some grain of truth in the words they published about him; perhaps this man fell in the moment of truth; perhaps he did not

> always fulfill his obligation. But all of these things are mere speculation, while what is sure is that this man was a vigilant and tireless writer, a prolific and passionate worker from his youth until his old age and, as the saying goes, "In the case of sure and perhaps, sure has it." . . . It seems to me that among the Jews of the Exile there is found an exile within the Exile. Men like Rodkinson are born of changes, of the changing of masks, of suffering—and of talents. He passed from one land to another, he changed names, changed professions, he inflicted himself with all types of mortification, he took up every type of work, he became a printer at a time when such flawless Hebrew was a rarity—he wrote, he published, he collected, and he spent his strength also as a researcher of the Talmud, in deep learning gained through great effort. . . . A man like this is a walking melodrama.[26]

Sokolow's expression of esteem was exceptional for the age.[27] He acknowledged as much himself, and when in time he came to collect his scattered letters he included in the final edition only the words on Kohen-Tsedek, omitting his comments on Rodkinson.[28]

Another admirer of Rodkinson was Morris Winchevsky (1856–1932, known by his pen name Ben Netz), who worked alongside Rodkinson for a number of years and described him at length in some of his memoirs in Hebrew and Yiddish. In one of his essays, he wrote:

> Rodkinson did not understand the meaning of "principles" at all, neither in theory nor in practice. He had no clear, fixed philosophy. He was eclectic without knowing the meaning of the word. . . . I say this not to denigrate him, but rather to explain his character to any who wish to understand his life and work.[29]

According to Winchevsky, what drove Rodkinson was only his nature as a printer:

> Rodkinson lived almost all his life in want. Now and then his wife would describe his passion for his newspapers as his undoing. Indeed, he offered up on the altar of our daily press his portion in

> this world and the world to come, and if he did not offer more, it is only because he had no other worlds to give.[30]

Winchevsky did not try to find an ideology in Rodkinson's many letters; for him, Rodkinson was only a Hebrew printer who allowed free expression of ideas, especially those of the first Hebrew socialists.

Rodkinson was aware of the range of views on his work. On multiple occasions he defended himself, often sharply, but only once did he cross the line into incivility, and that was when Yosef Shmuel Bloch (1850–1923) accused him—wrongly—of ties to antisemites, particularly August Rohling.[31] On that occasion he released an emotional and derisive response to all those who had attacked him over the years. Printed in Vienna in 1886, the letter presented an alternate picture of Rodkinson and described the terrible damage done by Bloch's accusations:

> But please see, my masters, the difference between him and me. I am a simple, God-fearing Hebrew. I will not hide my face; I will not cower; I will not stand in fear of the court's wrath; and I will say to all: this young man who has maligned me with lies and calumny, saying that I have fled punishment in Russia—he is a liar, he is a scoundrel! By claiming in print that I gave Rohling citations for his book on blood libel, this man wished to cause a permanent rift between me and my fellow Jews and, may the Merciful One save us, sought to kill me and my wife and my children through hunger—for surely he knows that I live by my pen, and that my brothers would have no mercy on me, believing that I had done such a deed. He knows well that everything he has written about me is a baseless lie. He knows well the zealous vengeance I take on the antisemites with everything I write or publish. He knows that he is the terrible hypocrite and not I. I suffer only for the truth, my soul's beloved.[32]

Rodkinson did not stop until he had boasted (in his journal *Barkai*):

> You have done a great thing, you zealots, casting light on all my deeds and all my words, for before you raised your voices it never

> occurred to me to tell my own story, for who am I that others should care to read it? But now that I see that you will not give me rest, that a month does not pass without one of you harassing me, defaming my name and shouting and wailing in heartache, I can no longer forgo my honor. I have even begun to believe that readers will enjoy this story and benefit from it, which will be not only my own but that of all humanity since they first walked this earth. In the telling I will not abuse you or insult you, but the readers will recognize you and your schemes, which would be revealed to every generation even if I did not cry out against you. . . . Indeed, even if you shout in triumph, if you deride and insult me for decades to come, to my spirit and my words you will have done no harm at all.[33]

In a note he added, "I hope to complete my lengthy autobiography [*Fifty Year Jubilee*] by the Purim season of 1887, during which, God willing, I will celebrate my fiftieth birthday, and it will be a memorial for me and for you." Such a book was never published by Rodkinson, but his desire to be read and remembered differently remains clear.

Such was not to be Rodkinson's luck: the caricature drawn by his opponents was accepted as fact by most of those who would write about him, even up until our own time. Some see Rodkinson as a hypocritical swindler in pursuit of financial gain, while others see him as a pioneer of neo-Romantic Hasidic literature.[34] Regardless of their conclusions, both admirers and critics of Rodkinson drew on the sensationalist testimonies of his opponents, with no examination of his work's historical context, no questioning of his opponents' motives, and no serious reviews of his opponents' books. So anyone who reviews Deinard's books, for example, will find them full of distortions, historical errors, and specious conjectures (among them the claim that Jesus, R. Isaac Luria, and the Baal Shem Tov never existed, and were in fact created by their disciples in order to found "new religions"). A survey of the reception of Deinard's works reveals that they aroused considerable criticism, when they received any attention at all—yet, amazingly, his comments on Rodkinson have gone unquestioned. Even approbations of Rodkinson, such as that he was a harbinger of the neo-Romantic trend in Hasidic writing, still assumed the accuracy of Deinard's claims, only without adopting his value judgments about Hasidism and the merit of its revival. Deinard earned a reputation in America for enriching the country's libraries with tens of thousands of books, manuscripts, antiquities, and Judaica items; however, his polemical writings are almost forgotten, while Rodkinson remains infamous for writing what he did.[35]

What led to this view of Rodkinson, and who is responsible for it? What caused his opponents to write what they did, and what caused Rodkinson to write heartfelt words in his own defense? And when all is said and done, who was this Michael Levi Frumkin-Rodkinson? Only a systematic reading of his writings and an examination of his work as a publisher can answer these questions. This work has yet to be done, though many have called for it. The words of the bibliographer Eliezer Raphael Malachi still hold true:

> An entire literature was created around the person of Rodkinson, but aside from a small piece that Sokolow wrote after his death there is not even an article dedicated to the literary work of this man who caused such a storm in his lifetime. Many enemies have risen against him, but there were more than a few friends who supported him.[36]

Malachi himself only added a few general lines to the still-incomplete description of Rodkinson's work. Dozens of Rodkinson's books and essays, as well as his diverse activities in different countries, have never received the full review they deserve. Certainly, with the writing of a systematic monograph, a truer picture will emerge of his intriguing life, and the stormy lives of his opponents will also become a bit clearer.

1 The Life and Works of Michael Levi Rodkinson

Rodkinson as a Hasidic Printer: Chernovitz and Lvov

Michael Levi Frumkin Rodkinson was born in 1845 to a Habad family living in the town of Dubrovno (today in Belorussia).[1] His mother, Rodke, was the daughter of Rabbi Aharon of Starosselje, the leading disciple of Rabbi Shneur Zalman of Liady, the founder of Habad. Aharon of Starosselje was also the key opponent of the dynastic succession of Shneur Zalman's son, leading a small, independent branch of the Habad community in parallel to the main court in Lubavitch.[2] Aharon of Starosselje's elitist marginalism, also expressed in his writings, certainly had no small influence on the young Rodkinson, who for the rest of his life stressed his unique pedigree.[3] Rodkinson's mother died while he was still a child and his father remarried. From this second marriage was born Israel Dov Frumkin (1850–1914), later the editor of *Ha-Havatselet* (The Lily). In 1863 Israel Dov moved with his parents to the Land of Israel, where he married the daughter of the renowned Jerusalemite printer Israel Beck.[4] Rodkinson did not join in the journey to the Holy Land, instead involving himself from an early age with a number of printing houses across Eastern Europe. While his nephew was focused on publishing Aharon of Starosselje's abstruse manuscripts, Rodkinson chose to print a wide variety of short, popular books in Hebrew and Yiddish, which he referred to as his "little booklets."[5]

At the age of eighteen Rodkinson printed his first book in Chernovitz, *Urim ve-Tumim he-Hadash* (The New Book of Urim and Tumim, 1863), on divination.[6] That same year, and at the same press, he was exposed to the booklet "A Wondrous Tale of Rabbi Zalmina Vitepsker," describing the miracles that had occurred to Rabbi Shneur Zalman of Liady while he was imprisoned in St. Petersburg. According to Rodkinson, it was this little book that spurred him to take up writing Hasidic hagiography himself, driven by a need to "emend" such stories circulating about the founder of Habad, emendations he made based on his own family traditions and reports he had heard from elders in his community.[7] In 1864, as part of the renaissance in printing Hasidic stories occurring at the time (in which he was joined by Aharon Walden and Menahem Mendel Bodek, among many others), he published in Lvov a number of collections of Hasidic tales in both Hebrew and Yiddish: *Shivhei ha-Rav* (In Praise of the Master) on the founder of Habad (which also included stories about Aharon of Starosselje); and two collections not dedicated to any particular dynasty, *Eidat Tsadikim* (Community of Holy Men) and *Sippurei Tsadikim* (Tales of the Holy Men). These booklets merited wide circulation and a great number of editions up until our own time. (Other anonymous collections written at the same time, and in a similar spirit, were mistakenly attributed to Rodkinson over the years by his opponents and by scholars influenced by them.)[8]

Not satisfied with a single genre, Rodkinson also published books unrelated to Hasidism, such as the Kabbalistic ethical treatise of Rabbi Akiva Shalom Chajes of Tultchin, *Hitragshut ha-Nefesh* (Ecstasy of the Soul, 1864), which was published anonymously and written in an artificial Aramaic mimicking the Zohar, a medieval mystical tome.[9] Michah Yosef Berdyczewski would later write about this little book: "And even the Hasidim, who bore unbounded hatred for [Chajes] and persecuted him without cease, would recite chapters from this book in the month of Elul, weeping over the profound words in it which pierced their hearts."[10] It seems Rodkinson's decision to print the book was based on its appeal to a variety of audiences, as had been the case with his Hasidic titles.

Soon after, Rodkinson published a book on the laws of witnesses, *Luhot ha-Edut* (The Tablets of Witness, 1865), by Rabbi Ozer Tsazmir of Kamenets, appending a Printer's Preface explaining how the book had come into his possession.[11] He also printed a second edition of *Urim ve-Tumim he-Hadash*, changing the exterior design and interior arrangement.[12] His signature, as in other books, was accompanied by a detailed listing of his illustrious Hasidic family tree.

That same year Rodkinson printed two books of Hasidic homilies, very different in nature from his previous collections of tales. Together with Avraham Yehoshua Heschel Drucker, he printed the book *Tanya* of Rabbi Shneur Zalman of Liady;[13] he also edited and printed *She'erit Israel* (Remnant of Israel), which contained the teachings of the Hasidic master and wonder-worker Rabbi Israel Dov Ber of Vieldenik. The latter was a student of Rabbi Mordekhai of Chernobil who, upon the death of Aharon of Starosselje's son, claimed the master's place and was followed by a small number of the Starosselje Hasidim.[14] We can assume that Rodkinson joined those Hasidim who migrated to the new court and crowned their new rebbe (who was not from the Habad community).[15]

In these books we see the exceptional editorial style that would be Rodkinson's signature throughout his life's work. His edition of *Hitragshut ha-Nefesh*, unusual in both content and form, includes an introduction penned by Rodkinson in the same Zoharesque Aramaic. What's more, his edition of *She'erit Israel* follows a completely different structure from most books of its kind; perhaps influenced by the books of Shneur Zalman and Aharon of Starosselje, it is arranged not by the weekly Torah portion but by topic. Characteristics such as these became even more pronounced with time, as Rodkinson endeavored to introduce new and sometimes controversial methods into every field he entered.

Between Hasidism and the Haskalah: Zhitomir and Warsaw

The next stage in Rodkinson's editorial work occurred in Zhitomir, where he moved his press in 1866. He made contact with the printing house of Avraham Shalom Shadov, which had opened the previous year and published a wide variety of books from both Hasidic and Maskilic authors.[16] So we find, for example, Avraham Ber Gottlober's translation of Moses Mendelssohn's *Jerusalem* (1867) printed alongside Rabbi Menahem Mendel of Vitebsk's Hasidic book *Pri ha-Arets* (Fruit of the Land,1867); the books of Hayim Zelig Slonimski (1866), a leading Maskil of the age, along with the book *Imrot Tehorot* (Pure Sayings) of Rabbi Baruch of Mezhibuzh (1865), the grandson of Israel Baal Shem Tov; and Gottlober's critical *Toldot ha-Kabbalah veha-Hasidut* (History of the Kabbalah and Hasidism) along with the first two volumes of Eliezer Zweifel's defense of Hasidism, *Shalom al Israel* (Peace Upon Israel, 1868–1869).

Rodkinson quickly found his place in this pluralistic environment, in which the supreme value was not any particular ideology but the very act of publishing. Here he edited and published Rabbi Israel of Bahafoli's collection of Hasidic homilies, *Ateret Tiferet Israel* (Israel's Crowning Glory, 1867);[17] Rabbi Yaakov Emden's Halachic work *Iggeret Bikoret* (Critique, 1868);[18] and *Marpe La-Am* (Healer of the People, 1869), a book of popular medicine.[19] In 1869 he also published a slightly modified second edition of *She'erit Israel*,[20] and we can assume that he was involved in additional publications that did not bear his name. Rodkinson's publishing credits did not mark the limits of his familiarity with different ideologies and worldviews, however; he also knew a number of the authors personally, including Eliezer Zweifel and Avraham Ber Gottlober.

Rodkinson did not stay much longer in Zhitomir, moving on to Warsaw, where he remained from 1870 to 1872. According to his own later testimony, there he tried his hand at printing Yiddish wonder tales unrelated to Hasidism, as well as one of the stories of Isaac Meir Dik and the chapbook of Yoel Mikhel Kuperman. His name does not appear on these titles as either editor or printer, and it is not clear exactly what role he played in their publishing.[21] In Warsaw he raised the plan of printing "the works of the Rishonim," those Halachic authorities who predated the *Shulhan Arukh*, a fundamental legal code from the sixteenth century. The first such work was

She'alot u-Teshuvot Rabbi Joseph ibn Migash, a collection of rabbinic responsa (1870), to which he added a short introduction with a distinctly apologetic tone aimed at appeasing critics of Hasidism—or, more accurately, critics of his own earlier Hasidic hagiography. Rodkinson was aware of the revolutions in the genre (as we will see in more depth in the next chapter), just as he was aware of the criticism of it by the Mitnagdim, Maskilim, and even certain Hasidim. In the introduction he recounted that the initial idea for the project came to him in 1865 from Rabbi Zalman Frodkin of Pultsk, who suggested that he print the books of early scholars so that, in a time of schismatic tension, "your deeds should be fitting in everyone's eyes." The rabbi from Pultsk had promised him that, if he did so, "the people will not slander you and none of your enemies will find fault in you."[22] That same year he published, along with Isaac Finkelstein, Rashi's *Sefer Pardes ha-Gadol ve-Sefer ha-Orah* (The Great Orchard and the Book of Light, 1870).[23] This endeavor, which was also apologetic in nature, did not require much of Rodkinson's time, and he soon moved on to other and far different worlds.

"With No Flower in His Collar": The St. Petersburg Period

The year 1873 found Rodkinson in St. Petersburg. In the account by Gottlober, printed in the newspaper *Ha-Magid* [The Preacher]), we find intriguing references to Rodkinson's visit to the Russian capital that year. Gottlober had met Rodkinson while still in Zhitomir, and he was amazed to see the same man sporting new clothes:

> Mobs of fools thronged to the city from the ends of the earth, scheming and conspiring, barking like dogs and surrounding the city to work their cons. . . . One day, as I walked the city streets, a man approached me in fine European dress, his beard trimmed with scissors, in a shirt white as snow, a coat with blue fringe at the neck and shoulders as on an officer's uniform, and pants that reached down to his black shoes polished like a mirror. He approached me and offered his hand and said, "*Shalom*!" I stood dumbstruck,

> for he appeared to me as a Gentile and a stranger whom I had never met before in my life. "What business did he have with me?" "I am . . . F [Frumkin]," the man said to me. My astonishment only grew, for indeed I had met this man before, in the town of Z [Zhitomir]. . . . He had been dressed in filthy [Hasidic] clothes and there had been a button with no flower in his collar; he had been drinking and carrying on with a group of self-proclaimed Hasidim who were fawning all over him, as so many other commoners have done, because of his stories of the *tsadikim* [Hasidic rabbis] and their miracles, which he made up himself and spread throughout Israel. And when he saw that his stories had stopped earning him a profit, the world being already full of them, he changed his tune, and came to St. Petersburg and put on some fancy clothes and, *voila*, he is a Western Jew! And here he was, with yet another way to swindle the people.[24]

No doubt, this testimony is tinged by Gottlober's own ill will toward Hasidism, and there is no reason to accept his judgments prima facie.

Gottlober did not expand here on the nature of Rodkinson's new "swindle," but others have done so for him. Starting that same year of 1873, we find many articles deriding the shift Rodkinson had made and claiming that in fact he had not left his hagiographic tales behind but had only dressed them in new clothes befitting his new audience. Such opinions arose from the singular belief that it is outside the realm of possibility that such a Hasid as Rodkinson could have become a true Maskil, and so it must have all been a deception—just as in his first incarnation he had only ever sought financial gain, so too in this new incarnation.

We have no other accounts of Rodkinson's activities in St. Petersburg or of his manner of earning a living. According to his opponents (primarily Aleksander Zederbaum, who published a long essay about Rodkinson in *Ha-Melits* [The Advocate] at the end of 1878), Rodkinson had gotten into financial trouble in the stock market and was charged with counterfeiting, jailed, and brought to trial; he then fled to Koenigsburg in Prussia. Zederbaum made reference to various Russian journals, issued between 1873 and 1877, linking

Rodkinson to shady financial deals, though the facts are difficult to verify.[25] Rodkinson, for his part, denied these rumors, saying the man mentioned in the papers was not him and claiming that his exit from St. Petersburg was unrelated to any crime; in return, he accused his opponents of spite, jealousy, and incitement.[26] Whatever the truth of the matter was, it is clear that at this time he began to form much grander plans, which drove him to once again set out for a new city.

The History of Hasidism and New Endeavors in Journalism: Koenigsberg

In 1875 Rodkinson arrived in Koenigsberg with big plans. There he changed his name from Frumkin to Rodkinson, that is, "the son of Rodke," which has the same numerological value as Frumkin.[27] Within a year of his arrival, he had printed two books on Hasidism as part of a broader project aimed at a comprehensive history of all "the great men of Israel," under the general title *Toldot Ba'alei Shem Tov.* The first volume, *Or Israel* (Light of Israel), was a history of the reputed founder of Hasidism, Israel Baal Shem Tov; while the second, *Toldot Amudei Ha-Habad* (History of the Pillars of Habad), had as its subject Shneur Zalman of Liady, the founder of the Habad Hasidic dynasty. Neither was written in the style of Hasidic hagiography but rather in that of the moderate Haskalah, and they aroused fierce opposition from Hasidim and Maskilim alike. Though these books were never reprinted and the entire project was shelved,[28] they remain critical for our understanding of the changes Rodkinson was undergoing, serving as faithful literary expressions of the first cracks in his Hasidic world.

Hasidic history was not his focus while in Koenigsberg, however. Immediately upon his arrival, he worked to open a new newspaper by the name of *Ha-Kol* (The Voice, 1876–1881).[29] Rodkinson believed the time was ripe for such a move.[30] *Ha-Melits* (The Advocate), under the editorship of Aleksander Zederbaum, had been out of print since 1872; Samuel Joseph Fuenn's *Ha-Karmel* (Mount Carmel), published as a monthly since the same year, and likewise *Ha-Magid*, under Eliezer Lipman Zilberman and David Gordon, failed to give expression to certain new trends in the Jewish street; *Ha-Tsefirah* (The Morning or The Dawn), under Hayim Zelig Slonimski and Nachum Sokolov, hardly dealt at all with current affairs; *Ha-Levanon* (The Lebanon), published in Mainz by Yehiel Brill and Meir Lehmann, was a strictly Orthodox publication; and Perets Smolenskin's *Ha-Shahar* (The Dawn) appeared only once a month.[31]

On May 7, 1876, Rodkinson printed an example of his paper *Aleh Le-Mivhan* (Test Copy), in which he announced his plans. According to what he wrote there, the Jewish people was divided into three camps: Talmudists, Hasidim, and Maskilim. The core of his critique was directed squarely at the members of the "third camp," "old men leaning on their crumbling platform, to the disgust of their supporters." So he criticized *Ha-Shahar* and especially Pesach Ruderman and David Kahana, who wrote a regular piece for the paper on famous Kabbalists and Hasidic masters.[32] We can imagine that his critique brought the newspaper many new readers from the traditional elements of society.

Colorful advertisements announcing the new paper appeared over several months in *Ha-Havatselet*, a paper owned by Rodkinson's brother Israel Dov Frumkin, who certainly served as a role model for him in his journalistic endeavors.[33] The first edition of *Ha-Kol* was published three months later and printed over the next four years as a weekly (and briefly as a biweekly) paper, achieving relatively wide circulation.[34] Immediately after its appearance, the paper's competitors tried to tarnish its name, publishing various and sundry stories about Rodkinson's exploits in St. Petersburg, none of them verifiable. Rodkinson, for his part, did not let their words go unchallenged, and succeeded in not only winning many subscribers but also recruiting the best writers of the time. These writers—among them Mordechai ben Hillel Hacohen, Simon Berenfeld, Morris Winchevsky, Eliyahu Wolf Rabinowitz, Tsvi Cherchevski, Judah Leib Levin, Mosheh Leib Lilienblum, Yitshak Kaminer, Judah Leib Sossnitz, Yaakov Rabinowitz, Mosheh Reicherson, Nahum Sokolow, Zalman Epstein, and Naftali ha-Levi[35]—were rarely of one mind and in fact frequently quarreled with one another over the paper. Rodkinson was not above entering the fray himself: in addition to the editor's preface and occasional pieces in the newspaper, he added "Notes from the Editor" in the margins of many essays, which at times amounted to essays in their own right.

With the passing of the years, Rodkinson hired a number of assistant editors for the paper, among them Israel Efrat, Eliyahu Wolf Rabinowitz, Yitshak Kaminer, and Morris Winchevsky, who in fact served as the acting editors. In this capacity, the latter two strengthened the paper's existing socialist trend, one which was far from Rodkinson's own politics.[36] Eliezer Raphael Malachi wrote that Winchevsky had told him in jest how he and Rodkinson "exploited each other, Rodkinson leaving him all the drudgery of running *Ha-Kol*, and Winchevsky using Rodkinson's paper as a mouthpiece for the socialist ideal and a weapon against the capitalists."[37] It was just such cooperation between ideological opponents that made the paper so successful, despite its gossipy editorials, its poor organization, and the editor's pidgin Hebrew, none of which were uncommon for the time.[38]

The ideological variety that resulted, however, was not without its critics. Gideon Kouts dubbed *Ha-Kol* "a paper without a creed,"[39] while Fishel Lachover described the paper and its chief as "turning with every passing wind."[40] Indeed, over its lifetime, the paper included every passing trend and every opinion. Here we see the full paradox of Rodkinson as writer and editor: on the one hand he spoke harshly of the Haskalah, while on the other he established a platform for its spokesmen. This tension was ascribed by many to hypocrisy or a simple desire for financial gain, but the matter is in fact more complex. Rodkinson wanted his paper to reflect a variety of ideologies, from Jewish traditionalism to the radical Haskalah and socialism. In short, that is, he aimed for what would become the hallmark of all modern, objective journalism. Only one agenda remained consistent, and that was to satisfy all sides and give a voice to each. So the paper contained all things and their opposites, as when Rodkinson invited the earliest Hebrew socialists to write for his paper and then himself critiqued—and rather harshly—Lieberman's socialist paper *Ha-Emet* (The Truth).[41] This dedication to the plurality of expression was at once the paper's strength and its weakness, and ultimately brought about its downfall.

We can learn something about the editor and his style from Eliyahu Wolf Rabinowitz, who described the beginnings of *Ha-Kol* and his first meeting with Rodkinson in Koenigsberg in the following way:

> Engrossed in my studies and far from the world of Hebrew journalism, I did not know that there was such a man named Michael Levi Rodkinson living in my own town, or that a trail of vermin followed behind him. Even the appearance of *Ha-Kol* evaded me. One morning a knock came on my door, and a man of great stature, with glasses upon his nose, a beard flowing down his chest, a top hat upon his head, and with cane and satchel in hand, entered and stood before me. "I am Michael Levi Rodkinson," he said to me, offering his hand, and to my inquiry as to his business answered that he wished to ask me to be the editor for his journal *Ha-Kol*. Young in years and a bit of an idealist, I was not particular about the terms of employment. Only one question did I ask: "And what is *Ha-Kol*'s line?" And to his response that "*Ha-Kol* was founded to fight against the nihilists," I answered that in coming to me he missed his mark, for I was myself a half "nihilist," and under no circumstances could I accept the position. He answered me, "It is not worth giving up the position over that. If you will not fight against the nihilists, go and fight for them." I was astounded to hear such words, and in my amazement I forgot that I must also fight for a high salary and clarify the details of the job, and I accepted the position. It seems that the contract we made gave me almost complete freedom at the paper, so long as I was careful of the censor.[42]

Rabinowitz's report, if true, shows that Rodkinson wished his paper to reflect trends that he himself did not support, stressing the importance of the medium itself over any particular message.

This was to be the bane of his attempts to recruit subscribers and patrons. Among those he turned to in search of financial support for the paper were "The Society for the Promotion of Culture among the Jews of Russia," which supported a number of journals and newspapers between the years 1876 and 1879, including *Ha-Melits*, *Ha-Tsefirah*, *Ha-Shahar*, *Ha-Boker Or* (The Day Dawns), *Ha-Ivri* (The Hebrew), and *Ha-Mabit* (The View). Rodkinson's *Ha-Kol*, however, was not to be included on that list—to Rodkinson's request came the curt reply, "*Ha-Kol* does not share the goals of the Society."[43] Neither did Rodkinson find success with his frequent appeals to Judah Leib Gordon (who served as the Society's secretary), Michel Gordon, and others.[44] They were certainly influenced by the letters from the likes of Ephraim Deinard, who portrayed "that good-for-nothing Rodkinson" as a fraudulent Maskil.[45]

At the end of 1877, due to problems with the paper's agents, Rodkinson made the four-month journey to Russia and Galicia in search of subscribers.[46] According to his testimony, he succeeded in this trip in subscribing a number of Hasidic rebbes, among them Rabbi Shmuel of Lubavitch, Rabbi David of Tolna, and Rabbi Yitshak of Skvir. While we cannot verify these claims, we do know that *Ha-Kol* circulated widely among the Orthodox, and his faithful readers were not limited to Maskilim.[47]

In addition to *Ha-Kol*, Rodkinson published a paper in Yiddish titled Ha-*Kol La-Am*, which also earned wide circulation before it closed in 1879. The paper sought to emulate Zederbaum's *Kol Mevaser* (Bearer of Good Tidings), which was published in Yiddish alongside the Hebrew *Ha-Melits* (and which Deinard saw as the beginning of "the corrupted and jargonistic Haskalah").[48] Rodkinson almost succeeded in enlisting Mendele Moykher-Sforim as his coeditor, and an announcement about his participation was even published, but for an unknown reason that most famous of authors withdrew from the project. This news, bitterly received by the readers, was certainly a factor in the paper's subsequent failure.[49]

In a mighty effort to expand his journalistic reach, Rodkinson founded a literary monthly as a supplement to *Ha-Kol*, calling it

Asefat Chachamim (Gathering of Sages).[50] In an advertisement for the new journal, printed in *Ha-Havatselet*, he stressed its nature as an anthology and supplement to *Ha-Kol*, promising that "all who hear our voice will delight at this child born on the knees of a new age."[51] In the introduction to the first supplement, Rodkinson stressed its editorial "objectivity" and renounced all responsibility for its content. His words were not merely spurred by fear of the censor, but reflected the editorial approach he would take to all his work over the course of his career.[52] He hoped the monthly would include essays, sermons, and stories that exceeded the editorial bounds of *Ha-Kol*. So, for example, Rodkinson turned to Shlomo Buber of Lvov, a subscriber to *Ha-Kol*, and wrote:

> His honor will take no pleasure in *Ha-Kol*, which is directed at the people of Russia! Indeed, for them the paper was founded, and from them its owner earns his living—and, in my opinion, words of Torah should not be found on the pages of this journal. Nevertheless, I have designated a place for words of Torah among a gathering of sages, and I hereby request from his Torah eminence that he honor *Asefat Chachamim* with his works, and I will provide a crown for his head.[53]

Rodkinson's goals for the journal, as revealed by this request, were in complete contradiction to those of the acting editor, Morris Winchevsky, who stressed its socialist aims and in fact completely ignored the program Rodkinson outlined in his preface. From the fifth edition of *Asefat Chachamim*, the work of "reviewing and organizing the essays" was officially placed in the hands of Winchevsky, with Rodkinson acting solely as the printer.[54] According to Winchevsky's testimony, he decided while on an evening stroll with Eliyahu Wolf Rabinowitz to take control of Rodkinson's journal and to turn it into an organ of the socialists. Winchevsky added that "with Rodkinson's well-known attitude against socialism, the journal *Ha-Kol* as our advertisement, and the joke that he called it *Gathering of Sages*, we are guaranteed success." Rodkinson, for his part, accepted the suggestion happily, not because of any affinity for socialism but rather out of his desire to establish an additional forum that would gain *Ha-Kol* subscribers, and so, "over a drink, in the main bursa marketplace of Koenigsberg, the contract was written with the esteemed printer."[55]

Winchevsky recounted that Rodkinson had announced the new monthly even before the closing of Lieberman's *Ha-Emet*, after realizing that that modest journal was succeeding in rousing the masses. *Asefat Chachamim* succeeded in drawing subscribers from *Ha-Emet*, as well as some of its writers, becoming the second socialist journal to be published in Hebrew and ultimately publishing eight editions to the three editions of *Ha-Emet* published in 1877. The new monthly debuted a number of important essays by the first Jewish socialists, among them pieces by Yitshak Kaminer and the beginnings of the famous serial by Mosheh Leib Lilienblum, *Mishnat Elisha ben Abuyah* (Teaching of Elisha ben Abuyah [the most famous Jewish heretic]), written at the encouragement of Lieberman and initially intended for publication in *Ha-Emet*.[56]

While Winchevsky used the journal to promote socialist ideals, Rodkinson used it to attack his denouncers, primarily Ephraim Deinard. In one edition there appeared a brief essay by Shalom Warhaft deriding "The Traveler," as Deinard was known, concluding with a mocking ditty.[57] In return Rodkinson's opponents, like those of the Jewish socialists, rushed to find slurs for the new supplement, among them Kohen-Tsedek's "A Collection of Stutterers" and Deinard's "Gathering of Fools."[58]

In 1878 *Ha-Melits* returned to circulation under the editorship of Zederbaum, and Smolenskin began to publish *Ha-Mabit*. Even though *Ha-Mabit*'s circulation of 500 copies was far outpaced by *Ha-Kol*'s 3,000, Rodkinson used his paper to launch harsh criticism against Zederbaum, Smolenskin, and their associates.[59] Zederbaum responded with a biting essay in which he "revealed" Rodkinson's shady past—an essay that had tremendous influence on the image of Rodkinson that would later emerge.[60] In the essay's wake, large portions of *Ha-Kol* were dedicated to the dispute, Rodkinson himself contributing a number of polemical pieces, written in a mix of Hebrew and Aramaic reminiscent of the language of the Zohar.[61] The fact that portions had been erased by the censor in Vilna only led to increased public demand and a petition that the paper be mailed to its subscribers in closed envelopes.[62]

One of Rodkinson's writers who joined the fray was Yitshak Kaminer, whose cover article in *Ha-Kol* directed all kinds of slurs at Zederbaum while praising Rodkinson for his ideological openness.[63] In response, Avraham Shalom Friedberg composed a long essay for *Ha-Melits* slinging mud at *Ha-Kol*, which had "opened wide its mouth and spoken nonsense"—a criticism similar to that leveled against Rodkinson's books on Hasidism.[64] Zederbaum added the following note to the essay, revealing much about the nature of the argument and the language in which it was carried out:

> Only one profession does [Rodkinson] pursue, and at that one he excels—dealing in lies and falsehood, flattering whomever he believes can line his pockets and pouring out wrath and scorn and even blows of his fist on whoever recognizes him for what he is—a scoundrel, an inarticulate ignoramus who cannot even write properly in Yiddish, much less Hebrew, to say nothing of any European language. What is there to say about such a wanton and conniving good-for-nothing as this?[65]

Friedberg would later write in his memoirs about the impact of his essay: "From Koenigsberg came the call to war. A great band of writers, both the worthy and the unworthy, gathered around *Ha-Kol* and marched out against the mighty cedar [Zederbaum], led by a printer who was the most worthless of all. There gathered every bitter soul that had been insulted, wittingly or not, by the printer of *Ha-Melits* . . . and none more so than the Dr. Y. Kaminer." Friedberg summed up the episode—a little too neatly—by saying: "The matter ended with his writers and allies throwing up their hands, abandoning him one by one. It was not long before *Ha-Kol* had fallen, never to rise again!"[66]

The issue of socialism was one of the factors in the dispute. Yitshak Kaminer claimed that Lieberman's *Ha-Emet* had closed because of its criticism of the Hebrew socialists, while Rodkinson, for his part, was drawn into a defense of *Ha-Emet*, even if he stressed that his way was not identical to theirs and accused Zederbaum in turn of slander. To all appearances, *Ha-Kol* folded for similar reasons. Even those who wrote for *Ha-Kol* flinched at times from the editor's personal style, and even more so from the crude polemics that filled the pages of his paper. Judah Leib Levin, who participated actively in a number of Rodkinson's publications, describes him in one of his letters in the following way:

> While the printer of *Ha-Kol* was here he asked me to be one of his writers, and when I learned that he was none other than Frumkin, I recoiled, for I knew about all of the abominable things he had done in St. Petersburg and in every city and town he passed through, and my heart felt a shudder of disgrace to behold a man of such ignoble deeds. . . . I saw that he was a total ignoramus, a wagon driver from the market and a man of low morals who devoted all his strength to selfish ends . . . and afterwards, upon reading a few pieces in *Ha-Kol*, I saw how like a fierce dog he falls upon any who insult his imaginary honor or criticize the foolish vanities that he utters without end. . . . He involves himself in everything, even though he is a boor and has not the intellect to contemplate a single idea. He is a fool and a crude ignoramus, and so shall he remain.[67]

In 1879, when *Ha-Kol* and *Ha-Melits* were filled with the arguments and counterarguments of their fierce debate, Mosheh Leib Lilienblum wrote to Levin:

> It is true that I and Cherchevsky expressed our objections to *Ha-Tsefirah* concerning the despicable quarrel that broke out between *Ha-Melits* and *Ha-Kol*, for which the latter is particularly responsible, since it opens the door to every good-for-nothing jokester more and more, and in our protest we wrote that it is a disgrace for

> us to be party to the slanderous actions of *Ha-Kol*, which reduce it to the level of its lowest competitors.[68]

Despite their criticism of Rodkinson, both Levin and Lilienblum continued to contribute to *Ha-Kol*. One of the important essays Lilienblum printed in the paper was titled "The Beginning of Hope," which he wrote to express his high hopes for the rabbinical assembly that met in St. Petersburg in 1879.[69] In a letter to Judah Leib Gordon, Lilienblum explained his reason for printing it in *Ha-Kol* of all papers; his explanation reveals once again one of the reasons for the paper's popularity among both readers and writers.

> I sent my essay to *Ha-Kol* last week, and its first installment has already been printed in the 14th Edition. I did not wish to send it to Herr Smolenski, for *Ha-Mabit* does not address religious matters at all.[70] . . . And if I were to publish it in *Ha-Shahar*, the essay would appear for only a few monthly installments, while I wished it to be published in its entirety. Aside from this, *Ha-Kol* is more readily found among the Orthodox, and I have faith in its printer who, in his desire to keep me as a contributor, will not change a thing in my essay, which would not have been the case with Herr Smolenski or even less so Herr Slonimski [of *Ha-Tsefirah*].[71]

The essay was indeed printed in full in *Ha-Kol*—though Rodkinson attacked it from every side.[72]

One of those especially bothered by Lilienblum's participation in Rodkinson's papers was Ephraim Deinard, who confronted him directly. Lilienblum's answer reveals the secret of Rodkinson's editorial style that allowed him to enlist prestigious writers despite the gossip surrounding the paper:

> In answer to your question about my writing for *Ha-Kol*, which causes you so much anger, I will answer you what I have already answered others, and that is that I have no business with the authority of the editor-in-chief, whom I see as nothing but the printer and the vehicle for my thoughts and feelings. Ask Herr Hayim Zelig

> Slonimski if he would have accepted my essay "The Beginning of Hope" as I wrote it in *Ha-Tsefirah.* You and I both know how I toiled and suffered over this essay, and what is Herr Slonimski's prestige worth to me? If a man should come to me and ask, Which of these two printers is more prestigious?, I should not hesitate for even a moment, and would answer that the printer of *Ha-Kol* is like a baby before Herr Slonimski. But I am not betrothing myself to either one; I seek only someone who will publish my writing as I wish, a desire that will be met in full if I turn to the printer of *Ha-Kol*, but not to Herr Slonimski.[73]

Even Gottlober, who "revealed" Rodkinson's duplicity in his 1873 essay, participated in *Ha-Kol.* Zederbaum fumed at this, accusing Gottlober of "offering incense to Satan's firstborn" and calling *Ha-Kol* "the libidinous graveyard where satyrs dance" and its editor "the angel of destruction."[74] Gottlober's response was more moderate, and between its lines we can sense Rodkinson's power: "Yes, the printer of *Ha-Kol* is like all the rest (would that all their hearts were circumcised!), and many are the Maskilim of our day who are counted among his writers and allies. Rodkinson will be what he will be, for he has already been made the printer, and earned Maskilim as writers; the past is not important—he remains a printer."[75]

Rodkinson was not satisfied with these publications, and in 1879 he also founded *Ha-Me'asef* (a double entendre, meaning both "The Anthology" and "The Rearguard"), "a monthly journal dedicated to literary matters, homilies, and essays not appearing in *Ha-Kol.*"[76] In the opening of the first edition Rodkinson outlined his editorial style: "Living up to its name, *Ha-Me'asef* is a gathering of all camps and all opinions, and as such cannot have any single editorial line." He continued, "a journal cannot have any goal but to be a trumpet in the mouth of the community and to enliven the editor's soul." Newspapers with clear agendas (such as Perets Smolenskin's *Ha-Shahar*), he added, are not long-lived, and are useful only for individuals.[77]

Though Rodkinson's contribution to this short-lived monthly was slight—amounting to the preface, notes on the articles, and a few book reviews—he was able to find someone who would write against Zederbaum and *Ha-Melits* and come to the defense of *Ha-Kol* against the attacks of Avraham Shalom Friedberg.[78] The well-known satirist Yosef Brill (Iyov mi-Minsk), a contributor to Rodkinson's monthly *Ha-Me'asef*, wrote a piece for *Ha-Shahar* parodying contemporary newspapers and their editors for their controversies; the result was a call for his head and a flurry of recriminations from all sides that left no man unsullied.[79] Similarly colorful portrayals of that contentious world are found in Yehoshua Mezah's unpublished book *Controversies Not for the Sake of Heaven*, meant to catalogue all of Zederbaum's disputes from throughout his life, including those with Rodkinson; and in his satirical booklet published under the name *Tefach Meguleh* (A Handsbreadth Revealed), which derided Zederbaum's *Ha-Melits*.[80] It is no wonder that such fierce debates as these led in the end to calumnies of another kind.

In mid-1879, after Zederbaum's dispute with Rodkinson had led to the latter's personal defamation before the authorities, *Ha-Kol* was banned in Russia on the charge that it spread "revolutionary" ideas, while Rodkinson was imprisoned for three weeks for his "revolutionary activities" with the paper.[81] Rodkinson, Winchevsky, and others accused Ephraim Deinard, at Zederbaum's urging, of informing on Rodkinson and his paper to the authorities in St. Petersburg. Winchevsky even published an essay on the first page of *Ha-Havatselet*, edited by Rodkinson's brother Israel Dov Frumkin, recounting the whole episode in piquant sarcasm.[82] A similar description appears in the writings of Yaakov Lifshitz, who harbored no love for Rodkinson; according to his testimony, Ephraim Deinard arrived in Kovno at the same time as Rodkinson had, "[f]ollowing him there almost as a cat sniffs out a mouse, the fire of vengeance and murderous wrath already burning within him." Deinard had procured a copy of Zederbaum's well-known and slanderous essay from late 1878, "Bi-Gevurah ve-Lo be-Sheti" (For Strength and Not for Drunkenness), and provided it to the authorities, who wasted no time in jailing Rodkinson while the charges were investigated.[83] More concerned by Rodkinson's relationship with socialists than by his colorful lifestyle, the authorities ultimately limited the circulation of his paper in Russia, where most of the subscribers were found. Not only was Rodkinson jailed but they also jailed Winchevsky, who was acting editor of *Ha-Kol*. Both were later freed on bail paid by the banker Shlomoh Feinberg of Koenigsberg, one of the primary supporters of *Ha-Kol*,[84] after which Winchevsky traveled to the house of Naftali ha-Levi in London.[85]

It seems that in fleeing controversy, Winchevsky in fact brought it with him. Yosef Kohen-Tsedek, who was living at that time in London, used Winchevsky's arrival as an opportunity to publish his scathing book, *Mikha'el ha-Nehepach le-Sama'el* (Michael Who Has Turned into Samael, 1879), and its later edition titled *Sfat Emet* (Language of Truth, 1880). Dedicated in large part to character assassinations of Rodkinson and Winchevsky,[86] the book was a reply to Winchevsky's withering critique, published in *Ha-Kol* in 1878, of Kohen-Tsedek's book *Musar Haskel* (Fool's Rebuke), and to a review by Rodkinson describing how he "suffered terribly through the reading of [Kohen-Tsedek's] litany of vanities" and "revealing" the author's motives and checkered past.[87] Fearing that his allies had turned on him, Kohen-Tsedek wrote with great emotion to Samuel Joseph Fuenn, asking him to write positive reviews of *Musar Haskel*:

> About a year ago I sent my book *Musar Haskel* to my good sir to review it in the journal *Ha-Karmel*, and some two months ago I wrote to you, to ask if it was his Torah eminence who said to the owner of *Ha-Kol* from Koenigsberg that "Kohen-Tsedek is an ignoramus and a lunatic." Until today you have not honored my sincere request. Does such silence imply consent? What sin have I committed against you, that you compare me to an ignoramus and a lunatic? Have you too joined those who hate me without reason?[88]

His anger at the words of Fuenn and his other critics, first among them Rodkinson, drove Kohen-Tsedek to publish *Mikha'el ha-Nehepach le-Sama'el*.

In his critique of the book, Aleksander Zederbaum strove to compare Kohen-Tsedek to Don Quixote and his "tilting against windmills," since "any sensible person who reads two or three opening lines in the journals of Rodkinson will see that there is but one good thing to be said of them, and that is that they are printed on fine, soft paper." After claiming that "Rodkinson's writings have no relation to literature; such rags are found among every people, and they find their audience, made up of equal parts fools and ignoramuses," Zederbaum concluded: "For such as these I have found nothing so fitting as silence."[89] The publication of Kohen-Tsedek's book certainly did not silence the debate, however; indeed, it only raised the pitch.

In one of his last essays in *Ha-Kol* in Koenigsberg, Rodkinson criticized the "snakes" hiding "under the great cypress [Zederbaum], their hissing evoking horror and disgust in every mortal soul," writing "the essay 'Bi-Gevurah ve-Lo be-Sheti' published in *Ha-Melits* was the source [for] Deinard and Yosef Kohen-Tsedek of London as well; the former informed against him, while the latter placed him at the beginning of his book [*Mikha'el ha-Nehepach le-Sama'el*]."[90] Zederbaum denied all connection to the episode and distanced himself from Deinard, whom he described as "perpetually spreading the most loathsome slander" and inciting quarrels everywhere he went. He claimed to have only one goal: "the obligation to remove the inappropriate editor—not by ad-hominem attacks nor with the help of slander nor the power of the state and its laws, but only with the power and spirit of literature, by rebuking excellent writers who have mistakenly anointed such a man."[91]

"The Society for the Worldwide Proliferation of the Hebrew Language": Berlin and Hamburg

In the wake of the Russian ban on *Ha-Kol*, Rodkinson attempted to save what he had founded and traveled to Galicia and Romania in search of new subscribers. When he arrived in Lvov at the end of the winter, he met Simon Berenfeld, who became the new chief editor of *Ha-Kol*. The damage done by the Russian authorities' ban, however, was severe, and only occasional editions of the paper were published at the end of 1880. Berenfeld, who did not hold the position long, moved to Lek, near Koenigsberg, where he served as assistant editor of *Ha-Magid*.[92] This move already presaged the end of *Ha-Kol*.[93]

In Berlin, Rodkinson launched a journalistic enterprise aimed at a new audience, the paper *Ha-Medaber Le-Israel* (1881–1882). Officially published by Tsvi Hirsch Itskovsky, the owner of a printing house in Berlin,[94] the paper did not bear Rodkinson's name, and he was not involved in its content. In the first edition, however, he did explain his motives in publishing the paper. His essential aims, reminiscent of those in his earlier papers, were to spread the Hebrew language, to bring peace between opposing parties, and to create a central forum for the Jews of Berlin. In the preface to the twelfth edition (4 Nissan, 1882), he wrote that the paper had met with such success that it would increase in both frequency and scope, but this seems to have been the paper's last edition.

It may be that the paper merely changed names, however. At exactly the same time Rodkinson began to publish another weekly titled *Ha-Hozeh* (The Seer, 1882).[95] Below the name of the printer was listed the mysterious "Society for the Worldwide Proliferation of the Hebrew Language," a name that aroused the ire of his opponents. Many participants in the journal, however, while fully aware that Rodkinson was the editor, were not angered by the name, including Aharon Yehudah Leib Ish Horowitz, Y. N. Goldberg, Noah Luria of Minsk, Shlomoh Rubin, Avraham ha-Kohen of Posen, Morris Winchevsky, and Rabbi Yaakov Ettlinger.

Deinard summarized the history of the journal and its editor in the following picturesque way: "For this fool, the master of *Ha-Kol*, every abomination is but a game—forging documents, taking multiple women everywhere he goes, associating with missionaries and publishing in their name the journal *Ha-Hozeh* in Berlin, wandering the streets in a drunken stupor, traveling from town to town on false papers, changing his name over and again, and trading his religion the way a Gypsy trades his horse." He added, "At the top of every page was written, 'Society for the Worldwide Proliferation of the Hebrew Language,' when everyone knows there is no such society, except for the Bible Society and the Missionary Society." Deinard printed this description in the journal *Ha-Melits* as well, and in his other books he added as "proof" for his claim that Rodkinson was a tool of missionaries the facts that one of the editions of *Ha-Hozeh* included an advertisement for the book *Toldot Yeshu* (History of Jesus) and that Rodkinson was at that time in contact with Franz Delitzsch (who established the Institutum Judaicum in Leipzig for the training of missionaries to the Jews).[96] Kohen-Tsedek, without adding any new details to support his accusations, similarly claimed that *Ha-Hozeh* was financed by London missionaries.[97]

Rodkinson, for his part, attempted to gain the support of German Jewish scholars, stressing that the medium was well known to them. So he wrote to Moritz Lazarus, with whom he had been in close contact for many years, "I believe the project deserves support, if not for me then for the sages of Berlin";[98] and in writing to Morris Steinschneider he emphasized that the new publication was only a continuation of *Ha-Kol* under a new name.[99] His efforts were to no avail, however, and after the first year of *Ha-Hozeh* he moved the journal to Hamburg, attributing the move to his disassociation from the mysterious "Society for the Worldwide Proliferation of the Hebrew Language" and to a lack of Hebrew readers in Berlin.[100]

The move to Hamburg marked a shift in not only the journal's locale but its content as well. Rodkinson began dedicating large parts to matters of migration and advertisements associated with shipping companies. He also promised to print Hebrew manuscripts found in the libraries of Hamburg, a task he partially completed.[101] In one edition of *Ha-Hozeh*, Rodkinson, as if speaking for those emigrants passing through the city on their way to America, derided the idea of settling in the Land of Israel and called instead for a migration to the New Land:

> I will say this aloud, that in our opinion America is the only land that can at this time receive the dispersed of Israel, and in which they can be safe from the disgrace of hunger and extinction—America and nowhere else. We too are Lovers of Zion, and we long

> with all of our hearts for the settlement of the Land of Israel and its establishment as a nation, but we cannot advise the weary and harried masses to seek refuge in the uncivilized lands of Philistia and Syria, whose inhabitants remain half savage, or at least have not yet received the light of the Haskalah.[102]

The paper was never able to establish itself in Hamburg, and after the move only six more editions were printed. While details are scarce, it seems that Rodkinson made additional attempts at similar projects, such as a Yiddish paper by the name of *Israelitischen Anzeigers* (Jewish Newspaper).[103] Rodkinson saw these projects as a continuation of *Ha-Kol* and *Kol La-Am*, but they never achieved the same circulation as those papers did in Koenigsberg, when most of the subscribers came from Russia. It is no wonder then that he once again decided to pull up stakes, this time moving to London.

On the New Antisemitism and Religious Reforms: London

At the end of 1882 Rodkinson arrived in London together with his family, after a brief stay in the resort city of Karlsbad, where he tried to find subscribers for the resurrected *Ha-Kol*.[104] In London he tried and failed to integrate into the city's Jewish community, though a number of Reform rabbis (among them David Wolf Marx) supported him, as did local aristocrats, who provided all his financial needs. Ephraim Deinard painted a different picture, repeating his unsupported claim that Rodkinson was involved with Christian missionaries and summarizing his "iniquities" while in London by writing, "It is no wonder that the Jews of Britain, too, looked with disgust upon this Polish Jew."[105] Deinard's comments were based not only on Kohen-Tsedek's books but also on his letter from January 1883 reporting on Rodkinson's arrival in England, which included fabricated stories about his connections with missionaries there.[106]

Rodkinson recounts that during his time in London he immersed himself in the issues of religious reform, spending long hours in the library of the British Museum. His diligence bore fruit: while in

London he published a number of important books in Pressburg, books that won him admirers and angry opponents alike.[107] The first from this period was *Matsat-Mitsvah ve-Alilat ha-Dam* (The Commandment of Matzah and the Blood Libels, Pressburg 1882),[108] written in response to the accusations of modern antisemites, especially the Tiszaeszlár Affair, the blood libel of 1882 in Hungary.[109] The thirty-two-page brief levels a fierce and unprecedented criticism of the rabbinic establishment, charging that the "mystery rites" surrounding the preparation of *matsah shemurah* ("guarded matsah," a form of the unleavened bread kept under constant supervision by a Jew since the time the grain is harvested) had given birth to the charges of the antisemites; so it was that in the very places in which these "superstitious rites" were common, antisemitism was as well. While stressing that there was no truth to the blood libels, he argued for the abolishment of the strange rituals, which had no source in the Talmud but nonetheless gave credence to the antisemites' accusations.

Rodkinson opened with a study of the revival of the blood libel in his day, pointing out that despite official government opposition and continual apologetics from Jewish intellectuals, the masses still believed that Jews needed blood for the making of *matsah*. Written arguments in the defense of the Jews, no matter how articulate, had no effect, for the simple reason that the masses did not read them. So, Rodkinson concluded, "It is fitting that we inspect our deeds carefully; perhaps our methods of preparing and baking *matsah* are arousing these suspicions in the hearts of non-Jews; perhaps we will find in our own customs things that seem strange and irrational to those who are not of our faith, giving them reason to suspect things of us which are not true." He continued, "Consider well these customs, and recognize that sin crouches at their door. These methods are so bizarre, the customs so foreign to all human reason, that they almost demand the belief that something mysterious is hidden in this *matsah*!"[110]

So it is incumbent upon the Jews, he concluded, to reject these bizarre and harmful customs with no source in the Talmud and to erase them from the *Shulhan Arukh* (The Set Table, a foundational legal code)—precisely the opposite of the actions of local rabbis, whose stringencies only exacerbated the problem, especially for Jewry's most vulnerable members. In Rodkinson's eyes, this was only one example of a much wider problem: he concluded, "I have not even mentioned the other nonsense practiced by the wonder-workers and the Hasidim."[111]

Rodkinson's critique of the Maskilim was no less fierce. The ink they spilled in their apologetics was in vain, since the poor among the people never read them; even the legal victories they won were not enough to stop antisemitism. The problem called for a new approach, one he had hoped would take form on the pages of *Ha-Kol*.[112] To this end he had offered those pages to anyone with something to contribute to the conversation, from Reform-minded Orthodox Jews to antireligious socialists, but slander had brought about the paper's end, and its writers could find no place for such conversations in other papers (as evidence Rodkinson cited the silence of Yitshak Kaminer, Judah Leib Levin, and Winchevsky).[113]

Rodkinson's own contributions to that discussion were not limited to individual religious, social, and economic reforms; rather, he spoke of a fundamental change in Jewish society. According to his analysis of Judaism and its historical development, many customs had taken root that were not in accordance with the Talmud and derived instead from the proclamations of rabbis, who shaped Jewish law at will. He wrote that these rabbis had given the Jewish people "a new Torah, dictated by their whims; they have laid a yoke on us so heavy we will break under its load; they have made us appear like savages in Europe with our Asiatic customs; and yet by their word do we live—a life of emptiness and void, contrary to all the nations!"[114]

The first step of his proposed solution was for the Talmud to be cleansed of all its "superstition and nonsense," while the second was for it to be translated into various languages, and finally for these translations to be presented to the government authorities.[115] Rodkinson optimistically called for a gathering of sages, working with government sanction, who would compose a new *Shulhan Arukh* based on the Talmud, as well as annul various customs such as those surrounding the baking of *matsah*. This new *Shulhan Arukh* would thereby prove the fundamental purity of the Talmud to the nations, civilizing the Jews in their eyes.[116]

Rodkinson concluded his book with a call to the Maskilim to write about the *Shulhan Arukh* and the Talmud in pursuit of this goal, as he himself would do, devoting years of his life to distilling "the spirit of the true Talmud." In pursuit of the same goal, Rodkinson criticized studies of the Talmud being conducted in a more radical vein, such as the research of Yehoshua Heshel Schorr in *He-Haluts* (The Pioneer): "By the light of God we will go out in strength to war against those who would destroy our Torah and our faith, and not in the way of *He-Haluts*, which would deny the people of Israel their Talmud; rather, we will pave a new way, a straight and glorious way, removing the fences that they have cast around the Talmud and so restoring its purity."[117] In this essentialist reading of the Talmud, Rodkinson was much like the earlier Mosheh Leib Lilienblum, who had sought to bring reform through the composition of a new *Shulhan Arukh* based more closely on Talmudic precedent.[118] But by the time Rodkinson penned these words, Lilienblum had already turned to a radically different ideology (not to mention a far more sophisticated understanding of modern antisemitism).[119]

The arguments Rodkinson made in *Matsat-Mitsvah* were roundly condemned; many of his critics saw him as a "reformer" on the one hand and a foolish "dreamer" on the other, whose words could give ammunition to the antisemites, a critique validated by the many Maskilim who had already abandoned the hope of fighting antisemitism with internal reforms. Indeed, some figures had given up on any religious solution at all. Distancing himself from Rodkinson and other would-be reformers, Judah Leib Levin argued that only return to the Land of Israel could save the Jews,[120] and he complained to Perets Smolenskin that Rodkinson plagued him with letters about the matter: "I do not know what he wants, for I told the truth, that return to the Land of Israel is my life's goal, and religious reform is anathema to me . . . those who seek reform do not understand at all the importance of bread and life."[121] Likewise did Levin's correspondence with Eliyahu Wolf Rabinowitz, partially published in *Ha-Magid*, contain derogatory statements against Rodkinson, with Rabinowitz writing, "Only infrequently do I see Herr Rodkinson, and when he was in my house this past Sabbath I told him that his book *Matsat-Mitsvah* is not worth the ink used for its printing. You know my thoughts on religious reformers in general." Indeed, Rabinowitz lamented all Maskilim who had not "freed themselves" from religion and theological questions: "Only a few of our fellow Maskilim understand how critical it is for a free people to separate the prayer house from the jailhouse, and to remove the throne from the Holy Land, and so Hebrew literature is swarming with theology and philology, ten times more than in the books of Haskalah, though these too are full of talk of religion, even if in a new form."[122]

Other critics saw the danger not in preserving religion but in reforming it. So David Gordon, the editor of *Ha-Magid*, concluded his critique of *Matsat-Mitsvah*:

> And we shall never know if the author himself believes with a full faith that, should the Jews cease baking *matsah shemurah* and compose a new *Shulhan Arukh* as he has envisioned, then hatred and vengeance against Israel would cease! If the author's words became known then they might do great damage against our people by broadening the gap, as his other reforms would; in these times, it is unity that is required. But we are consoled by the knowledge that most Maskilim who bear genuine love for their people will pay no attention to him. Nevertheless, it saddens the heart to see one of our own trying to treat our people's ills by reforming their religion![123]

In a similar spirit did Kohen-Tsedek (undoubtedly bothered by his treatment at Rodkinson's hand) cry out against the entire category of religious reform, calling the book *Hamets u-Matsah* (Leaven and Matsah).[124] It is no surprise that Deinard also joined in, writing that Rodkinson sought to annul all the commandments out of fear of Israel's oppressors and, in the assumption that all reform derived from Christianity, claiming that the book was financed by London missionaries. Perets Smolenskin, writing in *Ha-Shahar*, repeated the charge that the book was financed by London missionaries and, in typical style, included particularly personal and biting remarks.[125]

Even those reviews that did not slander Rodkinson personally did not accept the proposals made in his book. Some called for return to the Land of Israel, an idea espoused by Aharon Yehudah Leib Horowitz, who had spent time in America, and was on friendly terms with Rodkinson, even having written for his paper.[126] In his review in *Ha-Tsefirah* he wrote:

> The book can be summarized thus: ease the restrictions on the baking of *matsah* by non-Jews, because in this way the nations will realize that the blood libel is entirely false. Anyone who knows me well knows that I am not particularly stringent in my observance of the commandments, and yet I see absolutely no benefit in this leniency. Those who hate us and do us wrong do not themselves believe that we need human blood, and only make this claim to stir up the rabble against us. . . . The libel will never cease from the earth so long as the wicked continue to hate us in their hearts, even should we bind ourselves to eating only leavened bread on Passover, and only pork all the year round. . . . In my eyes, a return to the Land of Israel is a better solution to the problem of the blood libel than having non-Jews bake our matsah, and if I were a writer I would write a book by the name "Return to Israel Is the Beginning of the Redemption, and If Not Now, When?"[127]

At the beginning of *Matsat-Mitsvah* Rodkinson mentioned his intention to publish another work on religious reform. Soon after, in 1883, *Tefilah le-Mosheh mi-Kutsi* (Prayer of Mosheh of Coucy, subtitled "The History of Tefillin"), was published in Pressburg.[128] The book tells the history of the commandment of *tefillin*, using religious and scholarly sources in Hebrew and German, including letters by a number of Jewish sages.[129] The essence of Rodkinson's claim is that not only did Jews' relationship with *tefillin* change over time, but that "the *tefillin* we wrap ourselves in have only been used since Rabbeinu Mosheh, the author of *Sefer Mitzvot Gadol* (Great Book of Commandments), who resurrected the tradition after it had been forgotten in Israel."[130] That is, the first Jew to wrap *tefillin* as a daily practice was the thirteenth-century rabbi Mosheh of Coucy, who essentially invented the practice.[131] At the beginning of the book, Rodkinson stressed, "You should know, esteemed reader, that I, like you, am a faithful Jew; my God is dear to me and I desire only to do His commandments—but not those that have been passed on to us by false teachers and gluttonous rabbis, for the commandments were given only to straighten the crooked of heart."[132] His conclusion is that not only is it no longer obligatory to wrap *tefillin* every day but that the practice in its current form perverts the original idea of the commandment and so does damage to the religion as a whole.[133]

In *Tefilah le-Mosheh mi-Kutsi* Rodkinson also responded at length to the critics of his previous book, arguing that the essence of his book was not his proposed solution to antisemitism but rather his plans for religious reform in the spirit of the Talmud. His critics had misunderstood his book, he claimed, and had no aim in condemning it but "to vex and to desecrate."[134] Again he concluded:

> Would that we lived according to the Talmud as it is understood by those who have studied it deeply, for then the enemies of our people could not cast aspersions on us and on the Talmud, which has recently been slandered in all countries by antisemites. And few are those, of our own people or of another, who defend the Talmud. . . . For the Talmud, our Oral Torah, is free of all superstition and vices that we have been accused of since the beginning of the Exile. We could not hope for the betterment of our situation in any country; colonization of Palestine will not help us, nor will exile to a new land. We must show all the nations and their princes the beauty of our religion, its purity from all superstition, and its forbidding of every vice. . . . Aside from this, we shall do a tremendous good to the poor and persecuted masses who follow wide-eyed after their teachers and masters, who blind their eyes and leave them to dwell in darkness, and they will not know that it was not the holy Talmud that laid these bonds upon them, but the rabbis who invented it themselves, and if they would only open

> their eyes and see a new light and strive to save themselves, then they would find the fight for their lives easier to bear.[135]

Rodkinson described the book's reception in London in the following way:

> My little book, published only a month ago and not yet widely spread among our brethren, has shown me how well I have hit the mark, for here too in the city of London, where Orthodoxy rules . . . my little composition has earned many honored admirers, more even than I could have hoped. And if they are indeed forced to conceal their identities to avoid disgrace, a day will come when they will reveal their hearts and stand beside their brothers, openly and not in secret.[136]

Rodkinson knew that not everyone would welcome his books: "I expected the slurs, the curses and the bans," he wrote, "the arrows and the stones from the zealots and the rabbis after they had read my book; from the start I could hear the uproar in heaven and earth; but I fear none of it, for I have already faced the likes of these."[137] He had foreseen correctly: his opponents pounced on the new book and its author, once again accusing him of collaborating with all sorts of religious reformers and even the London missionaries.[138] Kohen-Tsedek, who called the book *Tefilah le-Sama'el mi-Kotz* (The Prayer of Satan from Thorn), used its publishing as an opportunity to condemn not just Rodkinson but religious reformers as a group and to publicize his own conservative approach.[139]

There were some positive reviews of the book, including one written by Simon Dubnow in the Russian journal *Voskhod* (Dawn), Dubnow, who in those years tended toward radicalism, praised Rodkinson's latter books and dubbed him "a writer who cannot be ignored and a journalist of considerable literary talent" with "progressive aspirations." He praised the author for his fearlessness in critiquing Jewish society and for "denouncing what so many ignore and at our own peril—that the rabbinate does damage to the Jewish religion, segregating the Jewish people." Rodkinson's approach was particularly praiseworthy in Dubnow's eyes at a time when antisemitism was on the rise and the typical response to it was "conservative religious apologetics."[140] This was a rare positive review of the book by a fellow Jew. Dubnow would later write, surely after further reading in Rodkinson's Hasidic books and the critiques of them, "I welcomed the calls for religious reform made by Rodkinson, though his erratic ways leave room for suspicion."[141]

While in London, Rodkinson continued the program of religious reform laid out in his earlier books with *Al Israel ve-Al Rabbanan* (On Israel and Our Sages), in which he critiqued the rabbinate and Jewish law, outlined the development of Jewish prayer, described his persecutors, and announced the upcoming release of his book *Matsat-Mitsvahve-Alilat ha-Dam* in English translation. Both of these books remained unpublished.[142] At the same time he was pursuing a plan, as he mentioned in a number of his writings, to publish a journal by the name of *Ha-Talmud veha-Shulhan Arukh* (The Talmud and the Shulhan Arukh), but the journal never appeared, since neither the subscribers nor the regular contributors Rodkinson tried to enlist ever materialized; some of the more prestigious writers he courted let it be known that they did not approve of his previous work.[143]

The fact that the journal was never published did not prevent Kohen-Tsedek from attacking it and trying to prevent its release. In 1882 he described Rodkinson's activities in London by writing:

> He wandered from town to town and country to country attempting to gain supporters for his "Shulhan Arukh Journal," saying, "How long shall we remain the slaves of Rabbi Yosef Karo and Rabbi Mosheh Isserles? We are taking our leave of this 'set table,' and tearing the 'tablecloth' that is upon it into twelve pieces! . . . The time has come to throw out the old and make room for the new."[144]

Kohen-Tsedek derided Rodkinson's method of working as well:

> He goes through each page of the *Shulhan Arukh*, reading without proper study and without understanding. Wherever he finds the words "kosher—pure—permitted," he rules accordingly in his "Shulhan Arukh Journal," since these three are proof of his "progress." And should he, God forbid, come across the words "unfit—impure—forbidden," he erases them and writes in his journal, "On the contrary, it is kosher—pure—permitted!" And so, in a moment, a new Torah is made.[145]

Such critiques as these seem not to have sapped Rodkinson's will to continue writing and publishing. In addition to his compositions on religious reform, Rodkinson planned to print, in both Hebrew and German, the book by Yaakov Hayim ha-Levi Korn of Lvov, *Kisalon Ben Parnakh*, previously published as a serial in *Ha-Kol*. The piece contains an account of the debate over the rabbinate of Shelomoh Yehudah Rapoport that was held in Tarnopol in 1840, and includes some disparaging remarks toward Kohen-Tsedek. This, too, remained unpublished.[146] Rodkinson composed a number of other pieces while in London, however, and it was in pursuit of their publication that he returned to Germany.

The Struggle against Antisemitism: Berlin

In or around the year 1884, Rodkinson arrived in Berlin to print and promote his books, leaving his wife and children behind in London.[147] While Rodkinson's peregrinations during that period make it difficult to trace his path, we do know that his multiple attempts to establish journals and newspapers and the concomitant need to win new subscribers took him to far-flung locations. On his journey to Berlin he briefly visited Vienna as well, where he met Joseph S. Bloch. As we will see, Bloch, initially impressed by Rodkinson, later changed his estimation of Rodkinson and forced him to leave Europe; but first we will recount Rodkinson's endeavors in Berlin.

Despite the criticism it received, it was *Matsat-Mitsvah* that Rodkinson chose to translate into German in Pressburg in 1883, hoping that in this way the book would win new fans. This hope was never realized,[148] though, and slightly later he traveled to Berlin to publish the booklet *Even ha-Roshah* (The Keystone,1884) as the first part of *Avnei Milu'im* (Jewels of the Breastplate), dedicated to continuing the discussion on religious reform.[149] In *Even ha-Roshah* he defended himself and his books *Tefilah le-Mosheh* and *Matsat-Mitsvah ve-Alilat ha-Dam* against wide-ranging criticism, including the claims that he sought to do away with the commandments altogether and that he served the interests of London missionaries. Once again he posed his thesis on the development of antisemitism and his proposal to establish a multinational gathering of rabbis dedicated to reviving "the spirit of the Talmud" and adapting it to "the spirit of the times."[150] His treatment of *tefillin* in the book was the first in a series on the commandments of the *Shulhan Arukh*, the majority of which, he argued, are nothing more than "extraneous customs" defended by rationales that amounted to "pure idol worship" and that "aroused both ridicule and disgust" among the non-Jews.[151]

Avnei Milu'im was meant to include another five volumes in addition to *Even ha-Roshah.* The second volume, *Even Barkat* (Emerald), would collect all the responses to his books on reform, now with annotations and correspondences from various figures in Germany, France, and England. The third, *Even Sapir* (Sapphire, published in Vienna in 1886), would contain "new studies and addenda" on previously treated topics, while the fourth, *Even Israel* (Jewel of Israel), would treat "the question of Palestine." The fifth volume, *Even ha-Shulhan* (Jewel of the Altar [or Table]), would pitch the journal *Ha-Talmud veha-Shulhan Arukh* that Rodkinson had attempted to establish in London, with examples of laws from the *Shulhan Arukh* that ran counter to the Talmud. The sixth, *Even ha-To'im* or *Even ha-Sofrim* (Jewel of the Scribes), would contain "the history of a few Hebrew writers, their character, their words, and their work," along with some letters sent to him by Perets Smolenskin, Judah Leib Gordon, Judah Leib Levin, Eliyahu Wolf Rabinowitz, and others.[152] Rodkinson planned to publish a new volume every two months, so that the work would be complete by the end of 1885, but he turned to other projects and most of the volumes were never published.

In Berlin he returned to the subject of antisemitism and religious reform with a new booklet titled *Levaker Mishpat* (Criticizing the Trial, 1884), in which he countered various claims of modern antisemites, primarily the apostate Jew Aron Israel Brimann, known by his pseudonym Dr. Justus, who founded most of his attacks on the *Shulhan Arukh*.[153] Rodkinson analyzed two influential events that had recently occurred in Germany—the famous trial concerning the publication *Der Judenspiegel* (The Jews' Mirror) and the burial of a non-Jew who had married a Jewish woman—presenting the events in such a way as to conform to his reading of antisemitism: "Having finished my work on *Even ha-Roshah* and having already turned to the second volume, I was forced to dip my pen once again into the ink, dedicating two new essays to recent events that caused quite a stir in the (antisemitic) German literature."[154] He stressed that both events concerned "my overarching aim in all my later books," that is, "the reform of Judaism by the publishing of a new *Shulhan Arukh* and in the gathering of a standing synod that will rule on matters of religious law and, of course, wage a war of the pen against our enemies." His intent, he claimed, was "to show the antisemites their own lunacy, ignorance, and stupidity all at once,"[155] but he did not miss the chance to ridicule the performance of the Jewish defense attorney either.

In *Levaker Mishpat*, Rodkinson argued with especial ferocity his views on the Talmud and the *Shulhan Arukh*, claiming that the *Shulhan Arukh* was not a "living book" for most Jews (or in any case shouldn't be) and in fact stunted progress, soured relations with Christians, and imprisoned the spirit of Judaism.[156] His comments are particularly harsh in the following paragraph:

> We have been buried for some three hundred years in the cemetery of the *Shulhan Arukh*, which has no spirit of life but only dead letters: *forbidden, impure, permitted, kosher, unfit, and such is our practice and it is not fitting to deviate from it*. It is a

> cemetery in which is buried the life and spirit of Israel, while we Jews are reduced to gravestones standing in memory of the Talmud, that book that lived within us for seven hundred years! . . . These gravestones have been taken by the rabbis and made into idols to be served, and so we have become a curse and a disgrace to the nations.[157]

In the course of his arguments Rodkinson fiercely attacked the Orthodox, who had added baseless laws and statutes never imagined by their ancestors. What's more, he argued against their very claim to being the possessors of normative Judaism, proclaiming, "there has never been such a thing as the Orthodox Torah."[158] He also launched into a long polemic deriding the book *Lev ha-Ivri* (Heart of the Hebrew), directed "against the liberals" by "a certain fanatic," Rabbi Hillel Lichtenstein of Kolomea.[159] This attack aroused widespread anger, as when Kohen-Tsedek wrote:

> This self-righteous [Rodkinson] seeks to uproot the commandments of *tefillin*, *tsitsit*, and *mezuzah*, to permit leaven on Passover, to grant permission to bury a Jew and a Christian together in the finest of our cemeteries, arguing that, since they were beloved in life, let not death separate them, "for love is as strong as death." Such wise and efficacious reforms as these, and more, does he call for, all in the name of bettering the world![160]

Kohen-Tsedek realized the extent of the reforms Rodkinson proposed in his little book, but he never imagined that his demands were in fact even more far-reaching, calling for the renewal of Judaism through a reworking of all its canonical texts, as we will see below.

Some supported Rodkinson specifically because of his outspokenness. Simon Dubnow, who praised Rodkinson's scholarship (even if he did call him "an abomination in the Jewish community"), shared his sensibility that the Talmud is "our great religious encyclopedia," as opposed to the *Shulhan Arukh*, "which for nearly two-hundred years has held back the healthy spiritual development of the Jewish religion and until today, in certain circles, prevents any progress in our religious life."[161]

Rodkinson also found a friend and faithful patron in Moritz Lazarus, a member of the Jewish elite in Berlin with whom Rodkinson had forged a connection during his previous visit. In a letter to his brother, Israel Dov Frumkin, Rodkinson wrote that while in Berlin he worked for a number of months for Lazarus, receiving a fine salary for his work gathering sources for Lazarus's book *Die Ethik des Judenthums* (The Ethics of Judaism, 1898).[162] Lazarus also supported a number of Rodkinson's projects over the years, including his books on antisemitism and the Talmud, and even wrote approbations to a number of his books, one being printed at the beginning of *Tefilah le-Mosheh.* Even if Rodkinson did win a few such supporters as Lazarus, however, his books on religious reform earned him many more opponents, who raised suspicions that he was acting in concert with missionaries, was in contact with antisemites, and had converted out of Judaism—accusations made in the heat of the controversy that seem to have been totally unfounded.[163]

Charges of abandoning the faith had been leveled against other reformers of the time as well, and the charge of collaborating with missionaries was one of the most commonly spread about the early Jewish socialists.[164] Even though Rodkinson was by no means a socialist, he had provided a forum for them by founding *Ha-Kol* and even more so *Asefat Chachamim*, and in doing so had made himself the target of the same accusations leveled against them. What's more, the fact that the better part of Rodkinson's books on religious reform were composed in London was taken as a sign of connections with the missionaries there. Likewise, his criticisms of the *Shulhan Arukh* and Jewish law were understood as supporting antisemitic charges, and it was but a small step to connect him personally to the antisemites themselves, although any familiarity with Rodkinson's books and personal life shows that he was in fact their fierce opponent. For such criticism, it seems, Rodkinson had already prepared himself when he set out to publish his books; the events that followed in Vienna, however, could not have been anticipated.

Gleanings from Rodkinson's Opponents: Vienna

In October 1884, Rodkinson arrived in Vienna to publish the German edition of his book on the *Shulhan Arukh*. The book was in fact a reworking and translation of a number of earlier compositions written in Hebrew in London and Berlin, to which he added an abridged discussion of the relationship between the development of Jewish law and modern antisemitism that included ferocious attacks on Justus and Rohling.[165] The book included a dedication to Leopold Zunz and copies of a number of letters from David Slutsky, Moritz Lazarus, and others in the hopes of bolstering Rodkinson's image. One of these letters expressed encouragement not to submit to the "zealots" who sought to do him harm, adding the claim that "if the *auto de fe* has been abolished, its decrees have not, and even now the inquisitors among our brethren wrathfully pursue any they deem a reformer or innovator." Rodkinson added his own responses to his critics in the margins of these letters, writing of Kohen-Tsedek, for example, "I have come to realize that this hypocrite will not blush even when his lies are bared to his face."[166]

In letters to his brother Israel Dov Frumkin, who was then living in Israel, he recounted, "I now hope to dedicate myself to the work of writing a Talmudic encyclopedia under the approving eye of Prof. Heinrich Graetz, only there is no publisher for this sizable job. I do hope to publish a weekly journal in the holy tongue and in Yiddish in the coming year, and if I only desire it enough I will succeed."[167] While we have no further information about this Talmudic encyclopedia or his relationship with Heinrich Graetz, we do know that Rodkinson did indeed pursue his dream of reviving *Ha-Kol*, attempting just that in late 1884.[168]

We learn the extent to which Rodkinson went to enter the world of Viennese Hebrew journalism from a letter dated 1885, in which David Frishman writes to Judah Leib Gordon, "The owner of *Ha-Kol* asked me to come to Vienna to publish a monthly journal; it would bear only my name, while he would serve as my partner in publishing, paying me a salary. No one would know that he is involved, he tells me, and I need fear no embarrassment before my friends because of him. (I answered him on the spot: No.)"[169] (After a period of indecision Frishman joined up instead with Yehudah Leib Kantor in editing the daily journal *Ha-Yom* [Today] in St. Petersburg.)[170]

Rodkinson struggled to find financing for the renewed *Ha-Kol* and turned to various sources in search of aid. One of his faithful supporters was Salomon Buber, with whom Rodkinson had corresponded while in Koenigsberg, sending him each edition of *Ha-Kol* as it was printed. Rodkinson asked Buber to recommend him to the *Alliance Française* in Paris and Vienna and to the Society for the Promotion of Culture among the Jews of Russia in St. Petersburg, and so to enlist their aid in publishing the journal, a request that was apparently never granted.[171] Full of hope, Rodkinson declared that "the gates of Russia have been flung open," promising to bring him many subscribers.[172] He even intended at first to publish two different journals—*Ha-Kol*, dealing with politics and literature, and *Kol Ya'akov* (Voice of Jaacob), dedicated to "the Jewish question"—but Rodkinson found publishing even one to be difficult.[173]

On December 10, 1884, the first edition of the new *Ha-Kol* was published, now dedicated primarily to scholarly essays on Jewish studies (in the spirit of *Wissenschaft des Judentums*) and the struggle against the resurgent "fanaticism and antisemitism" of the day, which was breaking out in the form of ever-bloodier pogroms that "bring disgrace upon all of humanity."[174] His hope of enlisting the sages of Vienna was only partially fulfilled; in one edition, Rodkinson announced that Adolf (Aaron) Jellinek would be a regular contributor to the journal and he would be publishing "ancient and one-of-a-kind manuscripts" from "the archives of the sages of Kabbalah," including a Frankist manuscript from Prague and the writings of Moshe de Leon and Abraham Abulafia, though in actuality only a portion of the Frankist manuscript was published (and even that aroused the ire of the Viennese Orthodox community).[175]

At the same time, Rodkinson returned to the ideas that had consumed him while in London and Berlin, dedicating a long list of essays to the question of the Talmud and the *Shulhan Arukh*.[176] As he had announced he would the previous year, he published the second volume of *Avnei Milu'im*, *Even Sapir* (1886).[177] The book included discussions on *tefillin* by Mosheh Leib Lilienblum, Avraham Krochmal, and others, now with Rodkinson's extensive notes in the margins.[178] Though most of these essays had been published previously in *Ha-Kol* and contained no new information, one anecdote is worth mentioning. While Lilienblum agreed with the essentials of Rodkinson's theories, adding only a few philological and historical details to the conversation, at the end of the essay he inserted some words that reveal the unbridgeable gulf between them after the pogroms of 1882:

> I must exceed the goals of this essay, as you exceeded the goals of your book in saying that colonization of Palestine will not help us so long as the nations and their leaders do not come to appreciate the beauty of our faith. In my opinion, one settlement in Palestine is better than countless displays of casuistry before our enemies, who have no reason to change and will never do so, since they have the power and, as everyone knows, those with the power make the rules. For nearly two millennia already we have sought repose in the lands of our enemies . . . yet does it not say in the Torah itself, in which we claim to have faith, "Among the nations you will find no repose"? For my part, I believe in my heart that, even granted eternity, we would never find repose in lands not our own, and it is in vain that we change our ways in the hopes of earning the love of strangers.[179]

In his note to Lilienblum's essay Rodkinson expressed regret over the other's position but replied, "I will not argue with you over Palestine since I have already withdrawn from the whole matter." Rodkinson did abandon the national-territorial question to devote himself to the sole aim of explaining the Torah to any who would listen, which he saw as his own vital contribution to the struggle against antisemitism.[180] Such a shift countered the trend of many contemporary writers who, compelled by current events, sought other solutions.

Rodkinson dedicated the final pages of *Even Sapir* to a discussion of the Talmud. In an essay titled "Talmudic Literature, or The

Old, Short Talmud," he returned to his motif of "purifying" the Talmud in preparation for its reprinting. He declared this project to be his life's work and his sole purpose, and indeed we find entire issues of *Ha-Kol* dedicated to it.[181] Continuing the radical line drawn in his earlier books from the Berlin period, he stressed with increased fervor the incompatibility of the *Shulhan Arukh* with the purified Talmud, writing, "This one bears no relation to that one," and spoke fiercely against contemporary antisemites, especially Justus.[182]

This was not merely a restatement of old ideas. In three long essays, two of which were printed in special editions in Pressburg in 1885, Rodkinson developed the idea of reprinting the Babylonian Talmud.[183] He spoke not of a traditional printing but rather an abridged version free of what he saw as later additions and external influences, a version he presented as the "true" and "pure" Talmud (reminiscent of the plans of Mosheh Leib Lilienblum, who called for a return to "the spirit of the Talmud" through the removal of "superstitions" that had entered Jewish law through the Kabbalah and Hasidism).[184] Rodkinson announced that such work exceeded the ability of one man and called for a "gathering of great sages" who would take on the task. Such a gathering would be the first of its kind, presenting the Talmud in a new form adapted to the spirit of its time, with the goal of turning the Talmud into an orderly, modern, and living text. We are "Talmudic Jews," Rodkinson declared, and without the Talmud there was no value to the existence of the Jews as a nation; so the Jews must purify the Talmud in order to rightfully claim their title and redeem it from the antisemites who had turned it into a slur.[185]

According to his own testimony, Rodkinson was inspired to undertake the project after reading a pamphlet by Meir Ish Shalom who spoke about the different historical layers in the Talmud, as well as the impossibility of translating it, in the preface to a critical edition.[186] Rodkinson described the profound impression the pamphlet made on him: "I felt a spark in my soul flare up amid the ash, igniting my heart and setting my blood to boiling; I saw a light so bright I was nearly blinded."[187] Thus he was moved to compose his new manifesto on "The True Talmud," that is, an abridged Talmud rid of its later strata and the "hallucinations" that had crept in with them.

Rodkinson spoke harshly of the voluminous hermeneutical literature that had grown up around the Talmud and the *Shulhan Arukh*, and continued to grow with each generation in the form of commentaries and supercommentaries, declaring, "all the books, the responsa, the debates . . . amount to a giant heap of dry bones, a witness to the iniquity of the generation!"[188] Not only were the commentaries useless, he argued, but the original texts were so laden with additions and "so full of superscripts, asterisks, and circles" that they had been turned into volumes so enormous as to be useless.[189] The editing of the Talmud and, by extension, of a large part of Jewish literature would let the Jews call out to all their enemies:

> This is our Oral Torah, given to us by our sages of blessed memory, the masters of the Talmud; the rest will remain in the archives, bound and lying in a remote corner; whoever wishes to pick it up may do so. By this Israel will discover the Talmud they have never known, and will neither be ashamed of it nor fear to teach it to their children. Our enemies too will be forced to abandon it, since they cannot indict us for teachings that we have consigned to the storage shelf.[190]

In great naiveté Rodkinson declared that there was no more reason to oppose his plan than to object to the famous abridgements *Kitsur Ha-Shelah* (The Abridged Two Tablets of the Covenant) and *Kitsur Shulhan Arukh* (The Abridged Set Table)—which had effectively replaced the original texts—and he called on the rabbis to support his vision and take a hand in shaping it.[191]

Rodkinson knew that some would attack his idea, but he pointed out that such "zealots" would attack him regardless,[192] and he refused to abandon the project until he had seen it through to the end, proclaiming, "I hereby sacrifice and sanctify the rest of my days upon the altar of this work; it will be the delight of my nights and the labor of my days, which I am forced to spend fighting for my very existence and that of my household. . . . From this moment I have but one goal in life; I have love only for it."[193] Rodkinson would indeed devote himself to the project until his death, even managing to gain a few supporters along the way. By dint of sheer will he ultimately realized his vision, though on another continent and in a different form than when he had first announced it.

Rodkinson's proclamations about the Talmud were indeed opposed from the moment they were printed. Even Meir Ish Shalom, whose pamphlet had inspired Rodkinson to take on the project, recoiled from the suggestion to actually censor and abridge the Talmud; he published a statement in *Ha-Kol* that he agreed to the plan only in principle, that is, on condition that it be done according to the scientific system that he himself had outlined, but certainly not by presenting a new and abridged text.[194]

Others leveled harsh criticism against Rodkinson; in a piece published in the orthodox journal *Kol Mahzikei Ha-Dat* and written under the pseudonym "Ha-GeMaRA"—initials that could be read as those of the imagined rabbi "The Gaon MaRA" or as "the Gemara"—the anonymous author numbered Rodkinson among the "destroyers" of the religion and marveled that the other papers "listened to such shaming of the Torah and of the religion and did not return answer, as if their Creator had placed them in the world only to raise the banner of the Haskalah." Evoking Kohen-Tsedek's *Michael Who Has Turned into Samael*, he dubbed Rodkinson "Samael, the Troubler of Israel," "a detestable man infected by every abomination he touches," whose writings "rebel against the word of God, the Torah, morality, and common decency," bringing lengthy proofs that *Ha-Kol*'s articles were full of heresy, not to mention gross error in their understanding of Torah, science, and Hebrew grammar. He wrote, "Our heart was torn and our innards pierced as by an arrow; our spirit poured out when we saw how great had grown the bold-faced impudence and heresy in the soul of this Hebrew printer; it is but the spirit of missionism taken a new form in order to trap souls with its shiny new tricks." He went so far as to equate Rodkinson and his "New Talmud" with the notorious antisemite August Rohling.[195]

Rodkinson, unrelenting, responded with a biting Talmudic parody in *Ha-Kol* that deflected the attacks of the author along with those of Kohen-Tsedek on which they were based.[196] This barbed essay hinted at what was to come from his pen in later years. If such criticism did not turn Rodkinson aside from his self-declared mission, he was soon beset by troubles—of his own making—that would distract him from it for the time being.

When Rodkinson had passed some months in Vienna and had weathered his critics' anger, he was accused by Dr. Joseph S. Bloch (1850–1923),[197] the editor of the *Österreichische Wochenschrift* (Austrian Weekly Journal), of collaborating with August Rohling, author of the popular antisemitic book *Der Talmudjude* (The Talmudic Jew, 1871).[198] Rohling was involved in a number of trials, including the end of the Tiszaeszlár Affair, in which he testified that Jewish sources required Christian blood for the Passover holiday. Bloch pestered Rohling until the latter was forced into a libel case that took Vienna by storm. Bloch's methods of public debate ultimately led to Rohling not only abandoning his court claim but publicly submitting to Bloch, a fact that greatly tarnished his reputation and cost him his position at the University of Prague. Rohling gave up his case in June 1885 when he saw that the "experts" appointed by the court to check the Jewish sources had arrived at entirely different conclusions from his own.

The Bloch-Rohling affair appears briefly in many studies, but usually with no mention of Rodkinson, who was dragged into Bloch's polemics at the conclusion of the affair. But even those studies that mention Rodkinson accept Bloch's reports about him, without verifying the accounts written in the Hebrew newspapers at the time and without recourse to Rodkinson's own testimony on the events. These sources must be uncovered if we are to see the whole picture of the affair and the decidedly negative image of Rodkinson that found its way into scholarly literature.[199]

In his memoirs, printed in German, English, and Hebrew in the 1920s and 1930s, Bloch recounted the entire Rohling affair, including a colorful and damning treatment of Rodkinson based mostly on memoirs published in daily papers from the 1880s and 1890s, which he quoted in full with his own added notes.[200] The failing in Bloch's research is simple: relying on the vaguest of hints in a letter to Rohling, Bloch accused Rodkinson of aiding Rohling as a "second Justus." Dr. Justus, born Aharon Israel Brimann, was referred to by some as "a half-mad Jewish youth."[201] An apostate Jew and author of the book *Der Judenspiegel* (1884), he helped Rohling locate excerpts from Talmudic and Kabbalistic literature, which he then interpreted and translated to match an antisemitic agenda. In his correspondence with Rohling, Justus mentioned an unknown figure referred to only as "R.," which was reference enough for Bloch to include Rodkinson in the cabal. Bloch claimed that Rodkinson translated Kabbalistic texts for Rohling, adding the standard Orthodox polemical charge that Rodkinson had converted and was in the pay of the missionaries, it being inconceivable to him that a Jew could write such heretical things about the commandments or go so far in his reforms as to call for revising Judaism's foundational texts.

Bloch recounted that he was given such an impression of Rodkinson even before meeting him in person, through the writings of Deinard, Kohen-Tsedek, and Zederbaum. So when Rodkinson arrived in Vienna and began his intensive work on his Talmud, Bloch attributed the visit to finishing the research for the Rohling trial, which was occurring at that time.[202] Deinard, for his part, wrote that Bloch had written to him personally asking him to speak his mind on Rodkinson and Yehiel Tsvi Lichtenstein-Hirschenson (1831–1912), whom Deinard saw as a missionizing apostate who wrote books in the spirit of the Kabbalah and new Hasidism; and we can safely assume that Deinard provided Bloch with intriguing, even sensational information about the two figures whom he found so similar.[203] Kohen-Tsedek's polemical books and Zederbaum's essay, "Bi-Gevurah ve-Lo be-Sheti," further strengthened the negative impression Bloch had already received from Deinard's letter.[204] When Bloch came into possession of Rodkinson's books, among them *Matsat-Mitsvah ve-Alilat ha-Dam* and *Levaker Mishpat*, he declared, "This book presents the Jews in an even worse light than does Doctor Justus in *Der Judenspiegel.*"

Bloch stood by his opinion of the "special hypocrisy" of Rodkinson's books, claiming that "apparently the author did not write a single word against the Jews; on the contrary, it was all written in their defense; however, from this position among their ranks he fires arrows into their midst." These "arrows" were Rodkinson's claims about the development of the Jewish religion, his plans for religious reform, and his radical statements about abridging and "purifying" the Talmud and the *Shulhan Arukh*, in which Bloch saw a secret intention to missionize that would do greater damage to Judaism than the writings of actual antisemites.[205] Bloch described his first meeting with Rodkinson as follows:

> One day Rodkinson came to me to ask that I publish an advertisement for his new book [apparently his book in German on the *Shulhan Arukh*] in *Österreichische Wochenschrift.* I absolutely refused his request and told him that I saw his writings as damaging to the Jews. He replied, "It is your prerogative to disagree with me, and you can express that disagreement in the margin notes, as you see fit." I said, "I have no time for this, and what's more, I don't wish to draw the readers' attention to such writings." He came to me twice more but, receiving the same chilly reception from me, he ceased his visits, choosing instead to attack me in his newspaper, but I made no response.[206]

Bloch continued his account, writing that, on a trip to Galicia to report to the voters there on the parliamentary elections being held in Vienna, he saw Rodkinson following behind him every step of the way, saying "all sorts of obscene things about him." Bloch stated that he decided not to respond at the time. In his picturesque description he wrote, "The rumors quickly spread in Chernovitz, Lvov, and Kolomea that Rodkinson had been sent to Galicia by the missionaries in order to campaign for Dr. Bloch. This was false, however. Rodkinson was not an emissary of the missionaries but of my opponents, sent to damage my reputation, since the open war being waged against me had not brought them victory."[207]

While Rodkinson spent March to May of 1885 in Galicia gathering subscribers for *Ha-Kol*, he did indeed fiercely attack Bloch, portraying him as two-faced, passing as pious to win the favor of the voters, or, in his words, taking up "the diadem of Hasidism" and "donning the priestly garments as one of the Catholic priests with all their finery." Rodkinson warned that Bloch's ways strengthened the antisemites and called passionately for the support of his opponents in the elections.[208]

It seems that Rodkinson's opponents (among them Kohen-Tsedek and Deinard) had been spreading the word that he was a tool of the missionaries for some time and, in the heated political environment, Bloch was hung with the same label. We have here a very interesting fact: Bloch pinned on Rodkinson the very accusations that Rodkinson himself had leveled against Bloch in his political campaigning. This reversal would prove instrumental for Rodkinson's future in Vienna; while Bloch proved adept at exploiting the charges hung on him, Rodkinson would collapse under their weight.

Rodkinson would later elaborate upon the meeting between the two of them. According to Rodkinson, Bloch approached him first, and even helped with his writings ridiculing Rohling, but the relationship quickly soured due to Bloch's pursuit of glory and his reticence to criticize the Orthodox establishment.[209] Elsewhere Rodkinson portrayed Bloch as a glory-hound who entered the Rohling trial only to make a name for himself. Even if Bloch succeeded in his task, he argued, it would have been better had he never gotten involved at all, leaving the fight against Rohling to others such as Moritz Gutmann and Franz Delitzsch.[210]

Bloch was not satisfied with accusing Rodkinson of being a member of the opposition or even a tool of the antisemites. He quickly tried to prove, on the most circumstantial evidence, that Rodkinson had collaborated with Rohling, helping him find and translate excerpts from Kabbalistic literature that could be used against the Jews—an accusation of a different order from all the abuses hurled by the two sides up to that point. On November 13, 1885, he published an essay titled "Aharon Brimann and R." in which he speculated that there was a "third conspirator" in Rohling's cabal hinted at by the letter "R." appearing in one of Rohling's letters to Justus. He did not stop at this conjecture, and in a series of essays he intimated that this "R." was a Russian Jew involved in Hebrew literature and, what's more, known to everyone in Vienna.

His claims resonated with the public and were reported in German and Jewish newspapers: Adolf (Aaron) Jellinek's paper reprinted Bloch's words and called for the unmasking of this "third conspirator," and other newspapers (first and foremost *Die Yudishe Presse* [The Jewish Press]) declared that they had already deciphered the hints and identified "R." as none other than Rodkinson.[211] This frivolous claim seems to have arisen from antagonism toward Rodkinson based on his writings and his personal connections with Bloch's political opponents, first among them Emmanuel Baumgarten.[212] It is a wonder that Bloch's opinion was so widely accepted, since in all of Rodkinson's books from the period, as well as in the essays dedicated to the topic in *Ha-Kol* throughout 1885, he was fiercely critical of antisemites, and especially of Rohling and Justus (he described the latter as having "sold his soul" for financial gain, as a con man, and as a "common swindler who takes every opportunity to deceive his fellow men," not to mention an apostate many times over).[213] It seems that those who wrote about Rodkinson hadn't read his own writings and were informed primarily by rumors and the statements of his opponents. In any case, Rodkinson's politics were clearly different from those of Bloch, who had his own explanations for modern antisemitism and his own proposed solutions to it.[214]

Once Bloch had provided the shady evidence for Rodkinson's connection to Rohling and Justus, others pounced on his speculations with delight, not only accepting them at face value but elaborating upon them with their rich imaginations. The individual most responsible for spreading this gossip in the early twentieth century was Ephraim Deinard, and it was by his hand that the rumor entered modern scholarship—and, once again, without any checking of the sources.[215]

Rodkinson denied any and all connection to Rohling, sending letters to every German newspaper in Vienna and Berlin proclaiming that he was not the "R." mentioned in the letter, and even warning Bloch that if he did not stop spreading rumors he would take him to court.[216] Notwithstanding Rodkinson's denials, the damage from Bloch's accusation had been done. In the fallout from the affair, Rodkinson was forced to close *Ha-Kol* that very month.

In the last issue of the paper printed in Vienna, issued one week after Bloch's first accusatory essay, and even before any explicit connection between Rodkinson and Rohling had been made, Rodkinson heatedly attacked the reactionary "Ashkenazi [German] Orthodox establishment" for inviting antisemitism with their resistance to change, even going so far as to paraphrase the prophet Jeremiah, declaring, "from Ashkenaz will evil spread to all the inhabitants of the earth."[217] He also expressed his desire to print a new book titled *Ha-Ortodoksia ha-Ashkenazit ve-Totsaoteiha* (German Orthodoxy and Its Actions), which would take aim at German Judaism for abandoning the Torah and the Hebrew language, and especially of Samson Rafael Hirsch and his followers, whose separate communities founded under the banner of "Modern Orthodoxy" Rodkinson declared a disaster for the religion.[218] The book was never published and Rodkinson was forced to busy himself with the much more burning issues of proving his innocence and refuting his attackers. We hear the urgency Rodkinson must have felt in a letter he wrote to Samuel Joseph Fuenn asking for help against his opponents:

> My dear sir and esteemed rabbi! It is not my way to burden others with my own concerns, and so I ask his Torah eminence to believe me when I say it is against my will that I write to request that his honor please fulfill his promise to write about me in the journals, and with all due speed. Circumstances compel me to ask that his Torah eminence express his sentiments in writing, because even yesterday, upon returning home, I met Rabbi N. Broyde, who explained to me that he has spoken with others about me and seen that they honor me in their hearts but fear to support me before

> Bloch my accuser. He has spread the lie that I am collaborating with English missionaries, and so I do not exaggerate when I say that this is a matter of life and death. You yourself must admit that the moral obligation rests upon his Torah eminence to do this with all possible speed—not only because our sages have said, "The one who begins a commandment should finish it," and not only because Dr. Jellinek has requested that his honor write in his name all that he sees fit, but also because, in my opinion, there is no man in all of Russia who knows the truth of the matter and of my heart as you do. So I will take the liberty to say: Before his reverend Torah eminence we will reveal everything in our heart—and if his honor will not extend his hand to a drowning man it will be counted as a sin, and the blood of Rodkinson will be on his hands.[219]

Fuenn did send an open letter to the editor of *Ha-Magid*, though he stated that, while he had written to defend Rodkinson and to clear his name, he should take the hint to follow the path of moderation in his future work:

> To remove the gossip from the wise and blameless rabbi, our master and teacher Michael Levi Rodkinson, who has suffered the lies of his enemies, who say that he has joined with the enemies of Israel and with that persecutor Rohling and his band, teaching them how to wage war against us, I found myself compelled to publicly state that since the slander was heard in Vienna, I have turned to the great rabbi, our master and teacher Dr. Aaron Jellinek, who seeks the best for his people in the holy community of Vienna, and asked him if there is any hint of truth in this matter, and in his passion for truth he was quick to inform me that he knows for certain that it was never so. . . . And since I have full faith in the words of this great rabbi, and I am myself convinced by R. Michael Levi's essays and journals that, not only is he not an ally of the antisemites, but even one of those who points out their faults and reveals their shame, and has fought fiercely with these scoundrels—I am astonished to say before those who know my name that R. Michael Levi is clean of all suspicion and all the lies the devils have spread about

> him. May my prayer for him be received, that he be more moderate in his studies, and may the peace of the Lord God of Israel be upon him to guide him in His truth.[220]

Adolf (Aaron) Jellinek, who was a close associate of Rodkinson, also offered to help him. As the editor of the newspaper *Neitzeit* (New Era), he decided to print over a number of months the correspondence between Rohling and his lawyer Robert Patai, including the statement that Rodkinson was not known to him at all and that he is not the "R." hinted at in the previous letters. This statement was sent in special editions to all members of the Jewish community in Vienna and Jellinek reprinted them in translation in the Hebrew newspapers.[221] In the newspaper *Ivri Anochi* (I Am a Hebrew), Yaakov Werber summarized, "Our eyes have indeed seen that Dr. Bloch missed the mark with his baseless speculations that Rodkinson should be counted among our enemies, and he has brought much evil upon a fellow Jew by doing so." Werber further lamented that the statement denying Rodkinson's involvement must have come from the mouth of Robert Patai, Rohling's lawyer.[222] Wherever the denials came from, whether from Rodkinson or his opponents, they had little effect; Rodkinson's reputation had already been destroyed.

This did not keep Rodkinson from continuing in his literary endeavors, however. On the contrary, the closing of *Ha-Kol* in the aftermath of the controversy spurred him to publish more monthly journals and special editions. Even before Bloch's earth-shattering accusations, he had announced in the newspaper *Ha-Havatselet* a new journal titled *Barkai* (Dawn), which would include eleven different sections, among them "Daily News," "World News and Nature," "Life Stories of the Jews of Russia and Germany," "Review of Books," "Biographies of Famous Men," "Letters of Famous Men," and "Feuilletons."[223] Despite these grand plans, however, the first edition, titled *Barkai, or Light on the Eastern Horizon!* (1886), was mostly dedicated to debating Joseph S. Bloch and refuting his claims one by one.[224] Rodkinson distributed the journal in two forms with identical pagination, a portion of the copies bearing the headline,

"Arming Oneself against the Abusers." The edition was written as a single, continuous essay, and it is clear from the personal and emotional tone that Rodkinson wrote it in great angst.

Rodkinson saw himself as suffering personal and professional ruin at the hands of his opponents. Knowing that Bloch's accusations and their wide acceptance by the public were out of his control, he grasped at the last weapon available to him—his pen. He recounted his meetings with Bloch in a special edition, offering an alternative history of the hostility between them. According to his retelling, friendship quickly bloomed between them after their first meeting in 1883 and, what's more, Bloch even relied on Rodkinson's knowledge and experience in fighting antisemitism.[225] The rift between them was made when Bloch refused to publish a review of Rodkinson's book in German on the *Shulhan Arukh* (a detail Bloch himself confirmed), due to his Orthodox inclinations and his different understanding of antisemitism and its causes.[226] The rift only grew when Rodkinson joined with a number of Bloch's political opponents from within the Jewish community.[227] From that point on Bloch found reasons to oppose Rodkinson in other areas as well, as when he angrily tried to cancel the printing of *Ha-Kol* over Rodkinson's publishing of a Frankist manuscript from Jellinek,[228] and before long Bloch was accusing Rodkinson of relations with missionaries and antisemites.

Rodkinson's response was to initiate a court inquiry to bring the truth to light.[229] He analyzed Bloch's essays against him in great detail and refuted the accusations one by one, concluding his words with an emotional call to his readers to judge for themselves who was right based on their own readings of his books.[230] He was certain that the unbiased reader would be convinced that the truth was on his side and see that all the slander against him arose purely from fear and jealousy. He vowed that he would not flinch before his opponents and would continue in his literary pursuits.[231]

Rodkinson's arguments were well received in the world of Hebrew journalism; some journalists even expressed their anger at Bloch for being so quick to accuse Rodkinson, even if they themselves felt no great love for him and his unusual work.[232] Nevertheless, the seed of doubt had been sown. Even David Gordon, who had studied the events carefully and who, as editor of *Ha-Magid*, gave ample room to articles in defense of Rodkinson and his fellows, could not hold back from making certain implications. While praising Bloch's campaign against Rohling, he raised the matter of the unknown figure "R.," "the identity of whom remains shrouded in mystery to this day," commenting:

> Rabbi Bloch, and after him Dr. Hirsch Hildesheimer, the printer of *Die Yiddishe Presse* in Berlin, wrote that this "R." is Rodkinson, the well-known printer of *Ha-Kol*—he and none other—saying that among all the allies of Rohling there is no one conversant in the books of the Kabbalists whose last name begins with "R.," and Rodkinson was one of the first to rush to the study of the Kabbalah, before he became a proponent of reform. Rodkinson denies the matter and shouts that they have accused him for no reason. Only God knows the truth![233]

Those who were already inclined to see Rodkinson negatively were not moved by his arguments in *Barkai*. So, for example, in a review of the piece in *Kol Mahzikei ha-Dat* (Voice of the Defenders of the Religion), the anonymous author derided the piece, "which in our opinion will be the first and last of its kind," since "in truth it was created only as a way for its printer to take vengeance on his enemies and to quarrel with his opponent Dr. Bloch," concluding that "there is no blessing in this Michael turned Samael." It even seems, in fact, as if the author had not read Rodkinson's arguments at all, taking them instead as a confession:

> Whoever reads his words with attention will find no contradiction at all with the accusations of the great sages of Ashkenaz calling him a missionary and antisemite. Rodkinson has accomplished nothing besides informing the public of exactly which respected and well-known figures have, in unison, written against him, to the shame of his father who rests in Jerusalem and to the disgrace of his saintly mother.[234]

As an abridgement of the Hebrew language *Barkai*, Rodkinson printed that same year a sixteen-page special edition in German titled *Wahrheit gegen Lüge* (Truth against Lie), in which he gave a detailed summary of the various essays he had written in a number of languages, revisiting his essential arguments against Bloch, Kohen-Tsedek, and Zederbaum.[235] Here, too, we can sense the passion with which Rodkinson responded to the accusations of collaborating with Rohling. Shortly afterward, he printed another special edition of *Barkai*, reusing the subtitle *Light on the Eastern Horizon!*[236] He hoped to publish a new edition each month and promised all presubscribers a free copy of the German pamphlet *Wahrheit gegen Lüge.* This second edition of *Barkai* included various essays on Jewish studies, such as the beginning of the autobiography of Salomon Maimon, translated by Shlomo P. Berman (published previously in *Ha-Kol*), alongside essays discussing the Bloch-Rohling affair, now written in a more moderate style, such as the complimentary review of the German book by Yosef Kopp, who represented Bloch in the Rohling trial.[237] Rodkinson praised the author for revealing Rohling's perjury in misrepresenting Jewish texts, calling Kopp "a savior of Judaism and Jewish literature from the lies that have been printed in countless examples and spread throughout the world" and "a deadly plague on antisemitism."[238] This did not mean that Rodkinson was done attacking Bloch, however: he argued that, even if he was right in his case against Rohling, Bloch was not much better than his opponent, and that it was the way of history to fell one wicked man with another. Evoking the language of the Book of Esther, he wrote that Rohling had fallen

> at the hands of a man as wicked as he from head to toe, identical to him in every detail—for Bloch, too, "the LORD hath made for His own purpose, for the day of evil"—for no one was willing to muddy himself by wrestling with this contemptible [Rohling] until this shameless [Bloch] arose. But, as our sages said, "let the miracle come, no matter how," even at the hands of a Ben Talmion whom divine providence arranged in its mercy for this poor and persecuted

> people. Heaven forbid we be ungrateful to him; rather, we too shall proclaim, "May Bloch, too, be remembered for good."[239]

An additional reference to Bloch appears in a brief essay citing Jellinek's denial of any claim between Rohling and Rodkinson and proposing a fine solution to the meaning of the mysterious "R." that appeared in Rohling's letter, the only "proof" linking the two men: it did not refer to Rodkinson at all, but to Rome.[240] The two special editions of *Barkai* were not widely distributed; it even seems that their circulation was entirely forbidden in Russia.[241] Nevertheless, Rodkinson found a way to distribute them worldwide.

One of the articles in the second issue of *Barkai* portrayed the biblical patriarchs as merchants and Maskilim, a portrayal that Bloch interpreted as repeating depictions of the Jews as bearers of capitalism by contemporary antisemites.[242] It is clear, however, that it was not Rodkinson's statements about Abraham that angered Bloch but rather his criticism of Bloch and his role in the Rohling affair. The newspaper *Ha-Tsvi* (The Hind), which was happy to review the Rodkinson-Bloch affair, recounted that Rodkinson's fierce tone was part of a ploy to force Bloch to agree to a public trial, in which Rodkinson hoped to reveal the truth to the public—a reversal of what Bloch had done with Rohling.[243] No such trial ever occurred, however, and the whole affair was cut short when Rodkinson's past came back to haunt him.

Events from the original dispute with Bloch continued to create problems for Rodkinson. Even if he had succeeded in disproving any connection to Rohling, the rumor had already spread that his flight from Russia nearly a decade earlier had been to escape charges of forgery, a charge for which he was arrested and investigated. Bloch reported that news of Rodkinson's political agitating in Koenigsberg and Vienna had spread to St. Petersburg; this spurred an announcement by the Vienna police on March 9, 1887, stating, "By judicial order following a court-ordered investigation, the writer Alter Shmidrov Frumkin has been arrested. Born in Warsaw, Russia, he currently resides in Brigittenau district [Vienna] under the name Michael Louis Rodkinson, wanted by the court in St. Petersburg for the crime of forgery and sentenced to jail."[244] In the newspaper *Ha-Magid* the following brief announcement appeared:

> A righteous man is caught up in the iniquity of the generation: On the ninth of this month Herr Michael Levi Rodkinson (who for a number of years published the journal *Ha-Kol*, and was previously known as Alter Frumkin), was taken into custody by order of the court and put under guard. According to all Hebrew and German journals, Herr Rodkinson was arrested at the request of the judges in St. Petersburg, who have been seeking him a number of years after his conviction by a Russian court of forging documents and sentencing in 1875 to one year of labor in the czar's labor force, and his subsequent flight from Russia. He has since settled in Koenigsberg, Hamburg, and Berlin, and for the past number of years Vienna, without having informed the local police of his residence there, and has been considering emigration to America.[245]

Following the arrest, the German papers in Vienna allocated substantial copy space to analyses of Rodkinson's character based on different episodes from second- and third-hand accounts (most of them by Zederbaum, Deinard, or Kohen-Tsedek)—some of which were accurate but most of which were total fabrications. Rodkinson blamed acquaintances of Bloch for the slander and attributed the dispute not to his record, which he claimed was clean, but to personal disagreements.[246] In any case, Rodkinson was acquitted and released from custody after a brief incarceration during which no charges could be proven against him, and the entire episode was forgotten.[247] After these confrontations, however, Rodkinson gave up hope for his work's success in Europe and, after brief stays in Vilna and London, made the choice in late 1888 to immigrate to America.

The New Talmud and Reform Activities in the New Land: New York, Chicago, and Boston

A number of writers arrived along with Rodkinson from Europe to America that same year, bringing their running argument with them.

These included Ze'ev Schorr, who had arrived some months earlier and immediately resumed his criticism of Rodkinson; and Ephraim Deinard,[248] who described Rodkinson's emigration to the New Land in the following way:

> He saw from afar another land spread out before him, a rich and spacious land, a land to which all those baptized in the name of the son of Miriam [Jesus] in London turned for help. Their calls to the American missionaries were not in vain; many Reform Jews stand today with one foot already at the church house door. And so one bright day in 1888, Rodkinson appeared in New York, and the mission's journal *Edut le-Israel* (Witness to Israel) cried out "Hooray!" Rodkinson had appeared in all his glory, spreading the gospel among Israel. For me, on the other hand, he had spread a net, saying, "This Deinard, bitter enemy of the servants of the Messiah and their persecutor in Russia, has now come to America."[249]

Unsatisfied, Deinard repeated the charge that Rodkinson had served as a teacher to Rohling and was cooperating with the mission in London, and proclaimed that the mission in New York was eagerly awaiting his arrival, printing the claims in one of the first editions of *Ha-Leumi* he edited, printed on December 14, 1888, close to Rodkinson's arrival. Deinard feared his evil influence so greatly that he felt the need to warn "our innocent brothers" of America not to fall into his trap.[250] In another article he hinted at Rodkinson in speaking about his opponents "who had been vomited out by their European homelands, and there was no one in the land who knew them and their names except the bailiff at the jail, or those who frequented the doors of donors in the Old Country, and when they came to the New Country boasted at having done great things."[251] He would later present "The Chronicles of Samael" in great depth, portraying Rodkinson as an ally of the antisemites and an apostate who, once "the waves of the sea had cast him upon the shore of America," began immediately to spread "the sermons of Delitzsch his master and Rohling his student, while every scoundrel and good-for-nothing, every false prophet and rabble-rouser, every friend to the London missionaries was gathered unto him."[252]

Behind Deinard's words we find another piece of the story: the criticism he himself had received in the Hebrew missionaries' journal *Edut le-Israel*. The journal ran a long article on Deinard, serialized over 1888 and 1889, mentioning along the way a number of less-than-flattering episodes from his time in Eastern Europe and portraying him as "a doomsayer who has never known peace, born to incite quarrels" and full of "snake's venom and spite." The anonymous writer also mentioned the Rohling affair and argued against Deinard as if on Rodkinson's behalf, refuting the charges of his collaboration with the missionaries.[253] It was certainly easy for Deinard to connect Rodkinson to the article and its source, portraying him as one of the mission's many heads.[254]

We find a similar tone in correspondence between Deinard and Ze'ev Schorr from the early 1890s, describing Rodkinson as "Rohling's master" who aimed to publish a newspaper that would serve as "the organ of the missionaries." This criticism only gained strength with Rodkinson's successful revival of *Ha-Kol* in America:[255] Deinard repeated it in every newspaper that he edited, while Schorr went so far as to dedicate an entire special edition of *Ha-Pisgah* (The Summit) to blackening Rodkinson's name with such "facts," describing him as "a drunken Cossack," "a Hasid, a Mitnaged, a religious reformer, a nihilist, an anarchist, a missionary, and an antisemite." Deinard crowed about the issue:

> This week a special edition of *Ha-Pisgah* has come out against the owner of *Ha-Kol*, showing everyone this man's true nature and his true intent, although for the Russian Jews and especially the Hebrew-readers among them this is no news. The reformers became believers in this son of Rodke, and for such as these we must make it clear that it is a crime to associate with him. And the names of his supporters will go down in disgrace in the history of the Jews in the United States.[256]

Despite the ferocity of such attacks, Rodkinson renewed his journalistic activities, fearing neither failure nor the sting of his longtime opponents. He founded *Ha-Kol* anew, vowing that it would "conquer the Jewish world"; once again he stressed its ideological and political neutrality, stating that his only agenda was "to unite the separated." The paper was published serially between the years 1889 and 1893, first in New York and then Chicago.[257] Despite the financial support of a number of Reform rabbis, he did not have the means to publish the paper continuously, and it never achieved the same circulation it had enjoyed in Eastern Europe. After twenty-one editions, the paper fell into bankruptcy due to lack of subscribers (a fate similar to Deinard's *Ha-Leumi*, published at the same time, which folded after its twenty-third edition). In order to satisfy the subscribers who had not received all the yearly issues, Rodkinson printed a supplement titled *Tchunat Ruah ha-Israeli* (The Israelite Spirit, 1889), and Rodkinson noted at its beginning that from then on he would publish the articles that had not been printed in full in *Ha-Kol* in a special edition. He also accused 500 nonpaying recipients of the paper of bringing about its downfall, declaring, "Every single one will carry the blame when the Hebrew language no longer bears fruit in America."[258]

The single edition that he printed consisted of two of his own essays. The first was titled "Tehunat Ruah ha-Israeli," which had been published a number of years before, in slightly different form, as the lead article in *Barkai*; it had been fiercely attacked then by Joseph S. Bloch. The second essay was a homily for the holiday of Shavuot, 1889, in which Rodkinson revived the utopian ideal of religious reform while criticizing its current proponents, writing, "The reformers have acted without general agreement between them, each building a pulpit for himself according to his heart's desire and not according to the Torah of Moses nor the Talmud." These words served as an opening to a broader attack against reformers as a group, targeting the "reformers" and the "radical Maskilim" together with the "Orthodox."[259]

In New York, Rodkinson reprinted those books of Yiddish popular literature he had tried to publish in the 1870s—"good stories in the jargon spoken among our brothers here," such as the novel by Isaac Meir Dik mentioned above. This earned him a substantial income, and Rodkinson stated that he intended to publish two or three novels of this sort every month, including one by Perets Smolenskin.[260] It is safe to assume that he published a number of other chapbooks in Yiddish at the same time but omitted his name as printer.

In 1890 Rodkinson also launched a new paper by the name of *Ha-Sanegor* (The Defender), but it did not last long; only sixteen issues were printed, despite advertisements for the new paper made with his brother's help in *Ha-Havatselet*.[261] The bibliographer A. R. Malachi, who dedicated a detailed study to the short-lived paper, dubbed it, with some justification, "among the sorriest Hebrew papers in America"; nevertheless, he came to Rodkinson's defense and wrote that most of the charges leveled against him were total fabrications, such as his alleged connections with missionaries and antisemites and the stories circulated by Deinard about his shady love affairs.[262]

In 1894 Rodkinson tried again, planning a monthly titled *Asefat Chachamim*, the same name as the socialist paper he had printed in Koenigsberg. Even though he succeeded in acquiring a number of poems and essays, however, he did not manage to publish even a single issue.[263] It seems that he continued his attempts to found papers in Yiddish and English throughout the 1890s, even purchasing a printing house for the purpose, but his plans never materialized;[264] these false starts in the New Land read like a parody of his successes in Koenigsberg. One thing was common to both periods, however—his literary activities were always accompanied by personal controversy.

The competition among Hebrew and Yiddish papers in America was intense, and Rodkinson found himself matched against familiar competitors from his days in Eastern Europe, among them Ze'ev Schorr, editor of *Ha-Pisgah* and *Hathiyah*; Ephraim Deinard, who published *Ha-Leumi*; and Katriel Tsvi Sharhazon, the owner of the *Tagblat* (The Daily Post), *Yudishe Gazeten* (Jewish Gazette), and *Ha-Ivri* (The Hebrew). Most of the papers were not long-lived, and the more successful among them were dedicated to mutual mudslinging, often accomplished through biting satire and sarcasm. It seems, in fact, that there was not a single issue of a Hebrew paper in America during those years in which Rodkinson was not disparaged. In this context we can understand the illustrated satire by Ephraim Deinard on Hebrew papers in America, *Sefer ha-Ploiderzak, o Meorat Tzefaunim* (The Chatterbox, or Vipers' Den, 1890), parts of which had been published a year earlier in *Ha-Leumi*.[265] An American version of Josef Perl's satire *Megaleh Temirin* (Revealer of Secrets), the book was written in the style of Hasidic texts, with the names of Deinard's targets encoded in acronyms and gematria. Rodkinson merited several pages in a section titled "These Are the Chronicles of Samael," which included rumors about his connections with missionaries and antisemites as well as his shady affairs with women.[266] Eliezer Raphael Malachi epitomized the situation of Hebrew papers in America at that time by citing Ephraim Deinard's *Ha-Leumi* and Rodkinson's *Ha-Kol*, describing the papers as "filled with quarrels, recriminations, slander, and mudslinging," and their owners as intractable quarrelers who had brought their squabbles to America after being expelled from Europe.[267]

An identical picture appears in contemporary foreign sources. In a study on journalism in the Cracow paper *Ha-Magid le-Israel* (Preacher to Israel), for example, the anonymous author wrote condescendingly that "the havoc of Hebrew literature has grown in America, where it increases in breadth but not in depth." While describing the internal debates and quarrels filling American journals, the author went on to mention the trials of the new publicists of "the apostate Rodkinson (the brother of the Hasid and former heretic—Rabbi Dov Frumkin, owner of *Ha-Havatselet* in Jerusalem), whose name is already nearly forgotten from the writers' market."[268] The newspaper editors in America once again explained what little gratitude they received for their work and how hard it was in the New Land. So wrote Samuel Benjamin Shwarzberg, the editor of *Ner Ha-Ma'aravi* (Western Light), a special issue recounting the hardships of printing (or in his own words: "a faithful portrayal of the condition of our literature in the New Land and the relationship of the People of the Book to it"). Among other things, he wrote about the work of an editor, which "does not provide delicacies and which has the potential to satisfy its workers with road signs to weaken its powers and to harass it out of the world"; and that "in a land of such gluttony and indulgence and animal pleasures, where each man pursues his own profit and chases his own lusts," they pay no attention to the fate of the Hebrew language. The efforts might have been more successful had philanthropists supported the papers in a more organized fashion so that "the company of supporters" would have been paid back what was owed, and had the papers not been filled with vanities and quarrels.[269]

Whether due to personal quarrels or to public apathy toward his agenda, Rodkinson's attempts at Hebrew journalism in America met with failure, and so he decided to switch to writing in English. His first book in English, titled *The History of Amulets, Charms, and Talismans: A Historical Investigation into Their Nature and Origin*, and dedicated to Aaron Jellinek, was published in New York in 1893, and dealt with the history of amulets, spells, and talismanic magic.[270] He recounted that he came to write the book after his studies of the commandment of *tefillin* and the responses to his Hebrew book *Tefilah le-Mosheh*. While that book had touched on the roots of the commandment and its connection to amulets, here he deepened his treatment; what's more, the Reformist polemics disappeared and in their place was a historical-philological study.[271] At the start of the book he reviewed the responses to his book *Tefilah le-Mosheh*, providing a long list of journals that had referenced it. At the same time he expressed his regret that up to that point the book had not merited a serious review by the Maskilim, much less the Orthodox community. If they would not critique the book, Rodkinson stated, he would do so himself, judging anew the ideas he had raised. The fault that he found in his own work was the lack of historical analysis, a fault that, at the advice of Shlomoh Rubin, he decided to address in a new series of books.[272]

Toward similar ends he published a number of essays in the journal *American Hebrew*, among them an English essay about the

Karaites.[273] An additional booklet was printed in Chicago in 1894 titled *The Pentateuch, Its Languages and Its Characters: A Treatise upon the Original Language and the Early Translations of the Pentateuch into Greek and Aramaic*, bearing a dedication to the London Reform rabbi David Wolf Marx, thanking him for his help in the 1880s; it discussed the Torah and its various translations.[274] These subjects, which Rodkinson had already treated more fully in his Hebrew books, were now presented in a historical overview written without the earlier polemical tone. The only controversy noticeable in the book is in statements against the German scholars who themselves derided Russian Jews from "the East" who now pursued their scholarship in English in America.[275]

Without a doubt, the publication of these books cost Rodkinson dearly. In a letter to Moritz Lazarus he lamented his situation, writing, "It was God's will, with which I will not argue, that I was forced to sell all my household goods, even the pillows and quilts from my bed, and thanks to God my wife did not stop me—and yet it was still a struggle, for I was besieged by troubles, and my eyes nearly rotted in their sockets." The melodrama notwithstanding, Rodkinson doubtlessly faced different hardships than he had in Europe.[276]

To the last book Rodkinson appended a chapter from a Hebrew work on the Talmud; and on the dust cover he wrote that he possessed a second volume of *The History of Amulets*, composed of 200 pages. The two works mentioned were never published, and it seems that he decided to focus on the project in which he had invested much of his energy since he had arrived in America—an abridged version of the Talmud. As early as the 1880s Rodkinson had proposed such a plan; now in America he raised the idea of publishing an English translation of the same version. This was an interesting challenge; according to Rodkinson, any translation of the Talmud was impossible without first drastically editing and abridging the text to befit the new era. He presented his plan for such a project in an essay in *Ner ha-Ma'aravi*, listing two goals: "to purify the Talmud of all extraneous content" and "to make it both suitable and worthwhile for translation into a modern language."[277] In 1895 he proposed a similar plan, now framed in the context of religious reform, in an English essay that earned positive responses in a number of papers.[278]

After making his proposal in the press, Rodkinson presented the actual work: the first volume of his Talmud "for the new age," a dual-language edition of Tractate Rosh Hashannah, was published in 1895; and Tractate Kiddushin was released as a second volume in 1896 (the remaining volumes were published in English only).[279] The translation, as noted on the front page, was done by the Reform rabbi Leonard I. Levi and the final editing by Rodkinson; their portraits were displayed at the beginning of the first volume. Isaac Mayer Wise checked the quality of the translation and then gave his sanction to the project, praising the writer at every opportunity as "a great Talmudist" whose work was trustworthy, and providing Rodkinson with a number of letters of recommendation so that American libraries would subscribe to the entire series.[280]

At the opening of the first volume Rodkinson restated the importance of a new and abridged version of the Talmud in silencing those who would condemn the book and the Jews along with it. He revisited the essential arguments of his Hebrew pamphlets from the 1880s and described his methodology in great detail.[281] In the end of the introduction he expressed his gratitude to those who had proofread and corrected the book, and presented a number of letters sent to him over the past decades from such figures as Moritz Lazarus, Meir Ish Shalom, Binyamin Ze'ev Landau, Marcus Jastrow, Isaac Mayer Wise, Benjamin Szold, and Bernhard Felsenthal, who had written to him personally in support of the project.[282] Rodkinson sent a number of copies of the new edition to writers in Eastern Europe who had supported the plan; these included Salomon Buber, whom he also asked to express his opinion on the idea in theory and in practice.[283] He tried to sign presubscribers for the forthcoming volumes (which would appear in three separate series: a dual-language edition, a Hebrew edition, and an English edition), meeting with some success.

It seems that Rodkinson planned to print the coming volumes with the New Amsterdam Book Company: in 1896 the firm printed a special issue with samples of his dual-language work, a list of presubscribers, and evaluations of Rodkinson's work as editor. Rodkinson was named as the project's editor-in-chief, while the list of translators included rabbis and scholars such as Josef Stolz, Louis Grossman, and Isaac Mayer Wise (who was responsible for the overall quality of the translation), as well as one of Rodkinson's own sons, Norbert M. Rodkinson. The series was meant to consist of between ten and twelve large volumes;[284] the first volume, printed in 1896, contained an English version of Tractate Shabbat without parallel Hebrew text (after which began a new numbering of the volumes).[285]

It seems that the plan quickly changed, however, and Rodkinson founded an independent company named "The New Talmud Publishing Company" with the aim of enlisting money and presubscribers. A special advance copy printed by the company in 1898 announced a new format for the project, with the English translation at the center of the page in larger format. The special issue presented examples of the work (now only in English) with, once again, praises of the earlier volumes and a list of positive references from the daily press.[286] Rodkinson was presented in all the issues as one of the great scholars of the Talmud and his name was inevitably followed by the title "Doctor of Theology" (a title picked up by the English daily press and included in most of his published articles as well).

While "The New Talmud" did not go without critical praise, most of the press was negative, including harsh attacks launched against the project immediately upon the release of the first volume. Some of the condemnations were attached to Rodkinson's adventures in Europe, and his erstwhile opponents from his days in Europe raised their heads once again, broadcasting the old accusations of Rodkinson's connections with Rohling and his involvement with missionaries. The criticism was extensive enough that one of his sons was compelled to draft a letter in his father's defense, citing a translation of Adolf (Aaron) Jellinek's statement from the 1890s denying all connection with Rohling, while Isaac Mayer Wise decried all of Rodkinson's slanderers as reactionary Orthodox Jews who feared the radical conclusions that arose from his various studies.[287]

In this environment, Deinard's and Schorr's newspapers became an open arena for attacks on Rodkinson and his project, most of which were aimed not at the quality of the work but at the character of its author. Yosef Leib Friedkin, for example, called the work an "abomination" born of Rodkinson's own iniquity, crying out, "*He* shall provide you with 'The New Talmud'? He, who has profaned the honor of all Israel with his abominations, could do no more for the Talmud than clap it in irons and desecrate it before the nations!" Hillel Malachowsky spoke about Rodkinson's affinity for those he referred to as "the dead Hasidim" and portrayed the whole endeavor as an attempt to spread Hasidism in the New Land.[288] Others hewed slightly closer to the details of the work itself in their criticism, noting, for example, that the translation was full of gross errors and was not even Rodkinson's own work (a fact that Rodkinson himself made clear at the start of each volume and in his essays on the Talmud).[289] On the other hand, another of his opponents charged that Rodkinson had previously translated the entire text into Yiddish, from which translation the final English version was produced by a committee of writers.[290] Others argued that, while the idea was a worthy one, it would be better realized by "a gathering of the greatest minds of the age, or at least someone besides this man who is not even a rabbi and whose profession is not the Torah."[291]

Leading the criticism of the project were Judah David (Julius) Eisenstein, Nehemiah Shmuel Leibowitz, and Ephraim Deinard, who saw the entire project as taking aim at the authority of the Talmud and the Halachah as part of the Reformist agenda, and they pointed out the Reformist biases in the translation.[292] In a series of essays, Eisenstein conducted a detailed study of the defects of the translation in the two dual-language volumes about to be printed, pointing out several errors and textual corruptions.[293] According to Nehemiah Shmuel Leibowitz, Rodkinson's work made it clear that "he has not even the most basic understanding" of the Talmud; Leibowitz criticized Rodkinson for being too quick to cut the text[294] and called on all the projects' backers to withdraw their support, as when he wrote to Salomon Buber: "With all my heart I wish to spread Talmudic literature among our brothers and fellow Jews here in our new land; but many are those who rebel and scheme against me—such as these have come to quarrel not only with me but with Talmudic Judaism itself . . . let sin cease from the earth."[295]

Leibowitz succeeded in convincing a good many of Rodkinson's supporters to withdraw their support, including some who were not opposed to the idea of an abridgement and translation of the Talmud. For example, in the journal *Ner ha-Ma'aravi*, which published both Eisenstein's critiques and Rodkinson's response, Leibowitz brought a batch of letters from the likes of Meir Ish Shalom, Kaufmann Kohler, and Bernhard Felsenthal, the very scholars whose backing Rodkinson had touted at the start of the first volume.[296] In another issue he presented a letter from Shlomoh Rubin, who had been close with Rodkinson at different stages in his life, calling the work meaningless "prattle" and arguing that "if everyone who doesn't understand something in the Mishnah or Gemara declares it a fraud and erases it, then the unfortunate Talmud will be left bare from one end to the other; there is no end to such a matter."[297] Kaufmann Kohler, who had certainly been influenced by Eisenstein's and Leibowitz's statements, went even further and wrote a detailed critique of the first volume he saw in English (Tractate Shabbat), concluding: "This work is a disgrace to Jewish studies in America and it is a sin to encourage it or support it."[298] Meanwhile Rodkinson carried on with his work, pausing only to respond with timely but moderate rejoinders.[299] The damage inflicted by the criticism, however, was severe, and Rodkinson lost many of his supporters. He himself reported that the Jewish Publication Society of America had refused to finance him—despite the warm recommendations he had received and his own fervent pleas—due to the unjustified criticism leveled against him by his Orthodox opponents.[300]

Rodkinson's critics were justified in claiming that his translation was far from accurate and unfaithful to the original text, a criticism emphasized by modern scholars as well. This should come as no surprise, though, since Rodkinson's stated aim was not to present the original text at all but rather to create, in his own words, an "Old-New" Talmud rewritten to suit the spirit of the times—a "corrected" text to support the religious reforms he had been calling for since the 1880s that could also serve in the fight against the antisemites who armed themselves with excerpts from the Talmud. It was a far cry from other translations made in response to modern antisemitism, such as the literal translation into German by Lazaras (Eliezer) Goldschmidt.[301] Rodkinson's translation was in fact part of an anthology project and edited according to different criteria. The choice to direct criticism against not only the many errors found in Rodkinson's translation but against Rodkinson's own colorful life shifted the focus from the work and its goal—turning the Talmud into a living text for the modern Jew.[302]

Having lost so many of his supporters, Rodkinson was forced to significantly limit the scope of his project, abandoning the dual-language edition with its parallel Hebrew text. The full English edition, however, was published in New York in eighteen volumes between 1896 and 1903.[303] To these volumes Rodkinson appended two volumes of essays on the history of the Talmud: its inherent creativity, its reception, criticism of it from various sides, and a review of all translations across the generations.[304] It seems that this was the only project in his life that Rodkinson succeeded in completing, even if in the end only a third of the Talmud was translated. With the completion of the project (and shortly before Rodkinson's death), the New Talmud Publishing Company released a brochure including a table of contents for the coming volumes, a long list of supporters and pre-subscribers, a facsimile of Moritz Lazarus's 1902 letter in praise of the project, and a detailed portrait of Rodkinson beside a facsimile of the prize he received in 1900 for "the first translation of the Talmud into a modern language."[305]

Rodkinson's final years in America were fraught not only with controversy but also with a keen sense of loneliness, evident in his many letters to friends and acquaintances from Eastern Europe who had also come to the New Land. In one of them he invited his friend Avraham Dov Dubzhevitz to share "a Hasidish drink," "the kind we used to drink in Russia before the circle dances on Shmini Atseret night," while in another he pleaded with his friend to help him bury the wife of his youth.[306] Another time Rodkinson begged the help of Judah Leib Sossnitz in the ceremonial letting of a drop of blood for the son born to him in his old age (born without a foreskin, the boy could not undergo circumcision). He wrote that this custom was very important to him, "even if I am not careful with other laws for obvious reasons," but that he feared to ask any aid regarding a ritual matter from the mohels of the city, who harbored no love for him.[307] The extent of Rodkinson's dislocation from the worlds in which he had lived is evident in a letter he wrote to Salomon Buber, with whom he had kept in close contact over the years: he told his old friend that, "due to all of my involvement in my work [of translating the Talmud], I am left with no time to read the Hebrew papers, and I lack all knowledge of goings-on in Europe."[308]

In these personal letters, as in others from the same period that remain in archives, Rodkinson expressed a sense of longing for and exile from the cultural world of Eastern Europe in which he had once bloomed. Despite his prediction that the Hebrew language and its literature had no place in the modern world and would in fact disappear within a few years,[309] shortly before his death he wrote to Nahum Sokolow that he longed for it still, and that his wish was "to join in a great work of Hebrew literature." Sokolow summarized:

> Finally, in his old age, all the facades have fallen away—even the name Rodkinson has fallen away—and all that is left is an old Jew from the old study hall who was once named Frumkin. An old Jew who loved to write Hebrew, and was forced to suffer in some place called America, to toil away at the translation of the Talmud into English—in short, he lost his mind![310]

Rodkinson's wish to return to the world of Hebrew letters, or more precisely his plea not to be erased from it, is just as clear in his choice to include in one of the volumes of his *New Talmud* a list of all his writings from his days as a Hasid until his coming to America; the list even mentioned unpublished pieces still in his valise, including an eight-act drama about the patriarch Abraham and a Hebrew autobiography. These compositions have since been lost.[311]

Morris Winchevsky, one of the regular contributors to *Ha-Kol* and *Ha-Kol la-Am* and editor of *Asefat Chachamim*, described Rodkinson as offering up his whole world "on the altar of the press."[312] Winchevsky's words ring true. All the days of his life, wherever he found himself, Rodkinson devoted his time and energy to writing and publishing in Hebrew, Yiddish, German, and English.

Frumkin-Rodkinson died at his home in New York on January 6, 1904, from pneumonia, at the age of fifty-nine.[313] Obituaries in the English press mentioned primarily his Talmudic project and crowned him with the name "grandfather of the Russian Maskilim in New York." A brief announcement in his memory in *Luah Achi'asaf* (Tablet of Achiassaf) closes with the words, "He was a tireless worker, a long-suffering man, and a wanderer all his days."[314] The words Rodkinson wrote upon the death of Perets Smolenskin are fitting to his own life: "Those who enter into Hebrew literature return not to a life of equanimity and honor, but rather to a life of wandering and an ignoble death in a strange and foreign land; such is the fate of a Hebrew writer."[315]

2 The Beginnings of Hasidic Hagiography

If the name of Rodkinson is known in America today, it is mostly due to his English edition of the Talmud, ubiquitous despite its many failings, and for the fierce attacks launched against him by such critics as Ephraim Deinard. Rodkinson's *New Talmud* was the only major project he ever completed in his lifetime and, despite all the criticism, its impact on the English-speaking public was significant. In the Jewish Orthodox community, the name Rodkinson (or, more accurately, Frumkin) is well known for an entirely different body of work: the Hasidic collections he published. These books continue to be printed in our own time and by now have seen dozens of editions, at times issued anonymously. The influence of his books is evident not only on Hasidic writers but also on those who later dipped their Romantic pails into the wells of this literature—such writers as I. L. Peretz, Shmuel Josef Agnon, and Martin Buber. Rodkinson's own tendencies were of an entirely different nature from both his Orthodox contemporaries and these Romantic writers of the early twentieth century.

Throughout the many twists and turns of Rodkinson's life, a concern with Hasidism seems to have been a common thread. Though his relationship with Hasidism changed from one period to the next, he never ceased writing about it in one form or another. In the following two chapters I have attempted to throw some light on Rodkinson's life story as it relates to his ever-changing relationship with Hasidism, analyzing the central trends of his Hasidic literary works and their impact on the world of Hasidism and beyond. As in his other endeavors, in his Hasidic writing Rodkinson was a pioneer as both a stylist and a publisher—and, just as in those other endeavors, his pioneering spirit aroused much controversy. This chapter in his life is one of the most fascinating in the history of Hasidic literature, and one of the most important for our understanding of the complex relationship between Hasidism, Haskalah, and modernization in Eastern Europe.

The Imagined Sanctity of *Shivhei ha-Besht* and the Silence of Print

The year 1814 marked the beginning of the printed Hasidic tale, for that year saw the publication of the book *Shivhei ha-Besht* (In Praise of the Baal Shem Tov), a collection of hagiographic tales about the mythic life of Rabbi Israel Baal Shem Tov and a number of figures surrounding him. While several editions of the book, in both Hebrew and Yiddish, were printed between 1814 and 1860, during that time we find a parallel "silence" of almost fifty years in which no other book of Hasidic hagiography was printed.[1] This fact does not indicate, as some have written, the marginal place of such literature in that period. On the contrary, to a large extent, the essential experience of Hasidism was grounded in stories and sermons that were first delivered orally and only later put into writing (a process similar to that undergone by the tales of *Shivhei ha-Besht*).[2] What's more, we find traces of such stories in print even before 1814, and many homiletical works printed afterward included short tales.[3] The existence of hagiographic tales in this stage of the Hasidic movement is also confirmed by anti-Hasidic literature of the time, which mentioned (with derision) the many stories circulating orally. This literature provides us with records not only of true stories but also of new wonder tales being created, wherein true events were exaggerated in their retelling. The power of these stories, whether told or read, was recognized by the Maskilim, who continually sought to counter that power.[4] Such facts indicate that, even if entire collections of hagiographic tales were not being printed, the stories were being told and set down during the so-called period of silence, and a closer look will reveal the extent of the tales' role in the social and ideological development of Hasidism.

That being said, the lacuna in the printing of this literature demands our attention, as does the sudden explosion that occurred in the 1860s—a phenomenon in which Michael Levi Rodkinson played a key role. One explanation for the nearly fifty-year-long "silence" in printing suggested by Joseph Dan was that the aura of *Shivhei ha-Besht* was so great that none dared compete with it. Other explanations offered by him were pressure from censors; the logistical difficulties of printing Hasidic books; and the ridicule the Maskilim poured on *Shivhei ha-Besht*, which might have left the Hasidic community hesitant to print new stories and open themselves up to more such ridicule. Like Dan, Chone Shmeruk claimed that we can attribute the silence in part to criticism of *Shivhei ha-Besht*, pointing out that this criticism often came from within the Hasidic camp.[5] Dan himself, however, wrote that these explanations cannot completely account for the extended silence, and he concluded that the question remains an open one.[6]

It is difficult to accept these explanations, even with Dan's qualifier. First of all, fear of criticism could not have been the preventive factor, since hagiographic tales were included in many homiletical books from the same period, and they were continuously being told orally as well. Discomfort, if there was any, was a personal matter, and did not prevent the printing of such a popular literary genre. Second, it is untenable that censorial pressure was able to silence the presses, since despite other obstacles collections of Hasidic homilies were being printed; if the Hasidim had wished, they would have found a way around the censors for their hagiographic works as well. Third, Zeev Gries has already claimed in his detailed studies on the character and role of hagiographic literature that there is no reason to ascribe the "silence" to any sense of "the sanctity of the book." Gries argued that we should look instead to the historical circumstances surrounding the appearance and development of the genre and the new possibilities provided by the Hebrew press.[7]

Taking a different angle, Yehoshua Mondshine criticized the very way the question of the "silence" was posed, claiming that it was based on false assumptions about the place of hagiographic literature in Hasidic life. His criticism was particularly sharp against such researchers as Simon Dubnow and Chone Shmeruk. In his opinion, "the sanctity of the book," or any reference to *Shivhei ha-Besht* as "holy scriptures," was the creation of Josef Perl, the author of *Megaleh Temirin* (Revealer of Secrets). This mislabeling, he contended, was accepted by modern scholars, especially Dubnow in his book *Toldot ha-Hasidut* (The History of Hasidism).[8] Mondshine went on to argue that *Shivhei ha-Besht* played no essential role in the development of Hasidism, and the wonder tales should be seen as "light reading material and not as Hasidic literature," a point of view in line with the late Habad's Hasidic tradition.[9]

Mondshine's contentious claim that modern scholarly research on Hasidism is actually a continuation of nineteenth-century anti-Hasidic satire merits further attention. It is true that Maskilim such as Josef Perl, concerned over the tales' power to seduce new "believers," dedicated much ink to them (and other Hasidic printing ventures) in their attempts to denigrate the movement.[10] Furthermore, as we will see, the Maskilim overestimated the role of *Shivhei ha-Besht* and other books in the spread of Hasidism, a result of their own conceptions of books as agents of change and of the struggle between Hasidism and the Haskalah as a "war of the books."[11]

While the notion of *Shivhei ha-Besht* as a "holy scripture" that imposed a moratorium on further hagiography demands emendation, this is not to say that such tales did not hold a central place in some streams of Hasidism and did not aid in the spread of the movement as a whole. In fact, Mondshine's own claim that hagiography is a low literary form, a folk literature, is itself a Maskilic motif well known since the days of Josef Perl, one that Habad Hasidim internalized in response to criticism of Hasidism.[12] The critiques of

Gries's and Mondshine's arguments notwithstanding, these scholars changed our conception of hagiographic literature and demanded a more nuanced picture of its genesis. The outlines of such a picture begin to appear upon investigation of the literature's "revival" in the 1860s.

The Revival of Hasidic Hagiography in the 1860s

There is no disputing the fact that in the 1860s there occurred a renaissance in the printing of Hasidic tales, one comparable to what occurred in the early twentieth century in Warsaw and Piotrków and in recent decades in Jerusalem and Brooklyn. This renaissance occurred in a number of places, among them Warsaw and Chernovitz.[13] But the most notable location in that period was Lvov (Lemberg),[14] where Michael Levi Rodkinson printed three collections—*Shivhei ha-Rav* (In Praise of the Master), *Eidat Tsadikim* (Community of Holy Men), and *Sippurei Tsadikim* (Tales of the Holy Men)—all published within a short time and in several Hebrew and Yiddish editions, amounting to thousands of copies in total. Aside from *Shivhei ha-Rav*, which contains stories of Rabbi Shneur Zalman of Liady and his disciples, the remaining books were not dedicated to a particular figure, instead containing tales about a number of early Hasidic heroes as well as pre-Hasidic figures.

Rodkinson was not the only one involved in printing hagiographic tales of this type: in this period Menahem Mendel Bodek published the books *Ma'aseh Tsadikim Im Divrei Tsadikim* (Tales of the Holy Men with Sayings of the Holy Men), *Pe'er mi-Kedoshim* (Splendor of the Holy), *Kehal Kedoshim* (Holy Congregation), *Mif'a lot ha-Tsadikim Im Divrei Meisharim* (Wonders of the Holy Men with Upright Sayings), *Seder ha-Dorot he-Hadash* (The New Order of the Generations), and others;[15] the Warsaw bookseller Aharon Walden published a large number of books, including *Kehal Hasidim* (Congregation of the Pious, published anonymously) and *Shem ha-Gedolim he-Hadash* (The New Name of the Greats).[16] According to Walden's own testimony, he printed tens of thousands of copies at a time; it was not for nothing that Ephraim Deinard repeatedly referred to him as "the crazy Hasid."[17] The same period saw the publication of *Sippurei Kedoshim* (Tales of the Holy Ones), a collection of unknown authorship,[18] and the small but important book of praises *Rahamei Av* (A Father's Compassion) by Yaakov Katina.[19] To this list we could add scores of authors and an even larger number of books, all published as part of the same trend (a complete and accurate list of this literature in print has yet to be compiled).[20] Due to a number of factors—some of the books were printed anonymously, some of the authors were not well known, and Rodkinson was among the first to print in this genre—some of these books have been wrongly attributed to Rodkinson (e.g., Aharon Walden's *Kehal Hasidim* and Yaakov Kaidener's *Sippurim Nora'im* [Awesome Tales]). As we will see, however, the primary factor in these false attributions were the waves Rodkinson made when he left Hasidism for the Haskalah a decade later.[21]

From a preliminary review of this rich literature, it seems that the overall intent was not to strengthen a particular court or stream within Hasidism (excepting a number of publications associated with the Habad and Bratslav communities), for most of the books included a variety of stories about holy men from previous generations, in which every new or veteran Hasid could find something of interest. This eclecticism continues until our own day, although since the 1980s a subgenre of the literature has developed of books dedicated to a particular Hasidic rabbi, known as the *tsaddik* (holy man), or to a dynastic line of such rabbis. These books are predominantly written by faithful Hasidim or even personal assistants to the *tsadik*, who convey the mythos of their own master and his court as part of a clear authorial agenda.[22]

It is worth mentioning the particularly notable place held by Habad Hasidism in the printing of hagiographic books. Habad, well aware of the power of the printed word to spread ideas in this age, has taken advantage of the press to spread its teachings (particularly obvious in the "history" of Hasidism that the sixth Lubavitcher Rebbe, Rabbi Yaakov Yosef Schneerson, published at the start of the twentieth century). Abraham Meir Habermann wrote, "Up until today, Habad is set apart from every other Hasidic group in their tremendous diligence and energy in spreading their teachings."[23] Already at an early stage Deinard made a similar observation, even dubbing the Habad Hasidim "Jesuits."[24] Since *Shivhei ha-Besht* this group played an important part in the printing of Hasidic hagiography, and surely Rodkinson, who came from a Habad family, was influenced by this trend.[25] The fact that the Habad Hasidim would later distance themselves from Rodkinson and in some cases from the entire genre of hagiography does not mitigate this early influence. It is also important to remember, of course, that the literary phenomenon was far broader than just the Habad community.

On the "Revival" and Its Causes

There were many factors in the publishing revival of the 1860s. There is no doubt that it was tied to the rapid spread of Hasidism in the second half of the century and the concomitant creation of a new audience for books of Hasidic homilies, and even more so for the collections of wonder tales and hagiographies of famous rabbis. In addition, Zeev Gries has tied the revival in printing hagiographic works to the spread of Romanticism in Europe and to the burgeoning nationalism of the time, which renewed interest in printing national epics and hero tales.

These Romantic trends in Europe at large, along with Maskilic ones within Hebrew literature, had an influence on the Hasidim and their writings as well, so much so that it could be said that the collections of Hasidic tales that appeared from 1864 on were "no more than an adoption of the contemporary literary style of the Maskilim," being "an inseparable part of the contemporaneous development of the Hebrew story and a response to the Haskalah and to new trends in anthologizing, printing, and reading." Thus the revival of Hasidic hagiographic literature was part and parcel of the larger renaissance in Hebrew literature occurring in Eastern Europe at the time.[26] We might also add that in the mid-1860s the Russian censorship of

Hebrew books was greatly reduced as part of a general trend toward liberalization, a fact that certainly prompted many Jews to take up new publishing ventures.[27] These facts bring us to the clear conclusion that the conversation about the exclusive "sanctification" of *Shivhei ha-Besht* and the "shocking silence" that followed its printing is not accurate, and new explanations must be sought. In beginning to do so, we will note a number of broader historical processes of which the printing of Hasidic hagiography was part.

Contemporary Historical Processes

The Beginning of Orthodox Historiography

Beginning in the 1850s, several publications appeared that can be categorized as Orthodox historiography, a genre that arose in response to the histories being produced by the *Wissenschaft des Judentums* school, a group of German-Jewish scholars, who developed the academic study of Judaism. These Orthodox historiographers did not see themselves as innovators but as continuators of a tradition, even if they adopted some new methods in their work.[28] This trend may have influenced the appearance of Hasidic hagiography, which aimed to present anew the "history" of Hasidism from an insider's point of view.[29]

A Revival in the Printing of Hasidic Homilies

In the middle of the nineteenth century we find not only collections of homilies being reprinted but also the publishing of many manuscripts that until then had been kept in Hasidic court libraries.[30] This phenomenon seems to have gone hand in hand with the revival in printing Hasidic tales; indeed, a clear distinction between the two literatures was not always maintained by the printers. While there existed two different (if not mutually exclusive) readerships, the printers of both genres were frequently the same figures: almost everyone who dealt in printing Hasidic tales was also involved in printing homilies. First among them was Rodkinson himself, who in 1864 published the book *She'erit Israel* (Remnant of Israel) by Rabbi Israel Dov Ber of Viednik and a year later Shneur Zalman of Liady's *Tanya*, both in Lvov (which was the publishing center of both homiletical and hagiographic works). The interpolation of stories into homilies that we find in almost every Hasidic book continued, as well a widespread practice in reverse—the insertion of brief homilies between stories.[31] An example of this is Yaakov Katina's *Korban he-Ani* (Poor Man's Offering, 1882), a collection of teachings that also included a number of tales, one of which recounts the "fall" of the Seer of Lublin, tying it to his longings for the redemption.[32]

Maskilic Printing Programs

We cannot describe 1860s Lvov as a publishing center for Hasidic books alone; rather, there existed in the city a number of parallel centers. It was there, for example, that Mikhel Wolf launched his unique, grandiose plans to edit and print anthologies of Maskilic and classical Hebrew literature,[33] beginning with Rabbi Nahman Krochmal's book *Moreh Nevukhei ha-Zeman* (Guide for Today's Perplexed, 1863) and the books of his son, Avraham Krochmal. Wolf's publishing credits make clear his aim of producing a literature to counter the ever-growing Hasidic corpus, as do his introductions to the polemical works of Rabbi Yaakov Emden (1870–1876)[34] and to the reprinted *Megaleh Temirin* of Josef Perl (1879). This process, of course, was reciprocal, with the Hasidim printing works of their own in return.[35]

Controversy, Satire, and Debate

Maskilic opposition to Hasidism only grew as that movement spread.[36] One expression of that growth was the renewal of anti-Hasidic satire; the literature, which had been launched by the publication of *Megaleh Temirin* shortly after the printing of *Shivhei ha-Besht*, enjoyed a second wave in the mid-nineteenth century in journals, dailies, and special editions that extended to the Yiddish press and literature. The return of the genre is testified to by the wide distribution and popular demand for Yitshak Yoel Linetski's book *Dos poylishe yingl* (The Little Polish Boy), previously published as a serial in Aleksander Zederbaum's paper *Kol Mevaser* (Bearer of Good Tidings);[37] and the popularization of Maskilic literature such as the writings of Isaac Meir Dik, Israel Aksenfeld, and Judah Leib Gordon. Large portions of this literature were directed against Hasidism and provided an alternative to its printed and oral hagiography. While the anti-Hasidic satire was described by one Maskilic author as "an elixir of life, healing the soul more than all shouts and protests combined,"[38] it was not without its critics within the movement. As Avraham Uri Kovner wrote in 1873 about the stories of Judah Leib Gordon:

> Herr Gordon's stories deal again with the *tsadikim* that everyone is laughing about in the satires, even if some of them are bad authors. . . . Are the *tsadikim* a plague on the body of the Jewish people, that we should speak of them without cease if we wish to be rid of them? Rather, our belief is that all of this mockery and jest will be of little help. Mocking the *tsadikim* and ridiculing the Hasidim only to rouse a sneer from their readers is a demeaning task for Hebrew writers. . . . This is precisely what Herr Gordon is doing by poking fun at the *tsadikim* and their followers, telling the most cynical jokes about them, assuming that in doing so he will rid us of this wicked pestilence . . . a most naïve assumption![39]

This critique is typical of the fierce tone Kovner took in criticizing his fellows in Hebrew literature; he had no interest in the obstinate struggle of those who based their very identities as Maskilim on their opposition to Hasidism and its hagiography. Despite criticism like Kovner's, it seems that there were few Maskilim at the time who did not try their hands at writing a satirical essay or story.[40] The two literatures, Maskilic and Hasidic, continued to feed off of one another, resulting in what could be described as literary inflation.

Though a comprehensive study is still needed, this outline leads us to conclude that there were many factors in the revived printing of hagiographic literature, among them new possibilities in opening printing houses, the easing of censorship, opposition from various Maskilim, the spread of Hasidism, and the expanding audience. As we will see, a number of these were explicitly mentioned in that literature itself.

Hagiographic Books by Rodkinson

We turn now to an examination of Rodkinson's first Hasidic works, which played a central role in the 1860s publishing revival. Rodkinson wrote these hagiographic works when he was close to the age of twenty, as a member of an elitist stream of Habad that broke off from the leading dynasty. Having already traced the many turns of Rodkinson's life in the first chapter, here we will only briefly review some of the major points.

By the time he was eighteen, Rodkinson had already begun his involvement in printing and publishing. The first book he brought to the press in 1863 was *Urim ve-Tumim he-Hadash* (The New Book of Urim and Tumim), dealing with matters of divination, which he printed in Chernovitz at the printing house of Eliyahu Eigel and Yosef Haas.[41] At the same time he was printing books of an entirely different nature, such as the Kabbalistic ethical treatise by Rabbi Akiva Shalom Chajes of Tultchin, *Hitragshut ha-Nefesh* (Book of Ecstasy, 1864), written in a Zohar-esque Aramaic that Rodkinson mimicked in his own introduction to the book;[42] and Rabbi Ozer Tsazmir's *Luhot ha-Edut* (The Tablets of Witness) on the laws of witnesses (1865). That same year, Rodkinson, along with Avraham Yehoshua Heshel Druker, reprinted Rabbi Shneur Zalman's *Tanya*,[43] and he edited and printed the collected teachings of the Hasidic master Rabbi Israel Dov Ber of Vilednik, *She'erit Israel*.[44] He also printed a second edition of *Urim ve-Tumim he-Hadash*, having reordered its contents and redesigned its cover.[45] Even though these latter books achieved wide circulation, it seems that Rodkinson only earned his reputation as a printer after publishing his own works of Hasidic hagiography.

In 1864 Rodkinson published in Lvov three such works. First, *Shivhei ha-Rav*, recounting the life story of Rabbi Shneur Zalman of Liady, appeared in both Hebrew and Yiddish editions. An unknown number of editions totaling thousands of copies were published over the following years (including a number of reprints between 1865 and 1866), most often without the author's name or introduction and at times with various additions, including a pen-and-ink portrait of the rabbi. A large portion of the book reappeared in *Kehal Hasidim*, a fact that led to its faulty attribution to Rodkinson.[46] The second work, *Eidat Tsadikim*, was printed in Lvov in the summer of 1864 and sold well enough to merit a second edition within a few months; it saw many reprints, most of them anonymous. The book includes twenty-three mostly original tales and an introduction revealing the influence of the one found in *Shivhei ha-Besht*. Large portions of the book were soon reprinted in other collections, primarily the popular *Kehal Hasidim*.[47] The third work, *Sippurei Tsadikim meha-Hut ha-Meshulash* (Tales of the Holy Men from the Three-Fold Cord), was first printed in Lvov in 1864 and printed again in 1865 with a new title, *Sippurei Tsadikim me-Arba'ah Meitivei Lekhet* (Tales of Four Holy Men); the only other change was the inclusion of the name of Rabbi Leib Sarahs on the book's title page. (Gedalyah Nigal has prepared a critical edition of these two books as part of his series of Rodkinson's writings.[48]) Though these small books were printed on low-quality paper and quickly wore out, leaving only a few surviving copies, their circulation at the time was enormous. Not only were they printed again and again, year after year, but each printing ran into the thousands of copies, the pocket-size penny editions being snatched up as fast as they could be printed.

The Sources and Their Reliability

Hasidic hagiographic literature, especially its literary aspects, has received much attention from scholars. I wish to add here a few conclusions about the nature of this literature and the way its authors and printers understood the act of printing these works. In such a discussion, the question of the reliability of the sources holds a special place. In his introduction to *Shivhei ha-Rav*, Rodkinson made the following statement regarding his sources:

> From my youth I have grown up among sages and Hasidim who basked in the holiness of our master, the venerable Rabbi Shneur Zalman of Liady (blessed be his righteous and holy memory) and his disciples. Every year on the 19th of Kislev, when we celebrate the miraculous redemption of our holy rabbi from prison in Petersburg, I would seek out stories from the faithful elders and the sages, who would not lie about what had happened to the rabbi while in prison, for I wished to investigate the roots of the matter . . . and once I had learned any detail of the story to be sure and true, I longed to engrave the words with a stylus of iron, so that this awesome event should not be forgotten by our progeny, for it stands as a lesson to anyone who listens with a discerning ear.[49]

This testimony is reminiscent of the "Printers Introduction" to *Shivhei ha-Besht*, which describes that book as originating in the tales exchanged by Israel Baal Shem Tov's followers,[50] who would later pass on those stories to the author himself.[51] Rodkinson stressed that he was not printing all the stories he had heard, due to "a lack of knowledge and a shortage of paper."[52]

Despite his stress on the reliability of the stories, Rodkinson's promise to identify the teller of every tale was not fully realized. If he wrote at the start of *Eidat Tsadikim*, "Before every tale I have included who told it and from whom he heard it," at the end of the book he confessed, "I must apologize before you, dear reader, for failing to do that which I declared I would do in my introduction . . . for in many cases I left out the name of the teller. Know, my friend, that it is only because these men would not agree to have their names written down."[53] It seems that there were additional reasons to stress the reliability of the sources, one being the fact that the book was printed in the 1860s after the stories had circulated orally for years.

Oral Tales, Written Tales, and Emendation of Tradition

In his introduction to *Shivhei ha-Rav*, Rodkinson revealed one of his incentives for writing the book and his reason for dedicating it entirely to Rabbi Shneur Zalman of Liady:

> I feared until now to approach the work, lest I besmirch the honor of the rabbi, heaven forbid. But when last year I saw the story had been printed in Yiddish (called "A Story of Rabbi Zalmina") and that it was full of lies and nonsense (for it was written by a native of Buchovina who knew nothing of the rabbi and who wrote down the story as he had heard it from some child, without distinguishing the good from the bad) . . . I said that to write this book would be a fulfillment of the verse "It is a time to act for the Lord."[54]

This book that prodded Rodkinson to write *Shivhei ha-Rav* (which was printed in the same printing house and in the same year) was "A Wondrous and Awesome Story of Rabbi Zalmina Vitepsker," by Rabbi Elazar Margaliot of Skolit, which recounted, with much exaggeration, the Habad rabbi's sufferings in prison.[55]

Rodkinson presented himself as setting the record straight based on his own reliable sources, though his own account stretched the limits of credibility. Such a self-understanding, which appears in multiple places in Rodkinson's works, reflects the confusion that existed within the Hasidic community about their own history. Contradictory traditions about the founders of Hasidism multiplied in the early decades of the movement, when the stories had not yet been printed. We detect Rodkinson's self-understanding as setting the record straight again in the above-mentioned introduction when he addresses the reader, saying:

> Only one small thing do I have left to ask of you, dear reader. Perhaps you will find in this book some matter which you have heard slightly differently, or some detail I have omitted or added. Do not be hasty to judge me as a liar (heaven forbid!). Know that I have

> carefully sifted through all the stories and removed all the chaff; the fine wheat I have presented to you, and I myself heard them from the mouths of pious, righteous, and learned men.[56]

That is to say, different traditions were circulating, even in print, and Rodkinson was presenting the "correct" and "authentic" versions. Likewise in his introduction to *Sippurei Tsadikim*, he wrote that one of his reasons for writing was that "the stories have become very corrupted in the mouths of the masses, each man adding and subtracting to what he had heard."[57] Beside this claim, which reappears in a number of places, he stressed that the stories he had collected were no more than a small part of a much wider body of literature, and that nothing he wrote could fully convey the greatness of the *tsadikim*.

An investigation into Rodkinson's relationship to *Shivhei ha-Besht* in these collections yields intriguing results. Even though he introduces *Eidat Tsadikim* as a complement to *Shivhei ha-Besht* that includes stories not told there,[58] he later states that not everything in that book is to be believed. Again he presents the correct version based on the traditions he possesses, writing:

> In *Shivhei ha-Besht* a story is told of the Baal Shem Tov visiting the arrendars of the community of Slutsk, and it is not told correctly. But the author is not guilty in this, for many things changed in the story as different people told it across the great distance from that city to the author of *Shivhei ha-Besht*, who wrote it down as he heard it, whether true or false. But I heard the story clearly from the beginning to the end, and I now present it to the reader. And the truth will be known.[59]

The printing of hagiographic literature in the 1860s is therefore a part of the project of "correcting" "faulty" traditions and expunging inaccurate or fabricated stories.[60] The same aim finds expression in Aharon Walden, who did not hesitate to say that the editor of *Shivhei ha-Besht* invented stories from whole cloth:

> The printer who put down the praises of our master and called it *Shivhei ha-Besht* did so without knowledge or understanding, for what praise could he offer the king and the light of the seven days with his exaggerations? What's more, he invented a number of things from his own imagination, and in doing so strengthened the hand of the sinners and gave fodder to the mockers who doubt the miracles. How did he not know that all the praises he told there do not reach even to the ankles of our master? And he has not even told the half of it.[61]

A gentler articulation of the same critique can be found in other Hasidic sources.[62] While this is no basis for deciding whether the traditions in *Shivhei ha-Besht* were considered "holy" or not by the Hasidim, it does show that, in the course of time, someone felt the need to "correct" a number of things printed in that book in light of other, more "reliable" traditions. Acting on the same need, Rodkinson stressed again and again that his sources were reliable, his stories "clear and true and fit to be spread among Israel," and "most if not all of them were told by wise-hearted men who were righteous, holy, and pious."[63] Later, however, the traditions Rodkinson brought in *Shivhei ha-Rav* would be contested specifically on this point.[64]

A Response to the Literature of the Haskalah

Rodkinson noted an additional factor leading to his decision to take up the pen, one that motivated the entire genre of hagiography in his time—the spread of the Haskalah.[65] We can find hints to this effect between the lines of Rodkinson's writings, and other editors were more explicit about their motivations. It is possible to see the entire emphasis on "faith in the sages" as a response to the influence of the Haskalah at the time, one example being the acrostic that Rodkinson composed for the opening of *Shivhei ha-Rav*: it is full of remonstrations to his readers to stay true to the traditions of the sages, as in the line, "Faith in the sages will save witless souls from crooked plots."[66] An even clearer example is found at the opening of *Eidat Tsadikim*:

> In this orphaned generation in which hearts have shrunk, the blessed Lord has planted *tsadikim* in every place to strengthen and unite all the people in their faith in the sages, each man according to his ability, thus fulfilling the verse, "Those who fear the Lord, the small with the great." And we need this now more than the earlier generations, for in our many sins the plague has spread from the free-thinkers among our people, who have given their hearts over to vanities that they call Haskalah, to destroy all the foundations of the religion. And were the sages not in every place, ready to halt them, we would all be lost, heaven forbid.[67]

Rodkinson went on to say that the "plague" of the Haskalah was spreading because "God made it to be the evil counterpart of holiness," and with the revelation of Israel Baal Shem Tov the "so-called Enlightenment" had also spread, all the more so now in his days when "the footsteps of the Messiah" could be heard, bringing the redemption. Rodkinson saw his stories of the *tsadikim* standing in the breach against the Haskalah.[68]

Rodkinson knew that Maskilim were likely to mock his book as they had mocked *Shivhei ha-Besht*. Perhaps it was because of their criticism of "the stammering" of the Hasidim, in contrast to the "pure language" of the Maskilic ideal, that Rodkinson wrote in his introduction to *Shivhei ha-Rav* the following words: "Neither be surprised at the low and simple style of these stories and of this introduction. Believe me, dear one, that I could write them in a refined and flowery style, but I wished for every reader, small and great alike, to be able to read it with ease."[69]

Similar language appears in Menahem Mendel Bodek's book *Mif'alot Tsadikim* (Wonders of the Holy Men), published a year later, and it seems that Bodek was taking his cues from Rodkinson. Bodek wrote, "It is for your own benefit, dear reader, that I composed the stories and the holy teachings within the book as well as in the introduction in a low and simple style, even though with God's help I could write them in a refined and flowery style, but I wished for every reader, small and great alike, to be able to read it with ease."[70] While it seems that Rodkinson was sensitive to the Maskilim who mocked "the language of the Hasidim," he was well aware of the needs of his intended audience, and so he chose readability over eloquence.

In *Eidat Tsadikim* Rodkinson once again emphasized the importance of this literature in opposition to that of the Haskalah, as well as the need for accessible language:

> This too the reader will see and discern, that the stories collected here are full of ethical rebuke and fear of the Lord. So I have presented them in the simplest language so that every reader, young and old alike, can read them easily. What's more, it is fitting reading for the children whenever they are not studying, so that these words can take root in their hearts while they are still soft as a reed . . . and even if when they grow up they study philosophical books or any other kind, they will know how to eat the fruit and throw away the peel.[71]

Again in his introduction to *Sippurei Tsadikim* he stresses both the message and its medium, adding:

> It is not only for the learned that we have gathered these stories, but also to educate their little children while they are still under their parents' care, to engrave faith in the sages in their hearts so that they do not stray from the Lord's path when they grow up. For in these times we must pay special attention to this, so that those of our youth who know the holy tongue do not cast their eye upon the books of the Maskilim and go astray after their opinions.[72]

Without a doubt, clarifying the relationship of other editors of hagiographic collections to the literature of the Haskalah will teach us much about the development of the genre. An intriguing example can be found in Walden's introduction to *Kehal Hasidim* (Congregation of the Pious; Lvov, 1866). The editor copies entire passages from Rodkinson's books similar to those we saw above,[73] but to Rodkinson's general statements Walden adds details about the wayward Maskilim whose books had recently been published, crafting his response not to the Haskalah as a movement but specifically to those books that the Maskilim had reprinted in the 1860s. Due to its importance, I cite the passage at length:

> Now, because of our manifold sins, the plague of the Maskilim among our people has increased. . . . They are "wise to do evil" and have given their hearts to the debauchery that goes by the name of Haskalah in order to destroy all the foundations of the religion and to insult the angels of the Lord and His righteous ones. They have written books full of vanity that mock our holy Torah, and in our manifold sins their writings have multiplied, such as *Moreh Nevukhei ha-Zman*,[74] *Ha-Holets* [= *Ha-Haluts* (The Pioneer)],[75] *Ha-Tsofeh* [The Watchman],[76] *Darkah Shel Torah* [Way of the Torah],[77] *Masekhet Aniyut* [Meager Offering],[78] and many more of the type. They are troublemakers and lawless wantons, patriarchs of impurity, may their names and their memories be blotted out for all generations. All of their books are written only to mock the words of the holy Talmud and the Halachists, and hidden within them vipers lie in wait to disparage the words of our holy sages and to pour disgrace on their honor, heaven forbid, and to lead the poor among our people to teach their children to follow in their ways. (May God remember for good the rabbis and leaders of Russia who put a ban and a curse on those merchants who would trade in these abominations—them, and those who would trade with them, and those who would trade with any who have traded with them—any and all who deal in such foolishness and those who read it, may their names be an eternal disgrace.) And were it not for the sages of every province who lead the people to go after the Lord and not to stray after their hearts and their eyes, as our sages have said, "'after your hearts' refers to heresy," we would be lost, heaven forbid. And so I have selected and gathered together from all the books all the stories of what the *tsadikim* in Israel have done, in order to astound and amaze the Jewish soul to follow the Lord and those who fear Him. . . . And these precious books will strike root in their hearts to follow those who fear and serve God faithfully. And the Children of Israel will not go astray after the

> emptiness which will do them no good; they will see how great is study of the Torah and the keeping of the commandments and they will say, "The Lord has done a great thing for us" through His faithful *tsadikim*. And I have presented these tales in a very simple style so that every reader, young and old alike, can read them with ease, and it is also fitting for the sweet youth of Israel when they are idle from their studies to read these tales and not waste their time reading the books of the Maskilim, words of debauchery and foolishness and lusty songs.[79]

This introduction aroused the wrath of Aleksander Zederbaum as early as 1867 (about a year after the printing of *Kehal Hasidim*), and he rose to the defense of the Maskilim, especially Rabbi Nahman Krochmal.[80] It is clear, then, that responding to the Haskalah was one of the key factors in the renewed printing of Hasidic hagiography, a fact expressed not only by Rodkinson but by others as well.

Faith in the Sages, Tales of the Tsadikim, and Mussar Literature

One of Rodkinson's primary reasons for producing his books, emphasized at the opening of every collection he edited, was the strengthening of "simple faith" and "faith in the sages."[81] While also consistent with his criticism of Haskalah literature and the growth of the movement, this religious value had very deep roots in all Hasidic literature,[82] and was part of a larger effort toward strengthening religious life in general.[83] Rodkinson compared the role of Hasidic tales in this effort to that of actual Torah, with no less impact.[84] This point appears as well in the introduction to *Shivhei ha-Besht* and other collections from the genre.[85] As part of this trend, Rodkinson added moralizing introductions and epilogues to a number of his books, such as *Sippurei Tsadikim*, in which he wrote, "And you, reader, pay attention not only to the externals of the story, which will delight your physical heart, but also its innerness, delighting in the spiritual pleasure of its moral"[86]; and *Eidat Tsadikim* included a note that "[t]he reader will see that all of the stories collected here are full of rebuke and fear of the Lord."[87] Like many of his contemporaries,[88] Rodkinson also included stories of non-Hasidic figures in his books, even calling one section *Shivhei Ha-Rama* (In Praise of Rabbi Mosheh Isserles, the Halachic annotator of the *Shulhan Arukh*).[89] In keeping with his own understanding of these stories and their import, Rodkinson did not evaluate them for their historicity or even plausibility but rather for their faithfulness to the traditions he possessed and for their implicit ethical value.

Rodkinson as Hasidic Author, His Intended Audience, and the Reception of His Books

A study of Rodkinson's published collections clearly establishes him as a Hasidic author in every sense, even if his writings were inspired by external literary trends. So too does the content of his stories locate him in that world. His wonder tales about the feats of the *tsadikim* and the various anecdotes from their lives and those of their students are entirely representative of contemporary Hasidic literature. Rodkinson addressed the Hasidic society in which he lived, answering that society's needs; there is no reason to describe his doing so as duplicitous or hypocritical or as a sign of personal instability (as some modern scholars tend to think as well). As already noted, these books were popular enough to merit multiple printings, most of them anonymous, revealing the delight with which they were received by most of Hasidic society.[90] The following critique by Rabbi Avraham Hazan of Tultshin, an important Bratslav Hasid from the late nineteenth and early twentieth centuries, is an exception, as was his critique of Hasidic hagiography as a whole:

> I will now present to the reader a brief retelling of the signs and wonders that we saw from our master and rabbi [Nahman of Bratslav], may the memory of the righteous be a blessing . . . as light and dark are these tales beside those stories written in recent

> books—*Eidat Tsadikim*, *Kehal Hasidim*, *Pe'er mi-Kedoshim*, *Shivhei ha-Tsadikim*, and all the rest—which passed from mouth to mouth and ear to ear among the water carriers [poor people] who have multiplied in these times.[91]

Next to the title *Shivhei ha-Tsadikim* in this passage, R. Avraham added the following interesting note:

> Even though they include many tales of the Baal Shem Tov, of blessed memory, and many other true *tsadikim* who performed awesome feats of supernatural power and displayed their knowledge of the future, they are not like the tales written in the books mentioned above, most of which were told at the table between the teller's third and fourth cups of wine while the listener sat dozing, until more than nine parts are false and a little of the truth is mixed in and mixed up and mixed around (except for *Shivhei ha-Besht*—that book is true from start to finish, as I heard from the mouth of my father [R. Nahman of Tultshin] who said it in the name of our master and teacher, of blessed memory [R. Nahman of Bratslav], except for a few stories, which were not well written).[92]

Rabbi Avraham's singling out of *Shivhei ha-Besht*—even though in his opinion that book is not without its faults—was meant to distinguish between the hagiography being printed at the time and the praises he himself told about Rabbi Nahman of Bratslav. This criticism sharpens the distinction between Hasidic hagiography as a whole and that of the Bratslav community, as formulated by Rabbi Natan of Nemirov and his disciples.[93] In any case, it is impossible to learn from these words anything about the relationship of Hasidim as a group to Rodkinson's books, beyond the unique case of Rabbi Hazan and Bratslav Hasidism.

A hint of later opposition to Rodkinson's stories among the Habad faithful can be found in the words of Shmaryahu Schneerson, the son of Rabbi Levi Yitshak Schneerson. Schneerson composed the introduction to Mordechai Teitelbaum's book on Shneur Zalman of Liady, published in Warsaw in 1910, in which he wrote:

> The authors of *Shivhei ha-Rav*, *Kehal Hasidim*, and other such books veiled the shining face of the rabbi [Shneur Zalman of Liady] in a cloud of wondrous legends, and attributed to him primarily supernatural feats, in order to present him as a "wonder-worker" only, and imagined that in doing so fulfilled their obligation.[94]

This critique was aimed not only at the hagiographic writing about Shneur Zalman but at the entire genre, full as it was of "wonder tales" and far from the Hasidic path of the writer. Schneerson's comment was characteristic of a number of the writers and spokesmen of Habad Hasidism, who opposed most Hasidic hagiography and so too the works of Rodkinson.

Such critiques came not only from Hasidim; we find similar ones in a number of letters by Maskilim from the end of the nineteenth century. Hayim Zelig Slonimski, for example, wrote, "These are not like the former days, when there were pure-hearted Hasidim among our people, meek and humble of spirit; they would see us merely as opponents to their philosophies, and no more." As evidence of the change, Slonimski pointed to Aharon Walden, whose *Shem ha-Gedolim he-Hadash* (reissued in Warsaw in 1889) emphasized sensationalist wonder tales over genuine religious teachings. Even in his praise of Shneur Zalman of Liady, Slonimski noted, Walden had barely mentioned the master's book *Tanya*, "since it contains no miracles or hidden secrets."[95]

Though Rodkinson's stories were reprinted in many later Hasidic collections, it is important to distinguish between the early stage of hagiographic literature discussed here and the later stage, which drew criticism from various Hasidim as well. The collections being published nonstop at the start of the twentieth century contained a disorderly mix of tales that were intended to support a particular dynasty or to entertain the reader. On this note, Chaim Bloch's comments on the genre, made around 1920, are of particular interest:

> A number of these hagiographic booklets were printed time after time under different titles, revealing the great poetic creativity of

> the first Hasidim. They wrapped the holy men of the land in legends almost like those we find in the Talmud and Midrash, and it is no wonder that today's writers [modern Jewish authors] should delight in them so much, for as Hasidism has declined, so has their power of creativity grown less. The tales printed in recent decades are empty of any unadulterated idea and most are full of nonsense; I see them as profaning Hasidism.[96]

Bloch also pointed out the influence of Hasidic hagiography on the new Hebrew literature. His own portrayal of Hasidism was in the neo-Romantic vein, citing many Hasidic anecdotes throughout his books and emphasizing the sublime nature of Hasidic teachings. He edited his own anthologies of Hasidic tales, reworking them and translating them into German, always taking pains to explain the differences between them and others common in his day.[97]

Rodkinson's stories held an important place in the early Hasidic hagiography that Bloch favored, and they influenced other Romantic writers from the late nineteenth and early twentieth centuries who waxed nostalgic over Hasidic tales, though most of them stood outside of that world.[98] Despite this influence, there is no reason to see Rodkinson's early writings as part of the Romantic movement, which developed later and drew criticism from both Maskilim and Hasidim.[99]

The turns of Rodkinson's later life, as well as hostility and jealousy directed at him from many of his competitors, cast a pall over his early books and left them subject to unfair judgments. In the 1870s and 1880s his opponents saw a Maskil writing in defense of Hasidism, and judged the early works by the character of their later author. Surprisingly, such specious judgments by Aleksander Zederbaum, Yosef Kohen-Tsedek, Ephraim Deinard, and others found their way into modern scholarship, with Joseph Dan writing that "hypocrisy and avarice are the hallmarks of his long and winding life story," and Hannah Handler stating that "the incentives behind the literary endeavors of Frumkin and others like him were not pure: the primary goal seems to have been profit; his identification with

Hasidism was at most partial, and his personal ideological stance was a combination of confused vacillation between opposite ideologies and blatant hypocrisy." In a similar spirit, all other editors of story collections, such as Menahem Mendel Bodek, are portrayed as "the exact opposite of Rodkinson."[100]

Such descriptions deserve renewed examination. We are certainly not dealing with "a writer of doubtful credibility," nor with a "hidden Maskil" who was creating "neo-Hasidism" and slyly hiding "Maskilic morals" in his stories, nor with a "typical Maskil" whose "motivations for publishing the stories were no different from any modern writer."[101] A close reading of Rodkinson's life makes it clear that at this stage he was a Hasid who simply adopted the new genre being created around him, and there is no reason to doubt his belonging to the Hasidic movement, as many Habad Hasidim suggest today, paradoxically adopting the claims of the Maskilim.[102]

It is important to stress that there are no direct references to Rodkinson's early books by Maskilim in the 1860s. If they related to these writings, it was as to the writings of a wayward Hasid, and there was still no special interest in attacking Rodkinson more than any other Hasidic writer or printer. We see this in the comments of Aleksander Zederbaum from 1866, and from one of the stories of Judah Leib Gordon from 1870 that mocked one of Rodkinson's tales without any mention of its author—apparently due to the fact that they did not know who he was, not because of any special emphasis on the stories themselves. In contrast, Aharon Walden was given a full (and derisive) treatment by these authors in those very same pieces.[103]

Their compatriot in the attacks on hagiographic literature at the time was Eliezer Zweifel, the well-known author of the multivolume defense of Hasidism, *Shalom al Israel* (Peace upon Israel, 1868–1873). In his opposition to the hagiographic writings, Zweifel made no explicit mention of Rodkinson, and his writings reveal similarities to a number of works by the Habad Hasidim, to whom he was close in one way or another and who came out against the entire genre of hagiography.[104] In the first volume of *Shalom al Israel*, published in 1868, Zweifel first praised Israel Baal Shem Tov and his early disciples and then criticized the Hasidism of his day, which he believed to be in a state of deterioration and atrophy, a motif he sustained throughout all the volumes of the book.[105] One of his examples was the radicalization in later generations of the casuistic form of religious study known as *pilpul*, in which participants pursue finer and finer (and often entirely theoretical) distinctions between different interpretations, contrary to the strident opposition of Israel Baal Shem Tov:

> In the place of *pilpul* and other such casuistry, which the early ones had expunged from religious life out of concern for the precious time it consumed, the masses of Hasidim of our generation have chosen to read entire books of nonsense and superstition, wasting their time on worthless tales and falsehoods that are not worth reading even as children's bedtime stories, like the books *Shivhei ha-Besht*, *Eidat Tsadikim*, *Kehal Hasidim*, and the like, by which they have flooded the fools, the naïve Hasidim, like a deluge, leading their hearts astray with nonsense, sinking their minds in superstition and lies and such things that never were.[106]

At the end of the second volume, published in 1869, Zweifel wrote, "There has never been a generation so replete with stringencies and strange customs, in superstitions borrowed from the non-Jews, in tales of wonders that never happened, which make the intellect recoil and one's hairs stand on end, as this generation here in our land."[107] This having been said, in a number of places in the book Zweifel appears as a defender of hagiographic tales that, though "fabricated" in the imaginations of their authors, nevertheless "delight the heart of the listener and plant in it proper beliefs and virtues."[108] On occasion he even cited tales he had heard himself[109] and found valuable, not because of any historical factuality but because of the morals they taught.[110] The excerpts mentioned above, however, point out the fact that Zweifel offered defenses only for early Hasidism and its homiletical literature, and that he found most of Hasidism in his day indefensible (a model adopted by many who wrote about Hasidism in a neo-Romantic spirit).

Zweifel alluded to Rodkinson only obliquely; in his critique of those contemporary Hasidim who had caused the deterioration of the movement by spreading nonsense tales, Rodkinson's name never appears. Among all the Maskilim, in fact, Rodkinson aroused special interest only when he left the Hasidic world at the start of the 1870s; then they stressed "his hypocrisy and his instability" and repeatedly mentioned "the books of nonsense" that "he invented out of his imagination." They circulated rumors that when he wrote the hagiographic tales he had already ceased believing in the way of Hasidism and wrote them only for profit. This criticism gained strength when he began to edit *Ha-Kol* in 1876. The first to make such a claim was Avraham Ber Gottlober, who described Rodkinson as early as 1873 as a hedonistic Hasid who had "profaned the masses with his stories about the *tsadikim* and their wonders, which he had made up himself and spread among hundreds and thousands of Jews"; Rodkinson, he wrote, had suddenly "put on some fancy clothes and become a German Jew! And now he deceives mankind with a different trick."[111] In an 1878 essay Zederbaum ascribed Rodkinson's efforts in the genre to "making a profit."[112] Pesah Ruderman made similar statements in one of his anti-Hasidic pieces from 1876:

> I heard from the mouth of a reliable man, the Maskil Rabbi Aryeh Leib Schalit, a wood merchant in Riga, that once on a trip from Petersburg to Riga he made friends with a man young in years, dressed in European clothes and eating unkosher foods in the hotel. From listening to him talk, Herr Schalit realized that he was the author of *Sippurei Tsadikim*, a collection of stories most of which he had invented from his own imagination and a few of which he had heard from the mouths of old women in Dubrovno. He had done so only to fill his pockets after having lost almost all his money to bad business.[113]

On the basis of such reports, which circulated both in print and by mouth after Rodkinson gained literary renown, Yitshak Yaakov Weisberg made a satirical comment: "[The heretics] have said that it was because of its sweetness that the lovely and lofty book *Kehal Hasidim* was translated into Yiddish and perhaps all the seventy languages, but this book too was made by a certain scoundrel in the holy community of Warsaw, and he is not one of our own."[114] Weisberg may have been aiming his insult at Rodkinson (who spent some time in Warsaw), even if he erred in attributing *Kehal Hasidim* to him, as did many others; if he was aiming at Walden, it is clear that the printer became a target only because of his connection to Rodkinson. Either way, the charge is parallel to the one that *Shivhei ha-Besht* was written by a Mitnaged in mockery of the Hasidim, a claim Weisberg made himself following the excerpt above.

Weisberg's comments are consistent with the justifications of the Jerusalem Kabbalist Menahem Menkin Halperin, who in 1901 rose to the defense of the book *Hemdat Yamim* (Delight of Days) against the charges of Rabbi Yaakov Emden and cleared it of suspicions of Sabbatian influence. Halperin cited a legend in *Shivhei ha-Besht* in which Israel Baal Shem Tov denigrates the book, writing, "this story of the Baal Shem Tov is a complete lie."[115] Thinking that the story appeared first in *Kehal Hasidim* and not in *Shivhei ha-Besht* (following the written opinion of David Kahana),[116] he wrote openly about "the joker who wrote *Kehal Hasidut* [*sic*]."[117] He did not know that the author was Aharon Walden, who in 1891 published together with him the book *Eits Hayim* (Tree of Life) by Rabbi Hayim Vital.[118]

Ephraim Deinard would later present a similar—and similarly inaccurate—picture: when discussing Rodkinson's early books, he confused them with other authors' and presented a fascinating but entirely fictional account of the young Rodkinson:

> At first, while still young and, like all Hasidim at that time, lacking wisdom or work experience, and as far from Torah and knowledge as a little child, he decided to make a fine and easy living by writing a second volume of the book *Shivhei ha-Besht*, believing that the

> Hasidim would "lick their fingers" over his wonders, and he called it *Kehal Hasidim*. Meanwhile, learned Hasidim, who considered such a book of nonsense to be a disgrace, often said that the author of *Shivhei ha-Besht* was a Mitnaged who only wanted to make fun of the Hasidim.[119]

Deinard also described how the Hasidic book *She'erit Israel* was brought to press by Rodkinson:

> For Hasidim of this sort he put together this bundle of rags, which is sold in Lubavitch for two coins a page, and which can earn a man a great fortune any day of the week, and printed it with the name *She'erit Israel*, named for the holy Israel of Vildenik. And as a Hasid, author, and scion of a distinguished family, he traveled to different cities to share his wisdom among the Habad Hasidim. However, in his travels he became convinced that Hasidim alone could not provide him with enough money, so he became a Maskil—that is, he was a Maskil in all his ways and a Hasid in all his deeds—like a Maskil he did not pray, but he drank his liquor like the finest of Kotsker Hasidim, and he traveled to all the fairs and mingled with both Hasidim and Maskilim. But he made no money for his trouble, and so he found a new living, one easy and fine and pleasant, selling to women.[120]

The key element in this picturesque and distorted description is the connection Deinard makes between the later hagiographic works and *Shivhei ha-Besht*. In his opinion that book, like others after it, was not favorably received by many Hasidim. Deinard also referred to the legend about its author being a Mitnaged who sought to poke fun at his subjects, a legend begun by Josef Perl and repeated in the 1870s in response to the second wave of Hasidic hagiography. Also deserving mention here is the fact that Deinard made no distinction between Hasidic homiletical and hagiographical literature, attacking both as the same animal. Elsewhere Deinard wrote in more depth about Rodkinson's "iniquitous" beginnings:

> He started out manufacturing some lies and debaucheries and wrote them in a book written in a pidgin Hebrew and called it *Kehal Hasidim*. . . . [T]he Russian censor had forbidden printing Hasidic books, and all the more so nonsense stories about their holy men, even forbidding the printing of the *Zohar* . . . so the Hasidim were hungry and thirsty for *Shivhei ha-Besht* and other such nonsense stories, which are very rare in print; and so *Kehal Hasidim* sold by the tens of thousands, and Michael Levi collected much money, and reaped honor as a Hasid from every member in the camp of "our people," until he had printed it again in Lemberg and divided it into sections, and gave every section a different name, and by selling these vanities he became a book merchant.[121]

Such descriptions comprised only part of Deinard's negative portrayal of Hasidism and its emissaries throughout dozens of his books. He similarly portrayed the Hasid Aharon Walden, author of *Shem ha-Gedolim he-Hadash* and *Kehal Hasidim*: "This man, whom we knew in Warsaw as a wild man, a debauched and crazed Hasid . . . owes all of his stories to old women and the idlers in the Hasidic prayer houses."[122] Nevertheless, he did distinguish between Walden and Rodkinson, writing,

> I will not speak now about Rabbi Aharon Walden's book *Shem ha-Gedolim he-Hadash*, which in truth is no worse than *Shivhei ha-Besht*, and better in any case than the books of the Hasidim-Maskilim, since he did not try to dress himself in the mantle of the Haskalah; we see him with naked eyes as an undisguised Hasid and fervent believer who decided to make a little money for his lies, at which he is no worse than his holy masters. But worse than him are the Hasidim-Maskilim [e.g., Rodkinson] who have recently emerged from their holes to repeat the nonsense that the Habad Hasidim were always uttering, that "Hasidism is pure philosophy, redemption payments [to the rabbis] is true charity, and the holy master is a genius and a saint." And should they want more stories such as those in *Shivhei ha-Besht* or find it inappropriate for a Maskil to tell such silly tales, they have invented new

> stories in the spirit of the new age, embellished with flowery language and fancy sayings.[123]

There is no basis to Deinard's analysis, and in fact there was practically no difference between Rodkinson's early stories and those of Walden or other Hasidic authors of the time. In any case it is clear that Deinard did not know exactly when the hagiographic works were published and had never seen their contents; there was no other way he could have consistently attributed *Kehal Hasidim* to Rodkinson.

Deinard frequently mixed past with present and truth with fiction when reporting on Rodkinson's life, and he provided forums in his papers for others' attacks. For example, in 1889 Yosef Leib Freidkin published a long, biting essay in *Ha-Leumi* (The Nationalist) describing Rodkinson as a "Maskilic merchant" who from the very start had "disguised himself in order to appear as a faithful Maskil and Hasid at one and the same time," and "just as he mocked the Hasidim in telling their praises in his books *Hishtapkhut ha-Nefesh* (Outpouring of the Soul) and *Eidat Tsadikim*, so too does he mock them now."[124] Such portrayals became common only after Rodkinson had left his native Hasidism for the Haskalah.

The claims that Rodkinson had written the Hasidic hagiographic works when already a Maskil (or at least half-Hasid and half-Maskil), and that he wrote them only for profit, are entirely baseless and assume that no reasonable person could believe in such fantasies—an assumption of the Maskilim that was surprisingly well accepted by modern scholars—and so whoever writes them is surely some kind of fraud. In fact, Rodkinson was a Hasid through and through when he printed his hagiographic works, and the later criticism against him came in response to decisions made only in his later life. The picture of Hasidism in Rodkinson's writings, as well as the disputes in which he was involved, turned even more complicated when he moved beyond the world of the Haskalah.

3 Images of Hasidism
History, Critique, and Religious Reform

Rodkinson wrote most of his Hasidic tales between 1862 and 1865. After wandering through various locales, he arrived in Zhitomir and then Warsaw, where apparently he discovered not only Maskilic literature but also the Maskilim active in those cities. It appears, however, that he did not fully enter the world of the Haskalah until his time in St. Petersburg; there he donned "European" clothes and forged relations with Maskilim.

Accounts of this period in Rodkinson's life can be found in the articles in *Ha-Magid* written by Avraham Ber Gottlober about his visit to St. Petersburg in 1873. Gottlober, who had met Rodkinson in Zhitomir, portrayed him as moving back and forth between the two worlds, deceiving the members of both.[1] From that year on we find numerous articles and essays mocking Rodkinson and the changes he was undergoing. The bulk of these attacks focused specifically on the hagiographic tales he had written. In at least one sense, Gottlober's testimony seems accurate: the transition was not absolute. Rodkinson did not became a "new man" in one moment but rather stood, for a certain time at least, with one foot in each world. This transitional period—the years between his career as a Hasidic author and his entry into the Haskalah in St. Petersburg—was ignored by his later opponents as well as by scholars. The full biography can be found in the first chapter, and we will now only revisit a few points in order to complete the picture.

In 1866 Rodkinson arrived in Zhitomir, where he made contact with the printing house of Avraham Shalom Shadov, founded the previous year.[2] Shadov published decidedly Hasidic and Maskilic books alike, such as Avraham Ber Gottlober's translation of Moses Mendelssohn's *Jerusalem* alongside *Pri ha-Arets* (Fruit of the Land) by the Hasidic master Rabbi Menahem Mendel of Vitebsk (both in 1867); the scientific texts of Hayim Zelig Slonimski (1866) alongside *Imrot Tehorot* (Pure Sayings), the collected homilies of Rabbi Barukh of Mezhbizh, the grandson of Israel Baal Shem Tov (1865); and Gottlober's critical *Toldot ha-Kabbalah veha-Hasidut* (The History of Kabbalah and Hasidism) beside the first two volumes of Eliezer Zweifel's defense of Hasidism, *Shalom al Israel* (Peace Upon Israel, 1868–1869). It was under Shadov's auspices that Rodkinson edited and published the collected teachings of the Hasidic master Rabbi Israel of Bahafoli, *Ateret Tiferet Israel* (Crowning Glory of Israel, 1867); Rabbi Yaakov Emden's Halachic work *Igeret Bikoret* (Critique, 1868); and the collection of folk remedies, *Marpe la-Am* (Healer of the People, 1869). In 1868 he also printed the second edition of *She'erit Israel* (Remnant of Israel) with minor changes and additions, and may have been involved in publishing additional books that do not bear his name. In Zhitomir he certainly would have discovered a greater array of Hebrew Maskilim and their literature, including Zweifel and Gottlober, a few of whom he even contacted.

Rodkinson nevertheless chose to leave the city, arriving in Warsaw in 1870. Once there, he announced a plan to publish the writings of the early Halachic authorities, and succeeded in publishing the first two books from a proposed series: *The Responsa of Rabbi Joseph ibn Migash* and Rashi's *Sefer Pardes ha-Gadol ve-Sefer ha-Orah* (1870). After a brief stay in St. Petersburg, Rodkinson arrived in Koenigsberg in 1875 with many plans in the making. There he changed his name to Rodkinson ("the son of Rodke," which has the same numerological value as Frumkin).[3] His first role in Koenigsberg, and the one in which he would invest most of his efforts, was as editor of *Ha-Kol* (The Voice), which he filled from 1876 to 1881.

On May 7, 1876, he published *Aleh le-Mivhan* (Test Copy), outlining his plans. In the issue's opening essay Rodkinson wrote that the Jewish people was divided into three parties: Talmudists, Hasidim, and Maskilim. The bulk of his criticism was aimed at the Maskilim, criticizing *Ha-Shahar* (The Dawn) and especially Pesah Ruderman and David Kahana (the latter wrote a regular piece on famous Kabbalists and Hasidic masters).[4] The first official edition of *Ha-Kol* was published August 8, 1879, and over the next four years the paper was printed as a weekly paper (and briefly as a biweekly one), achieving relatively wide circulation. During the same period, Rodkinson published a Yiddish paper titled Ha-*Kol la-Am*, which ran until 1879, as well as the monthly *Asefat Hakhamim*, which was in fact the second socialist journal published in Hebrew (after Aharon Shmuel Lieberman's *Ha-Emet* [The Truth]). Upon the appearance of these journals, Rodkinson's journalistic competitors attempted to sully his name by publishing reports of his exploits while in St. Petersburg and his past as a Hasid; these reports cannot be verified, and most of them seem to be fabrications. In either case, Rodkinson paid little mind to them and invested all his efforts in editorial duties and recruiting subscribers for his papers.[5]

Reprints of Hagiographic Works and the Haskalah Literature

During this stage, Rodkinson wrote prolifically about Hasidism, and the collections he published in the 1860s were later reprinted in a number of editions by others. *Sippurei Tsadikim me-Arba'ah Meitivei Lekhet* (Tales of Four Holy Men)[6] and *Siftei Kedoshim me-Arba'ah Meitivei Lekhet* (From The Mouths of Four Holy Men),[7] printed in Lvov in 1873 and 1876, respectively, were identical in content and were in fact only new versions of *Sippurei Tsadikim meha-Hut ha-Meshulash* (Tales of the Holy Men from the Three-fold Cord), first printed by Rodkinson in the same city in 1864.[8] Yosef Kohen-Tsedek pounced upon this fact with delight,[9] hoping to fault Rodkinson as a recidivist Maskil who was still drawn toward Hasidism or, in his words, “a hermaphrodite with the sexual organs of both a Hasid and a heretic.”[10] Kohen-Tsedek did not mention that the book was first published in 1864, and it seems he did not know of the first printing, believing that the book had only then been written. Rodkinson, in response to the book *Mikha’el ha-Nehepakh le-Sama’el* (Michael Who Has Turned Into Samael), claimed that he was not responsible for the new editions and in fact had never even seen them.[11] We can assume that he was correct in saying so, since he had sold the printing rights to his hagiographical works some years before.

Sippurei Tsadikim (Tales of the Holy Men) was reprinted a number of times in Rodkinson’s lifetime (including in 1873, 1876, and 1886) without inclusion of his name. Of special interest is the 1895 printing under the title *Sippurei Tsadikim meha-Hut ha-Meshulash*;[12] the edition was printed by the author and book merchant Elazar Shenkler of Turnov (1865–1940), who had previously produced his own works of Hasidic hagiography,[13] and was published by the Cracow printing house of Yosef Fischer, who also published many Maskilic books. Shenkler, who of course made no mention of Rodkinson, did not change a word in this edition, even keeping the preface with its ridicule of Maskilic literature. Yet, at the end of the book, the printer included an advertisement for his bookshop, noting that it included not only “books of ethics, Kabbalah, and stories of holy men” but also books of “scientific research, poetry, writings of Hebrew poetesses, all sorts of Yiddish books, wonder stories, novels,” and the like.[14] Such an advertisement is striking when attached to a book containing the words, “for in these times we must not let opinions multiply in the youth who understand the holy tongue, taking up the books of the Maskilim, about whom the prophet said, ‘They are wise to do evil, but to do good they have no knowledge.’”[15] The advertisement’s placement in this edition raises questions regarding the reading culture and the way in which hagiography was understood at the end of the nineteenth century, in contrast to the first and second waves of the book’s printing years before.

Shivhei ha-Rav (In Praise of the Master) and *Eidat Tsadikim* (Community of Holy Men) also merited additional reprints between

1870 and 1900, most often without mention of their author and sometimes without the introductions and epilogues.[16] In the 1880s, small books of Hasidic hagiography were printed in large quantities. While the exact number is very hard to estimate, it is clear that they were popular reading material. Nahum Sokolow was correct when he surmised, "Perhaps they are even more popular than the books of the Haskalah among the Maskilim."[17]

It is unlikely that Rodkinson was actively involved in all the reissues of the hagiographic works he had written a decade before, as his opponents claimed; the publishing rights were most likely owned by others, or perhaps the works were printed without permission. In that period such rights were routinely ignored and entire books were reprinted without authorization, as when Rodkinson's *Shivhei ha-Rav* was copied in Walden's *Kehal Hasidim* (Congregation of the Pious) within a few years of the original publication.[18] Even if Rodkinson was involved in reprinting these new publications, it is reasonable to assume that it was solely for financial reasons, since he himself criticized them, as we will see. His opponents, some of whom were not aware of the earlier editions (as Kohen-Tsedek was not), saw the new and repeated printings of his early works, with their worldview that he had since denounced, as evidence of his hypocrisy, duplicity, and avarice.

It is important to emphasize that it was not only Rodkinson's hagiographic works that were reprinted during those years; what's more, it is impossible to attribute all the printing activity to financial concerns alone. The homiletical work *She'erit Israel* (Remnant of Israel) by Rabbi Dov Ber of Vilednik, issued by Rodkinson in the 1860s, was printed a third time in Koenigsberg in 1877. Judging by the location, it is reasonable to assume that Rodkinson himself was involved in the printing, since at the time he had begun serving as editor of *Ha-Kol* in Koenigsberg, where few other printers were active in publishing Hebrew books. In this edition, which did not bear Rodkinson's name, the book's connection to Hasidism is also obfuscated, and it is presented as a book of religious philosophy.[19] Avraham Shalom Friedberg quoted extensively from the introduction to this edition in mockery of Rodkinson's affected literary style, concluding, "In it we see this good sir [Rodkinson] wearing a huge *shtreimel* [a traditional fur hat] that comes down right over his forehead to his nose and moustache."[20]

In any case, it is clear that when Rodkinson entered the world of the Haskalah he took Habad with him, and his ties to his ancestral traditions remained strong. That same year Rodkinson expressed his desire to reprint Sefer *Sha'arei ha-Avodah* (Gates of Service) and *Avodat ha-Beinonim* (Service of the Ordinary Jew) by his relative Aharon ha-Levi of Starosselje (a desire that was never realized).[21] These books, which were essentially theoretical discussions of Habad teachings, differed from the hagiographic works in many ways. Later we find that Rodkinson's praise of Habad teachings was derived from other Maskilim, such as Eliezer Zweifel and Senior Sacks,[22] and it seems that he saw the philosophically inclined Habad as categorically different from the Kabbalah and other forms of Hasidism.[23]

Even if Rodkinson maintained his regard for Hasidism, as evidenced by his continued efforts to publish Hasidic (and specifically Habad) teachings, it is clear that a shift did occur in his writing about Hasidism. His expressions of admiration, made as he was beginning his editorship of *Ha-Kol* and *Ha-Kol la-Am* in 1876, were no longer written as a Hasid but as a moderate Maskil, with the aim of providing a historical picture of Hasidism set in the context of the many and diverse streams of Judaism.

The New History of Hasidism: *Toldot Ba'alei Shem Tov*

In 1876 Rodkinson published two books on Hasidism as part of a more comprehensive project: *Toldot Ba'alei Shem Tov, Part I: Or Israel* (The Light of Israel), dedicated to Israel ben Eliezer, commonly referred to as the Baal Shem Tov;[24] and *Toldot Amudei ha-Habad, Part I: Amud ha-Rashi* (A History of the Pillars of Habad: The First Pillar), dedicated to Rabbi Shneur Zalman of Liady.[25] The larger project, which never materialized, was to be a series titled *Toldot Ba'alei Shem Tov*, and its intent is made clearer by the German title of the books: *Biographie Sammtlicher Rabbiner/ der Gouvernments Volhynien, Podolien, Ukraine, Gross—u. Klein-Polen und Galizien/ von Jahre 1695 bis 1876/nebst Geschichte der Frankisten* (Collected Biographies of Rabbis of Volhynia, Podolia, Ukraine, Greater and Lesser Poland and Galicia from the Year 1695 to 1876, Excluding the History of the Frankists). Evidently the series was meant to be a wide-ranging study exceeding the bounds of Hasidism. Given their importance to a broader understanding of Rodkinson's work, all the intended volumes will be explored in detail below.

Rodkinson wrote that the project would include six volumes, each further subdivided into sections: (1) *Or Israel*, dealing with the Baal Shem Tov and Jakob Frank; (2) *Amud ha-Torah* (Pillar of Torah), the biographies of Rabbi Dov Ber, the Magid of Mezritsh, and eighty of his disciples; (3) *Amudei Polin* (Pillars of Poland), the biographies of Rabbi Elimelekh of Lizhensk, Rabbi Israel of Kozhnits, Rabbi Yaakov Yitshak "The Seer" of Lublin, and their students; and (4) *Toldot Amudei ha-Habad* (A History of the Pillars of Habad), on the leaders of Habad from Rabbi Shneur Zalman of Liady on. The last two volumes are of particular interest: (5) *Toldot Geonei Israel* (A History of the Great Minds of Israel), on Rabbi Jonathan Eybeschütz "and all the sages of the Talmud and the Kabbalah from the year 5550 until today"; and (6) *Toldot Hakhmei Israel* (A History of the Sages of Israel), on Moses Mendelssohn "and all the sages of the Haskalah until today, with all the new literature."[26]

Of these, only the first two volumes were published. Rodkinson wrote in 1883 that the rest were never published due to the negative press the first two received, but he hoped to complete the series in the future, a hope he never saw fulfilled.[27] The first volume, *Or Israel*, was published in 1876 and dedicated to the story of the Baal Shem Tov, with an emphasis on the dispute with Jakob Frank. The second volume was published in the same year under the title *Toldot Amudei ha-Habad*;[28] it promised to tell the biographies, in three sections, of "the rabbis of Reisin starting with the year 5507, in which was born the learned and pious elder rabbi Rabbi Shneur Zalman of Liady, and his disciples, his sons and all his family until today": *Amud ha-Rashi*, on Rabbi Shneur Zalman of Liady; *Amud ha-Tavekh* (The Middle Pillar), "shedding light on the lives of his sons, his family, and his eminent disciple, the holy Rabbi Aharon Horowitz of Starosselje, their quarrels, their time in prison, their disputes, and everything that befell them, from the day of their birth until their ascent to heaven; and completing the changes in versions that are missing from *Amud ha-Rashi*"; and *Amud ha-Torah*, "casting bright light on the life of the learned and pious rabbi Menahem Mendel of Lubavitch, from the beginning of his forty-year reign, and everything that befell him, along with all of his sons and their descendants until today."[29] The published volume included only *Amud ha-Rashi*; the remaining two sections were never written, or at least never printed. The reasons given for its composition were entirely different from those outlined in the early hagiographic collections. While Rodkinson had previously addressed Hasidic society, he now turned to a much wider audience.

The Background to the Writing of *Toldot Ba'alei Shem Tov*

Rodkinson's book was not exceptional in its subject but rather was part of a broader trend in the writing of Jewish history, especially of the Kabbalah and Hasidism. This trend, which began in the mid-nineteenth century with the German writings of Peter Beer, Isaak Marcus Jost, and Heinrich Graetz, found expression in Hebrew as well.[30] A few years earlier, in 1867, Aleksander Zederbaum had published the book *Keter Kehunah* (Crown of Priesthood), which included an extensive description of the development of the Hasidic movement.[31] The 1860s also saw the appearance of Eliezer Zweifel's controversial book *Shalom al Israel*,[32] written in defense of Hasidism, for which Zweifel was labeled by other Maskilim as a "crazy man . . . who would strive to spread the teachings of the Baal Shem Tov among the Jews."[33] In 1870 Avraham Ber Gottlober published the first and only section of his planned comprehensive work, *Toldot ha-Kabbalah veha-Hasidut* (History of Kabbalah and Hasidism), written in response to Zweifel. The published volume addressed only the history of the Kabbalah, and was essentially a copy of Graetz's work with some additions.[34] Gottlober angrily contended that the book did not receive wide enough circulation (in contrast to Zweifel's book) and that even those who bought it did not necessarily read it, much less give it the thought required to understand it. He recounted a visit to the home of an acquaintance, where he saw a special edition of the book standing beside the Hasidic classic *Toldot Ya'akov Yosef* (The Generations of Yaakov Yosef)—"both of them in fine gilded bindings, practically identical, as if they were twins born of the same womb."[35]

Hebrew literature at the time was in fact replete with descriptions of Jewish mystical literature and its history. Many journals contained studies of the Kabbalah and Hasidism, including Pesah Ruderman's piece on Hasidism in *Ha-Shahar*;[36] and David Kahana's long compositions on the Kabbalah, Sabbatianism, and Hasidism, which had tremendous influence on his contemporaries.[37]

In the light of this variegated literature, it is worth examining Rodkinson's later work. *Toldot Ba'alei Shem Tov* was addressed to a different audience than that which read his hagiographical works. Rodkinson no longer stressed "faith in the sages" as the ethical value of his stories, but rather a historical view of the Hasidic movement as part of the diversity of the modern Jewish world. The schema of the multivolume *Toldot Ba'alei Shem Tov*, as outlined above, bore a clear similarity to those of contemporary Maskilic works, a similarity that was repeated in the book's interior design as well: the extensive footnotes (at times printed in Rashi script), the clear division into short chapters, the relatively precise identification of sources, the front page in German, the detailed table of contents, and the introduction all reflected Maskilic literary norms. The similarity even extended to the book's physical appearance: no longer one of Rodkinson's "little booklets," *Toldot Ba'alei Shem Tov* was a bona fide book, and one need only to look at its cover and that of *Toldot Amudei ha-Habad* beside those of *Shivhei ha-Rav* and the like to see the great difference between the two categories.[38] Rodkinson's adoption of contemporary Maskilic design standards for his books in the 1870s points to their nature and their intended audience. While some of his opponents claimed that the physical appearance was the only difference between Rodkinson's early and later books,[39] in truth Rodkinson's writing underwent more substantial changes.

Historical Preludes and the Case of Jacob Frank

The clear influence of Maskilic literature on Rodkinson is also recognizable in the historical introductions he penned for his later books, in which his intent was not to tell wonder tales but rather to write history. Already in the introduction to *Toldot Ba'alei Shem Tov*, titled "The Beginning of the Account," he presents his understanding of history—from Rabbi Isaac Luria through Shabbetai Tsvi, Jakob Frank, and the wonder-working *ba'alei shem* (masters of the Name of God) until the appearance of the Baal Shem Tov.[40] *Or Israel* opens with a chapter titled "The State of our Jewish Brethren from R. Isaac Luria to the Baal Shem Tov 5448 [1698]," which recounts the history in a distinctly Maskilic style;[41] *Toldot Amudei ha-Habad* also opens with a historical study of the partition of Poland and the start of the dispute between the Hasidim and its opponents, the Mitnagdim.[42] What's more, his lengthy discussions of changes in Hasidic liturgy, found in the last section of the second book, are of significant historical value.[43] In this sense, Nahum Karlinsky was correct when he described the change in Rodkinson's writings as a shift from "stories of the Rabbi" to "history of the Rabbi."[44]

One of the noteworthy features of *Or Israel* in this context is its varied ways of relating to Jakob Frank and the Frankist movement. This topic deeply engaged the Maskilim of the time, and it was typical of a Maskilic composition to tie the story of Frank to that of the Baal Shem Tov. Such ties were generally negative, contending that the Baal Shem Tov was only the latest of the "deviant cults" of which the Frankists were the most egregious example.[45] But Rodkinson tried to distinguish between the two movements in his study, fighting the widespread Maskilic identification of Hasidism with Sabbatianism and especially its Frankist form.[46] Such a conversation certainly would not be found in a classical Hasidic composition, but it was also exceptional among Maskilic books. Rodkinson attempted to show the greatness of the Baal Shem Tov in his struggle against Jakob Frank, as already alluded to in a number of stories in *Shivhei ha-Besht* and as Zweifel had already done in *Shalom al Israel*.[47]

While in his defenses of the Baal Shem Tov Rodkinson displayed his broad knowledge of Maskilic writings, his treatment of Jakob Frank was superficial and even derogatory. Rodkinson listed the sources he used in his description of the Frankist episode at the opening of *Or Israel*; aside from the polemical writings of Yaakov Emden and the anti-Sabbatian literature that were readily available to him, he made extensive use of the no less biased books of Heinrich Graetz and David Kahana. Rodkinson wrote that he accepted the latter's unfavorable conclusions only as they applied to Jakob Frank, but not to Hasidism.[48] Rodkinson dedicated many pages to discussing Frank, although he still left his description incomplete, promising to complete it in future volumes of *Or Israel*.[49]

A number of years later, in 1885, while Rodkinson was editor of *Ha-Kol* in Vienna, Adolf (Aaron) Jellinek published a Frankist manuscript from the start of the nineteenth century in Rodkinson's paper. Jellinek had received the manuscript from Wolfgang Wesley, along with the latter's notes, and published it in the original German, now spelled out in Hebrew letters.[50] In introducing the manuscript, Jellinek explained its importance for the understanding of the Frankist movement's ideology and the beliefs and hopes of its members. The piece did not appear in full in *Ha-Kol*, only two more installments being printed.[51] In one of the pamphlets that he published in Vienna in 1886, Rodkinson recounted how Shmuel Yosef Bloch, the one who had accused him of contacts with antisemites, "boasted continuously about the favor he had done for all Israel, since it was his criticism . . . that had made Jellinek retract the article."[52] So he rushed to print the real reason for the suspension of the essay: that "Most of our readers did not approve of our use of jargon in the newspaper, and we concede the point and promise to provide other essays in the holy tongue."[53] He attributed Bloch's statement to the elections in which he was involved and to his personal enmity for Jellinek. In any case, it indeed seems that the reason for discontinuing the article had no connection to its content, and we should not see Rodkinson's sanction in printing such an article as evidence of any change in his opinion of Jakob Frank and the Frankist movement.[54] As we have seen, Rodkinson's modus operandi as printer and editor was to be open to different and even contradictory ideologies, and the newspapers he printed did not necessarily reflect his own positions. The situation is different, however, when we come to analyze Rodkinson's own writings.

Rodkinson's Sources on Hasidism and His Critique of Hagiographic Literature

If, in writing about Jakob Frank, Rodkinson was informed by the books of Graetz and others who took a dim view of Kabbalah and Hasidism, when discussing Hasidism he repeatedly stressed his internal sources and their reliability, as in his opening to *Or Israel*:

> Until now, no single book has been dedicated to the story of this holy and exalted man [the Baal Shem Tov]. The many stories told among the Hasidim, whether in print or by mouth, lack all order; there is no tongue and no pen that can reveal his light. So too none among the masses of Israel have heard of his disciples who learned Torah from his mouth, or of their disciples. . . . So we took it upon ourselves as a holy duty to collect the history of this lofty and exalted man from the many books (and from what has been truly told), along with all his disciples who learned Torah from his mouth and who taught their disciples in turn; we place this book before the reader in proper form and order, so that every holy and righteous rabbi among his disciples may come to his proper place in peace.[55]

A number of important issues arise from this statement. Aside from the fact that Rodkinson selected material from both printed sources and "what has been truly told" off the page, he stressed the problematic nature of the many collections printed without proper order. Rodkinson's criticism of these stories was extensive, though he had written some of them himself in earlier years. Once again he stressed that his own work had been based on "authentic traditions" received from his ancestors, and he recounted his pedigree in detail. According to Rodkinson, this gave him both the ability and the license to criticize the literature on Hasidism and to forgo mentioning those stories that were "mere tales" and "exaggerations," presenting only "reliable" and "verified" stories, the teller of which he often noted.[56] It is important to stress that the nature of the stories is also different, there being few of the "wonder tales" that were so widespread in the genre to which he had contributed in the past.

His critique of *Shivhei ha-Besht* is especially striking, testifying that he referred to the book only in "matters that can be relied upon."[57] We have seen that in his hagiographic works he brought different versions of the stories presented in *Shivhei ha-Besht*, something he did here as well, if in a different spirit. So, for example, one of the praise tales that was thoroughly mocked in Maskilic literature is the account of how the Baal Shem Tov drank "concentrated wine" and then badly botched his citation of a Talmudic saying. Rodkinson explained this strange story by claiming that the author of *Shivhei ha-Besht* had a corrupted text in which the words were repeated in the wrong order—in which case the Baal Shem Tov had not misspoken at all. He concluded, "The story brought in *Shivhei ha-Besht* jumbled the saying of the Gemara, rendering it 'Fear diminishes harsh wine,' because he either heard it incorrectly or did not know the phrase, and we heard it correctly from our ancestors. And everything will find its proper place." Rodkinson was no doubt responding to the early anti-Hasidic satires of this tale that used it to mock the Baal Shem Tov.[58]

Rodkinson's criticism of *Shivhei ha-Besht* was very harsh, as when he noted that it contains "many exaggerations with no basis."[59] Nevertheless, he penned a long note attacking Pesah Ruderman for repeating a well-known Maskilic charge that a Mitnaged or Maskil had written *Shivhei ha-Besht* in order to poke fun at the Hasidim.[60]

This charge was repeated on a number of occasions by Ephraim Deinard, who used it, not surprisingly, specifically to attack Rodkinson, whom he saw as a prime target due to his financial motivations.[61] Rodkinson's criticism was directed, inter alia, against various stories in *Shivhei ha-Besht*, as when he wrote about the stories of the Baal Shem Tov before his revelation: "All of this is told at length in *Shivhei ha-Besht*, and with exaggerations . . . and we have made it a rule that every story without a moral need not be presented to the reader," and that the author of *Shivhei ha-Besht* "would tell us his revelation in different ways that contradict each other, and to fulfill our obligation to the reader we will copy his words at the end of the book."[62]

The criticism is even more obvious in his discussion of the series of stories dealing with the figure of Rabbi Adam Baal Shem. This series had already borne criticism from some Hasidim and was the butt of many Maskilic jokes.[63] Avraham Krochmal, who would later meet Rodkinson and work with him in promoting religious reforms, wrote a parody about the lost writings of the Baal Shem Tov, claiming that he had found them and that they were in fact nothing but the writings of Spinoza and the like.[64] Rodkinson was more subtle than most critics, citing the story but hinting that it had no reliable basis.[65] In this context he noted an additional matter requiring attention, that the "exaggerated tales" in *Shivhei ha-Besht* had been put by the editor in parentheses, and so he (Rodkinson) did not copy these stories at all.[66]

Rodkinson also critiqued the writings of Aharon Walden, with whom he was well acquainted and whom he had even met while in Warsaw.[67] The bulk of his criticism was aimed at the book *Shem ha-Gedolim he-Hadash* (A New Monument to the Great Rabbis), about which Rodkinson said, "we could not find a single true word in all the book, which is wrapped in darkness, and which confuses the holy one's disciples one with the other and counts among them many who never saw the light of his face."[68] The criticism is even fiercer in the marginal notes throughout *Or Israel*, where he wrote that if he needed to list all the errors in *Shem ha-Gedolim he-Hadash* his list would be thicker than the book itself.[69] He does point out a few errors, however, noting, "There is neither order nor rule to his writings, for he did not seek out the truth through any research into the stories or their sources," and concluding, "many of the stories in his book are based on lies." Rodkinson even called it a disgrace that the book was given the same title as the work by Rabbi Hayim Yosef David Azulai, who traveled through several lands in pursuit of his research, "which this dwarf did not do, though he would follow in the footsteps of the giant, filling his book with the talk of old women and with legends traded around the ovens in the study hall, and on this basis presumed to make a book for the House of Israel."[70] He further wrote that a number of the things Walden told must have been "seen in a dream," for they had no other source.[71] Rodkinson repeated this comment throughout his writings[72] while critiquing Walden's other book *Kehal Hasidim*, parts of which are taken directly from Rodkinson's own books.[73] We also find critical notes on the books of Menahem Mendel Bodek, who was publishing hagiographic works at the same time that Rodkinson was publishing his own.[74]

It is no less interesting that at times Rodkinson even leveled criticism against his own books, the authorship of which he did not deny. For example, after bringing the story of Rabbi Shneur Zalman's coming to Mezritsh, he wrote, "This story has already been published in the book *Shivhei ha-Rav* (Lvov, 1864) and later copied into the book *Kehal Hasidim*, and in general all the stories collected there need to be read carefully, for they contain some true things but many untrue, and the writer erred due to his lack of knowledge and his failure to tell truth from lie."[75]

Rodkinson's criticism was not only aimed at hagiographic literature as a genre but also at the anecdotes woven into the books of homilies being published in the same period. In one instance, for example, he expresses doubts about the reliability of those who published the sayings and tales of Pinhas of Korets, saying that they were "ignorant, heartless, and inarticulate" men who "wrote whatever occurred to them, spreading hallucinations and nonsense among the Jewish people in the name of this holy man."[76] Along with these criticisms, he repeatedly stressed that the stories he had published were reliable. At times he even presented a story and wrote beside it that he brought it only to teach a moral, and took no responsibility for its historical accuracy.[77]

Criticism of Haskalah Literature

While Rodkinson read Hasidic tales with a particularly critical eye, he no less harshly critiqued statements made by Maskilim on Hasidism, especially those who continued the anti-Hasidic line of Josef Perl and his school, expressed most clearly in those days in *Ha-Shahar* (which he also attacked, as mentioned above, in the first issue of *Ha-Kol*). The bulk of these critiques was directed against Pesah Ruderman and David Kahana, who published their work in that journal. He dubbed Ruderman "young in years and even younger in wisdom," and he attacked him a number of times for his statements against both the Baal Shem Tov and the Vilna Gaon, writing that "Ruderman spoke out of his own jealousy and hatred for the Hasidim, who expelled him from their community; his hatred is meant to make up for his stupidity."[78] David Kahana, too, Rodkinson accused of misrepresentation, driven by "his overwhelming and baseless hatred for Hasidism";[79] and we have already seen the nature of his criticism of Kahana as well as Graetz for their approaches to Jakob Frank. This did not stop Rodkinson from accepting their scholarship, as he frequently did; however, as he put it, he took the "kernels" and threw away "their peels."[80]

The Vilna Gaon and Hasidism

Another feature of these writings worthy of note is Rodkinson's favorable view of Elijah Gaon of Vilna. Already in *Shivhei ha-Rav* Rodkinson gave hints to this effect, in blaming the Gaon's opposition to Hasidism on "deceitful men" who misled the Gaon—a common feature of Habad historiography—and in his references to and citations from the book Sefer *Matsref ha-Avodah* (The Crucible of Divine Service).[81] But Rodkinson's relation to the Vilna Gaon comes to clearer expression in the later *Toldot Amudei ha-Habad* when he describes the Gaon's war against the Hasidim,[82] obscuring the ideological factors behind it. His treatment provided a basis for later Hasidic historiographies that attempted to justify or redefine the Gaon's opposition.[83] As a result, Hasidic hagiography would soon begin to include tales in praise of the Gaon himself, with no mention whatsoever of his war against Hasidism.[84]

Ephraim Deinard picked up on this immediately, portraying other books such as Yehoshua Heshel Levin's *Aliyot Eliyahu* (The Ascensions of Elijah, Vilna, 1856) as influenced by this Hasidic trend.[85] Deinard described this book as an attempt to blur the line "between light and darkness," between the Gaon and the Baal Shem Tov, by portraying the Gaon as a Hasidic rebbe, wrapped in wonder tales. The book's stories amount to a sort of biography of the Gaon, though the chapter on his war on Hasidism is missing; rather, the focus is on the Gaon's response to the radical Haskalah, a fact that incensed Deinard.[86] While some Hasidim praised the book,[87] other Maskilim shared Deinard's fury, as when Avraham Mapu wrote in 1857 to his brother Matityahu that "some swindler has published *Aliyot Eliyahu*, telling lies about the wonder-working Gaon of Vilna, and the rich fools among our people have made him rich."[88]

In his later writings Rodkinson did more than minimize the dispute between the Gaon and the Hasidim and adopted the notion of "The Three Shepherds"—the Baal Shem Tov, the Gaon, and Moses Mendelssohn—each of whom had an important and legitimate role in the development of modern Judaism. In this sense he was close to Rabbi Samuel Joseph Fuenn, Eliezer Zweifel, and others,[89] though, in contrast to such authors as Menasheh of Ilya and later Zweifel, Rodkinson did not suggest a compromise between the camps, nor did he attempt to mediate between them.[90] Rodkinson's adoption of this concept points to the place in which he stood: between the three worlds, and in each one in its time. This is the most striking feature of his work from this pre-1876 period, whether speaking of his historical studies of Hasidism, his articles for the press, or his editorship of *Ha-Kol*.

On the "Later" Rodkinson, His Intended Audience, and the Reception of His Books

Who was Rodkinson's intended readership? Were they Hasidim or Mitnagdim? According to Rodkinson's own testimony, he addressed all parties. He claimed "objectivity" in his theories and so his writings were appropriate, in his opinion, for any and all who wanted to hear the "pure truth." At the start of *Or Israel* he even noted that whoever did not want to hear this "truth" or wished to first know if the author was a member of his own party should not continue reading the book, "for such a book as this will find thousands of readers even without you."[91] Elsewhere he hinted that his books were intended for the Hasidim and not the Maskilim, a claim that his own work does not support and that seems to have been made only to arouse the reader.[92] These compositions were written in the spirit of the Haskalah, as we can see from their literary style, their contents, and the books that served as their sources. It is difficult to imagine that he believed this type of publication would find many readers in the Hasidic camp.

While his emphasis on the reliability of his Hasidic sources and his attacks on Maskilim who wrote against Hasidism were likely to strengthen his arguments with Hasidic readers, these books, more complex than the hagiographic collections he had written, had no impact whatsoever on that camp. We find evidence of this in the fact that they were never reprinted, in contrast to all his other books, which have been reprinted and copied from repeatedly until our own day.

In this context, Ephraim Deinard's mocking comments on Rodkinson are particularly interesting, as these comments reflect the reception of his later books in Hasidic society:

> After the Hasid Rabbi Eliezer Zweifel, there arose the well-known *tsadik* and grandson of holy men who, in the stories of *Toldot Amudei ha-Habad*, *Kehal Hasidim*, and other such rags, raised the Hasidim and Hasidism up unto the heavens. Yet every man who has come across these books has spat seven times, and though

> in Barditshev he sought booksellers who would pay six coins for every copy of his book *Toldot Amudei ha-Habad*, not a single man took him up on his offer.[93]

It is likely that Rodkinson's failure to sell this book among the Hasidim was due to its "Maskilic" tone, while his difficulty in spreading it among the Maskilim was due to the fact that it was too "Hasidic" and defended Hasidism. Similar claims were leveled against Rodkinson by at least one Mitnaged, Yosef Kohen-Tsedek:

> And he dwelled in Koenigsberg, and published there *Toldot ha-Besht* and *Toldot ha-Habad*, which even the most extreme Hasidim recognize as pure lies. It is as wondrous as the Parting of the Sea and as miraculous as the sun standing still in the Valley of Gibeon what he has done. . . . And even now he boasts that he has "ninety more of the same" in manuscript . . . which he has not printed, saying that this broken generation is not worthy of them.[94]

Rodkinson's critics even ascribed to him books that he had never written, blaming him for their contents. For example, Deinard wrote:

> Rodkinson had sold his people and his religion for ninety pounds sterling to the London missionaries, writing books like *Toldot Amudei ha-Habad*, *Kehal Hasidim*, *Seder ha-Dorot he-Hadash*, and other such nonsense, hoping to collect money from Hasidic communities with such lies, flattery, foolishness and licentiousness. . . . Even Hasidim, if they have any education, testify that all his words are lies.[95]

We find further support in other sources for fierce criticism of Rodkinson's later books by the Orthodox, who saw them as contrary to the faith (it seems that in this case his opponents' testimony had much truth to it).[96] It is no wonder, then, that they attributed others' books to him and accused him of forging Hasidic texts.[97]

If Rodkinson's later books earned criticism among the Hasidim, the criticism was harsher from the Maskilim. Many continued to see him as a Hasidic author through and through—having only slightly changed his form of expression—and so they fiercely attacked his later works as well. His journalistic activities did not aid the reception of his books and many of his attackers were counted among his competitors in that field. First among them, of course, was Ephraim Deinard, whose words have been so frequently cited here. He saw *Toldot Amudei ha-Habad* as merely a new guise for the same "nonsense and superstition" Rodkinson had printed in the 1860s. Only a "modern name" had been added to make the book "look like the books of the Haskalah," though in truth it was only "Hasidism in the spirit of the age."[98] The following comment by Deinard about *Toldot Amudei ha-Habad* reflects this transition from hagiography to the new style:

> Michael Levi Frumkin became the symbol of the Haskalah and Hasidism when he revealed that all the nonsense tales written in *Shivhei ha-Besht* . . . and all the old wives' tales told among the Hasidim about their rabbis . . . are not as they seem (heaven forbid!) but only sublime concepts and high philosophy wrapped in rags like the fruit inside the peel.[99]

Deinard also attacked Zweifel's books on Hasidism, claiming that the author wrote them only because the Hasidim bribed him to write in their defense. This accusation had been widespread since the arrival of the first volume of *Shalom al Israel*, and Zweifel responded to it with vigorous denials.[100] The lack of clarity in Zweifel's writings and his use of a variety of literary forms prompted Deinard to describe Zweifel too as "the son of an idle Hasid" who "was wont to poke fun at the Hasidim while in Maskilic company, and to mock the Mitnagdim in the confidence of the Hasidim."[101] It is no wonder, then, that Deinard would later write that Zweifel and Rodkinson were in his eyes cut from the same cloth, even if the difference between the two was great.[102]

Yosef Kohen-Tsedek, too, attacked Rodkinson's later books, and with even greater ferocity, first in the 1879 pamphlet *Micha'el ha-Nehepach le-Sama'el* (Michael Who Has Turned Into Samael) and later in his book *Ohalei Shem* (The Tents of Shem), published in 1883. He accepted the claim that Rodkinson was both (or neither) Hasid and Maskil, a bit of an antisemite and a bit of a missionary, and certainly a two-faced scoundrel. As we have already seen, he derided the reprints of Rodkinson's early hagiographic works when the author seemed to have already left that world, and added that Rodkinson's new books on Hasidism were not far removed in quality or content from the former.[103]

In the Hebrew papers, and especially those published by Rodkinson's opponents Aleksander Zederbaum and Perets Smolenskin, we find a criticism of his books that combined these men's personal enmity for Rodkinson with their dislike of Hasidism as a whole. Their favorite mode of critique, in good Maskilic fashion, was the satire. In a barbed essay mocking Rodkinson and *Ha-Kol*, Avraham Shalom Friedberg turned to Rodkinson's later books, pouncing on Rodkinson's recriminations of his fellow Maskilim: "In telling so many exaggerations and wonders to defame his good name, he spurns the sages Ruderman and Kahana," on whom, in fact, he based much of his writings on Hasidism.[104] Aside from noting the substandard style of the composition and its many errors, Friedberg described Rodkinson as duplicitous in his treatment of Hasidism: "He dresses in one guise and then removes it, dons the *shtreimel* [traditional fur hat] and doffs it, crawls out from his hole to fulfill his obligation to the readers of *Ha-Kol*, who are not all complete Hasidim, and then runs back, trembling in fear lest he anger his own people, upon whom he depends . . . so he changes the colors of his skin as the mythical *tahash* beast."[105]

We see a similar approach in the short study on Hasidism by Pesah Ruderman, in which the author recounts a few of Rodkinson's "iniquities,"[106] and in Perets Smolenskin's satirical review of *Toldot Ba'alei Shem Tov*,[107] in which Rodkinson is portrayed as running back and forth between the camps as he follows the money. Dripping with sarcasm, the piece refers to a number of other anti-Hasidic satires previously printed in *Ha-Shahar* ("Al ha-Torah veha-Emunah"

[On Torah and Faith], “Hitgalut ha-Yanuka mi-Stolin” [Revelation of the Child from Stolin] and “Milah de-Metika ke-Duvsha” [A Word as Sweet as Honey]), placing critiques of Rodkinson within the tradition of anti-Hasidic satires in the style of Josef Perl’s *Megaleh Temirin*.[108] Likewise did Mordekhai David Brandstetter, a close associate of Smolenskin who published most of his stories in *Ha-Shahar*, write Rodkinson into one of his stories, granting him the dubious moniker, “Rabbi Michael Levi Frumkin of the holy congregation of Koenigsberg, the last author of hagiography.”[109]

An only slightly different tone is heard at the start of the twentieth century in the writings of the first scholars of Hasidism, who attempted to place Rodkinson’s writings in their broader context. First among them was Simon Dubnow, who had the following to say about Rodkinson’s *Toldot Ba’alei Shem Tov*:

> In his two works he is half-Hasid and half-Maskil; he proffers the stories of *Shivhei ha-Besht* and *Shivhei ha-Rav* in a modernized Hebrew, adding to the latter a number of oral traditions about Schneurson as well as a few previously unpublished letters, using the books of Zweifel, Graetz, and Kahana, and uniting all of these into a popular lecture liable to capture the hearts of freethinkers as well. This is no piece of scholarship, but rather Hasidic hagiography in modern garb.[110]

In a letter to Shmuel Abba Horodecky, Dubnow used similar language and pointed out the need “to separate the wheat from the chaff” and to “emend” the legends in *Shivhei ha-Besht* as well as in the later literature “born in the minds of frauds such as Frumkin-Rodkinson or the countless scions of Hasidic families who fabricate stories to earn money.”[111] These words, marking the beginning of modern scholarship on Hasidism, were written under the influence of Deinard and others, only without the curses. They certainly do not reflect Rodkinson’s writing post-1876 and lack any clear distinction between the early hagiographies and his later work. Dubnow’s final critique could have been said of a number of his acquaintances, such as Avraham Kahana, Shmuel Abba Horodecky, and Martin Buber, whose histories of Hasidism written at the start of the twentieth century reflect the obvious spirit of Romanticism.[112]

On the Fate of *Toldot Ba'alei Shem Tov*

Rodkinson responded to the negative press his books received in an issue of *Ha-Kol* with his article "Me-Az Yatsa Matok" (Out of the Strong Came Something Sweet),[113] but made no mention of publishing more volumes of *Toldot Ba'alei Shem Tov* and said nothing substantial regarding his earlier hagiographic works. One point he emphasized that is relevant for our purposes is that he neither wrote the hagiographies published in the 1870s and 1880s nor had a hand in their publication. In his 1883 book *Tefilah Le-Mosheh* (Prayer of Moses), Rodkinson repeated his recriminations of his critics:

> My two works *Toldot Ba'alei Shem Tov* and *Amudei ha-Habad* blazed a trail for the many books that followed: the histories of all the Hasidic rabbis, of the rabbis who followed the great sages Rabbi Jonathan Eybeschütz and Elijah Gaon of Vilna, and of the Maskilic sages who came after Ben Menahem (Mendelssohn). It was our desire to offer them to the readers along with all the oral legends told by their followers, comprising in our estimation about ninety volumes—but then we intended to pull back the veil from the faces of all the legends . . . but this desire of ours remained unfulfilled due to a variety of circumstances, first among them that the booksellers in Russia never paid us for the books they received. What's more, to our deep sorrow these books were given to self-important critics who spilled much ink in attacking us, including one mischievous critic who went so far as to blame us for sins we never committed, ascribing to us holy books of which we had never heard.[114]

Rodkinson continued to fight back against his critics on the pages of *Ha-Kol,* but in the face of these harsh reviews he abandoned the publication of the remaining volumes; in fact, he may have never even begun to write them. It was just these volumes that could have completed the picture of Rodkinson's complex world and his understanding of the different streams in contemporary Judaism. As we have already seen, however, Rodkinson was never one to stand in one place for long, and he quickly turned to other plans. From 1876 until his death, not a single one of his many books was dedicated to Hasidism. In some of them, however, we can still discern hints about his relationship to the movement. In these books we encounter a new direction.

Kabbalah, Hasidism, and Religious Reform

Rodkinson's critics aimed most of their arrows at his two books on Hasidism from 1876, Toldot Ba'alei Shem Tov and Toldot Amudei Habad, continuing to write about them for years to come. His critics conflated all of his books into one body of work and judged them as such, revealing no sensitivity to or understanding of the transitions Rodkinson had undergone in his lifetime. While his works from 1865 and 1876 remained his central works on Hasidism, his later books cannot go without mention.

After 1876, Rodkinson did not dedicate any particular forum to discussions on Hasidism. Rather, he focused his energy on two areas: new attempts to found *Ha-Kol* and other papers in London, Berlin, Vienna, Chicago, and New York; and his writings on the interrelated topics of religious reform, modern antisemitism, the *Shulhan Arukh*, and the Talmud. In later years he focused more closely on his abridgment of the Babylonian Talmud and its translation into English, a project that would be published in twenty impressive volumes.[115]

The picture of Hasidism that arises indirectly from Rodkinson's later works differs from that found in his works from the 1860s as well as those written in the mid-1870s. For one, his calls to return to the spirit of the Talmud and to nullify certain commandments and stringencies that he claimed were inventions of the rabbis were certainly not typical of a Hasidic worldview. His new relation to Hasidism, and to Kabbalah as well, seems to have been closely tied to his arguments for religious reform. Rodkinson was not exceptional in this; in the writings of Mosheh Leib Lilienblum, Isaac Sobel, Judah Leib Gordon, and others, discussions of religious reforms were often accompanied by attacks on the "superstitious customs" of the Kabbalists and Hasidim.

This trend appears throughout Lilienblum's writings, for example in the satirical song "Kehal Refa'im" (Congregation of Ghosts, 1870), dedicated in part to satirizing a Kabbalist,[116] and in his notes to one of Rodkinson's books, in which he claimed that "all the Kabbalists are either swindlers or lunatics, and nothing can be learned from them."[117] Likewise, a long chapter of Yaakov Tsvi Sobel's biting satire *Ha-Hozeh Hezyonot be-Arba'ah Olamot* (Visions of Four Worlds, 1872) was dedicated to Kabbalistic literature. For these reformers, the Kabbalists and the Hasidim symbolized not only supporters of the "old order" but specifically the rabbinic establishment, which defended its stringent additions to Jewish law with superstition and nonsense.

Rodkinson, for his part, presented the Kabbalists' understanding of *tefillin* in his book *Tefilah le-Mosheh* (1883), where he wrote:

> Our sages of the Talmud trembled greatly lest this commandment become corporeal and idolatrous if they allowed all men to perform it, for the *tefillin* themselves might become the object of worship, being construed as the eye of divinity, the bearers of divine efflux, etc. Their fear was not in vain! For the Kabbalists, who have restored the worship of idols to its former glory by creating for themselves the figure of Primordial Adam with its many faces and personalities . . . have found fertile ground in the commandment of *tefillin* . . . infusing them with the sanctity of actual divinity.[118]

Rodkinson accepts the distinction between the early and later Kabbalists, meaning by "later" those from the time of Rabbi Yosef Karo and after.[119] These comments are a reversal of what he had said in 1876 when describing the different "camps" within the Jewish people, and he certainly did not describe the Kabbalists as "restoring the worship of idols to its former glory."

Rodkinson made even more extreme statements about Hasidism, bringing anecdotes in the spirit of the anti-Hasidic satires, as in his discussion of the era of Rabbi Yosef Karo:

> In his days the Kabbalah of Rabbi Isaac Luria had already begun to spread, along with the custom of the sages to kiss [the *tefillin*], yet no one lay the *tefillin* of Rabbeinu Tam except men of great deeds and the exceptionally pious, until the recent Kabbalists arrived, and after them the Beshtians [the followers of the Besht], who commanded their Hasidim to teach their sons to lay *tefillin* of Rabbeinu Tam from the age of thirteen; and since then the Hasidim have acted without restraint: the wagon drivers wear them pulling their wheeled chariots, and young Hasidim wear them drinking the wine of rectification and while offering the incense of their pipes, and the rabbis wear them while they drink their coffee; the common man rises from his bed, pours water over his fingertips, and while still in his undergarments rushes to kiss the *tefillin* . . . and such has become law in Israel.[120]

Rodkinson adds another note: "Those who know the ways of our people, our rabbis and Hasidim in Russia, and also the poor of our own country, will vouch for us that we have not exaggerated even by a hairsbreadth."[121] He even suggested the reader verify his words himself: "Go now, dear reader, and visit the study halls in Russia or anywhere that the Russian or Polish Jews have established their prayer houses, and see how they study their gemara crowned in their *tefillin* while the young Hasidim drink their alcohol with *tefillin* on their heads."[122] While these words must be assessed in their context—as brief notes within a comprehensive book attacking rabbinic stringencies and calling for a return to "the spirit of the Talmud"—it is impossible to ignore their scathing tone.[123]

Shlomoh Rubin, who had written much on the Kabbalah and its emissaries and who was close to Rodkinson at the time, drafted a letter in support of the author and his ideas, which included an anecdote of his own deriding the Hasidim. His harsh words were cited at the start of *Tefilah le-Mosheh*, without protest from Rodkinson.[124]

Rabbi Hayim Oppenheim, too, who added a number of notes at the start of the book, wrote, "If we will take seriously the hallucinations written in the hidden wisdom, and especially the *Zohar*, most of our fellow Jews would be even more appalled by what the rabbis of our own time say." Rodkinson added, "And I say that hallucinations uttered by the rabbis, even those who aren't Kabbalists, to whom we pay attention, whether willingly or not, are not better or worse than the hallucinations of the Kabbalists." Regarding the term "hidden wisdom," for which Oppenheim used a common acronym, Rodkinson wrote cynically, "I admit without shame that I do not know the meaning of this acronym."[125]

Again we hear Rodkinson speaking harshly of the Hasidim. Yet, in the very same book, he referred to his 1876 multivolume work *Toldot Ba'alei Shem*, apparently without reservations regarding its content, even if his opinions had changed somewhat.[126] Below we will see a further example of this change.

Hasidism, Philosophy, and Christianity

In the first part of his 1884 book *Even ha-Roshah* (The Keystone), Rodkinson described the opposition to his ideas on the Kabbalah and Hasidism. There he repeated:

> Yet another has grown angry "that I, born of the Kabbalah as well as the revealed Torah, am the greatest enemy of the Kabbalah and disparage it unashamedly." To this I will answer them that the truth does not show favor to parents or teachers. What's more, my ancestors were not admirers of the Kabbalah, but rather justified it only by understanding it as a philosophical system. Please read the precious books of the sage my maternal grandfather, *Sha'ar ha-Yihud veha-Emunah* [Gate of Unity and Faith] and *Sha'arei Avodah* [Gates of Service] or *Avodat ha-Beinonim* [Service of the Ordinary Jew], and you will see that he explains all the mystical unifications [of the Godhead] as the faculty of the intellect descending from the provider to the receiver, that is, from the teacher to the student, and removes all corporeality from these

> anthropomorphized names, and even though[, in his books, Rabbi Hayim Vital] warned against corporealization, my grandfather's ways were as far from the ways of the students of Rabbi Isaac Luria as east from west, for Luria's students' understood the unifications as spiritual but not intellectual. I will elaborate on this elsewhere, but in any case my ancestors were far from admiring and sanctifying the corporealized Kabbalah, which carefully follows the Christian system and its "Trinity." See the books explaining the Gospels and you will see that they are founded upon the Kabbalah. And see the books of Shlomoh Rubin and you will see that the Kabbalah and the Christian faith have one source, and what is in one is in the other. That is enough for one who understands.[127]

Rodkinson did more than differentiate between the Kabbalah and Habad Hasidism; he supported the extreme charge that the Kabbalah is identical with Christianity, evoking not only Shlomoh Rubin referred to above,[128] but also his nemesis Ephraim Deinard.[129] There is something exceptional to Rodkinson's opinion, however; he continued:

> It is hard to describe the matter, but the truth is as I said: the sage Rabbi Shneur Zalman of Liady, who understood that the ways of the Kabbalah hew close to idolatry, began to elaborate upon it with philosophical knowledge, which is the basis of the *Tanya*, and his words were explained by my grandfather the sage, Rabbi Aharon ha-Levi of Starosselje, may the memory of the righteous be a blessing.[130]

These words simply cannot be aligned with what Rodkinson had written a few years earlier. We sense here a certain discomfort regarding his earlier writings; on the one hand, a tremendous change had occurred in his relationship to Hasidism, while on the other he could not fully disconnect from the Habad tradition, which he continued to admire. The solution he found was the expropriation of the theoretical Habad Hasidism from the world of popular Hasidism by raising it to the philosophical sphere.[131] This trend was adopted and further developed by Zweifel, Senior Sacks, and Judah Leib Sossnitz, each of whom in his own way interpreted Habad thought as pure philosophy, with little to no relation to the Hasidism of the masses.[132] Deinard wrote in response that "the Jesuits of Habad" had managed to plant in the heart of many Jews the belief that "the teachings of Hasidism are true philosophy, and that Hasidism is the new and proper enlightenment to which all the wise of the earth will soon be drawn."[133]

It is impossible to ignore the sharp tone Rodkinson took in his book on *tefillin*, as in other writings from the same period, a tone entirely lacking from his earlier writings. While in his books from 1876 he attempted to cast the Hasidic movement in a positive light by focusing on its positive features, here the movement is wrapped in the same dark vision of the Maskilim from an earlier era. Rodkinson's goal here was not to analyze the historical development of different streams within Judaism, as it had been in 1876, but to outline a new path for the future. As such, Hasidism, along with the rabbinate, became the target of fierce attacks. The proverbial exception here was Habad, which, in Rodkinson's opinion, was closer to philosophy.

From the day Rodkinson set foot in America, we do not find him relating at all to Hasidism, aside from offhand comments. Even though in his English works he revisited a number of his earlier ideas on religious reform, they were expressed differently in their new American context, in which Hasidism had no place.[134] Now that he was acting in a spiritual terrain that was more accepting of his innovations, Rodkinson turned to other and grander projects, foremost his English translation of the Talmud in the spirit of religious reform.[135] In America Rodkinson focused on the writing of history, even if on sensitive topics, and he abandoned the polemics around Hasidism that had characterized the better part of his life up to that point.

Epilogue

Rodkinson and Neo-Hasidic Literature

We have seen that the first period in Rodkinson's life differed from the second in many respects, and these differences included the environment in which he pursued his literary endeavors of adapting and distributing Hasidic tales. In the beginning, Rodkinson was rooted in the Hasidic world and wrote exclusively for a Hasidic audience, even if he was influenced by outside trends. The following stage found him rooted in the world of the Haskalah; its influence on him is recognizable throughout his work from this time, and his writing on Hasidism became more nuanced as he wrote to both the Hasidim and the Maskilim. His roles in the development and popularization of the printed Hasidic tale and in the historiography of Hasidism were important in Hasidic society as well as in the Maskilic one.

If in his early years he was among the first to distribute the printed Hasidic tale among the Hasidim, in the second phase of his life he was among the first Maskilim to write positively about Hasidism—and he did so amid writers and thinkers who did not know what to make of his message and for the most part assumed the anti-Hasidic mindset of Josef Perl and his school. What's more, if Rodkinson was not the only Maskil to defend Hasidism, he was unique in doing so as a Hasid-turned-Maskil.[1] We may see in his later works a continuation of the efforts of Eliezer Zweifel and his associates in their attempt to reveal another face of this mass movement and to resist the automatic reflex of anti-Hasidism, often expressed through satire, that was the inheritance of most Maskilim. It stands to reason that Rodkinson, like Zweifel and the few others who wrote in a similar spirit, was speaking for others who found no voice in the Jewish press with its fierce statements and extreme positions.[2]

Nevertheless, shortly after writing positively of Hasidism, in 1876 Rodkinson shifted to an entirely different stance, making derisive comments toward Hasidism as he did toward the rabbinic establishment. His sarcastic comments, reminiscent of decidedly anti-Hasidic writers, place this period in Rodkinson's life in a different category. His attempts in later years to present Habad teachings as a form of pure philosophy disconnected from the phantasms of the Kabbalah are likewise intriguing.

In light of these facts, we must say that arguments made by Joseph Dan (among others) that Rodkinson was the harbinger of the Neo-Romantic movement that arose at the end of the nineteenth and start of the twentieth centuries ("Frumkinian Hasidism" in Dan's words), as well as some of Ephraim Deinard's more negative statements cited above (on "the new stream" in Jewish literature), are only partially correct. While they may apply to Rodkinson's second period, they cannot be said of his early years, in which he was still very much part of the Hasidic world and its internal renaissance in hagiographic literature, nor of the post-1876 period, in which he moved away from the Hasidic world entirely and reflected on that world in works that must be called sui generis, rendering it difficult to describe Rodkinson as the harbinger of any Romantic trend. Though Rodkinson stepped outside the Hasidic world and began to write about it from a "Maskilic" point of view, he did not leave it entirely for the world of the Haskalah, and after all is said and done he remained between the two worlds. There is no doubt that this intermediate point created an opening for those who would follow at the turn of the twentieth century: both those who mocked Hasidim in their anti-Hasidic satires and those who praised the movement and wrote about it in a neo-Romantic spirit.

Notes

Glossary

Bibliography

Index

Notes

Introduction

1. On Rodkinson, see Reisin, *Leksikon*, 4:70–77; Frumkin, *In Friling fun Idishen Sotsiyalizm*, 165–80; Kressel, *Leksikon*, 2:888–89. See also n. 35 below.

2. On Deinard, see Schapiro, "Ephraim Deinard," 149–63, where a list of his publishing credits can also be found; Schapiro, "Efraim Deinard," 622–23; Berkowitz, *Ephraim Deinard: "A Transitional Figure" (1846–1930)*; Berkowitz, "Ephraim Deinard: Bibliophile and Bookman," 137–52; and the bibliographic notes in Goldman, *Hebrew Printing in America*, 1:243–34.

3. Deinard, *Mashgei Ivrim*, 3, 7, 17. All translations are those of the author and translator.

4. See Deinard, *Kehilat Amerika*, 2:46, 54–55.

5. Deinard, *Zmir Aritsim ha-Rishon*, 4–5. See also Deinard, *Miflagot be-Israel*, 34–43. Israel ben Eliezer (1700–1760), commonly referred to as the Baal Shem Tov, was a folk healer and spiritual teacher who was considered the founder of the Hasidic movement.

6. Deinard, *Tselem ba-Heikhal*, title page, iii–iv, 183–84. The book (125) even includes an illustration of "the headstone carved by Dr. Yosef Klausner when he wrote his book *Yeshu ha-Notsri, Hayyav ve-Torato* [Jerusalem 1922]," on which appears a black cross and the inscription, "Died 1922, and he has yet to pass on to heaven" (ibid.). A similar dynamic appears in his polemical writings on Zionism, such as *Herpat Britaniyah*, in which he portrays the British Mandate as a missionary government with the conversion of the Jews as its goal.

7. See, for example, Deinard, *Meha'at Sofrim*; Deinard, *Kehilat Amerika*, 1: 1–2, 13–29. Deinard excluded Maskilic writers such as Erter, Mapu, Smolenskin, and Judah Leib Gordon, and directed his vitriolic attacks at those who came after them.

8. Deinard, *Le-Korot ha-Yehudim*, 30; Deinard, *Mashghei Ivrim*, title page. In a number of places Deinard extensively described Rodkinson's "life story," combining fact with fiction throughout. See, for example, Deinard, *Mashgei Ivrim*, 3–15; Deinard, *Tselem ba-Heikhal*, 153–57.

9. Deinard printed numerous anti-Hasidic manuscripts, most of them from the collection of Mendel Landsberg of Kramenets; see, for example, Deinard, *Megileh Afah*. For a synopsis of his views on the Kabbalah and Hasidism, see Deinard, *Alatah*; Deinard, *Am To'ei Levav*. Gershom Scholem wrote inside the cover of his own copy: "A wondrous book! Almost every line is a lie—and everything he says with added assurance, with 'facts,' dates, interconnections—is all bastardized, incomprehensible, or simply fabricated, and it is impossible to criticize sentence after sentence. Such a waste of fine paper!" (*Gershom Scholem Library Catalog*, 1:38). Deinard included many notes in his descriptions of Kabbalistic manuscripts that he put up for sale, which are in fact fabrications and colorful slurs; see Deinard, *Devir Efraim*, 9–11; Deinard, *Reshimah* (Manuscript), 71–73. In a letter to Schwadron he wrote that he inteded to write a book titled "Forgeries in Jewish Literature," focusing on Kabbalistic works [Deinard to Schwadron (Manuscript)].

10. Deinard printed a number of anti-Christian manuscripts with his own introductions. See Deinard, *Bitul Ikarei ha-Notsrim*; Deinard, *Hoda'at Ba'al Din*; Kahana, *Hokhmat Yehudah*. For a synopsis of his essential claims, see Deinard, *Herev le-Hashem ule-Israel*; Deinard, *Mikhtav Galui le-Yeshu ha-Notsri*; Deinard, *Ha-Ya'ar be-Ein Dov*; Deinard, *Devir Efraim*, 21–22.

11. Deinard, *Mashgei Ivrim*, 14–15. On his blindness, see *Kehilat Amerika*, 1:iii; Deinard, *Alatah*, 4; Grossman and Ahlborn, *Judaica at the Smithsonian*, 76.

12. Deinard, *Tselem ba-Heikhal*, 140.

13. Deinard, *Mashgei Ivrim*, 18; compare *Zikhronot*, 2:41; Deinard, *Kehilat Amerika*, 2:137, no. 884; Deinard, *Tselem ba-Heikhal*, 152.

14. Deinard, *Tselem ba-Heikhal*, 154–55.

15. Deinard to Kahana (Manuscript), Courtesy of the National Library of Israel, Jerusalem. See Kahana, *Rabbi Israel Ba'al Shem Tov (Ha-Besh"t): Hayyav, Shittato u-Fe'ulato*. Elsewhere Deinard criticized Kahana (Deinard, *Mashgei Ivrim*, 16; Deinard, *Herev Hadah*, 5–6). On Deinard's intent to write a comprehensive work by the name of *Hasidim ve-Hasidut*, beginning with the BaalShem Tov and ending with neo-Romantic compositions, see Deinard, *Zmir Aritsim ha-Rishon*, 5. For a summary of his conception of Hasidism, see Deinard, *Am To'ei Levav*.

16. On Kohen-Tsedek, see Amen, *Ba'al ha-Mevaser*, 86–88; Bader, *Medinah ve-Hakhameiha*, 119–20; Sokolow, *Ishim*, 205–13; Tsamriyon, *Die hebräische Presse in Europa*, 1:256–64; Wunder, *Me'orei Galitsiyah*, vol. 3, cols. 310–14. Avraham Yaakov Paperna ridiculed these publications founded by Kohen-Tsedek, writing, "Will not the heart of every Maskil quiver and fail when he sees such benighted men as these standing atop the literary height, with the keys to the gates of the Haskalah in their hands?" (*Kol ha-Ketavim*, 27–29, 50, 78–79).

17. Kohen-Tsedek, *Mikha'el ha-Nehepakh le-Sama'el*; Kohen-Tsedek, *Sfat Emet*. See also Kohen-Tsedek, *Ohalei Shem*, 73–74, 76–77.

18. Kohen-Tsedek, title page.

19. On Leibowitz see Eisenstatd, *Hakhmei Israel*, 62–64; Berenstein, *Nehemiah Shmuel Leibovits*; Goldman, *Hebrew Printing in America*, 1:245–46, 418–19; Kressel, *Leksikon*, vol. 2, cols. 251–52. Before becoming an opponent of Deinard, he wrote a number of anti-Hasidic pieces in his paper *Ha-Leumi* (1888–1889).

20. Leibowitz, *Ha-Mavet be-Panim Sokhakim*, 20, 37. Meir Ish Shalom corresponded with Rodkinson over a number of years and it seems that he took issue with Rodkinson's methods only with the publication of the abridged Talmud and its translation into English. So it was as a close associate of Leibowitz that he attacked Rodkinson so fiercely for his activities in America (Leibowitz, *Eikhah Rabati*, 10–12; Kahana, *Hokhmat Yehudah*, 52–53).

21. Leibowitz, *Ha-Mavet Be-Panim Sokhakim*, 20. The debate between Leibowitz and Deinard takes an especially coarse tone in the latter's letters to Schorr; see Kabakoff, *Me-Igrot shel Ze'ev Shor*, 311.

22. Leibowitz, *Mikhtavim*, 45–46. On these books, see the bibliography.

23. Ibid., 46–47; Berkowitz, *Deinard's (Or Mayer) Catalogue*, 65–67. Davidson, to whom the letter was sent, was a close associate of Deinard's and they even resided together for some time (Reizin, *Igrot Sofrim Ivrim*, 171–72). Elsewhere Leibowitz portrayed Deinard as a liar whose books were full of bibliographic errors (Leibowitz, *Mishpato Yiten la-Or*). On Deinard's proposed fraudulent activities concerning the book trade, see the comments of Rodkinson's nephew in Frumkin, *In Friling fun Idishen Sotsiyalizm*, 172–73.

24. Deinard, "El ha-Korim be-Eiropa," 1; Kahana, *Hokhmat Yehudah*, 53–54. Deinard would have surely been uncomfortable had he seen Leibowitz's books from the 1930s with their romantic and pseudo-philological treatments of the Zohar, such as *Midrashei ha-Zohar*, *Peninei ha-Zohar*, and *Tashlum Peninei ha-Zohar* (even if he printed in 1929 a new edition of the anti-Kabbalistic book *Ari Nohem* by Yehudah Aryeh Modena).

25. Sokolow, "Feuilleton," 94–97. This issue even included Rodkinson's portrait.

26. Ibid., 97.

27. Upon reading these words, Micha Yosef Berdyczewski wrote, "Sokolow's essay on Kohen-Tsedek and Rodkinson; a few smart comments. Nevertheless, the man understands something when he renounces the Europeans and dons the Jewish frock (Berdyczewski, "Pirkei Yoman," 53; Holzman, *Ha-Sefer veha-Hayim*, 138).

28. Sokolow, *Ketavim Nivharim*, 3:45–48; Sokolow, *Ishim*, 205–31.

29. Winchevsky, "Rodkinson," 61. On Winchevsky, see Kressel, *Leksikon*, vol. 1, cols. 659–61; and chapter 1 in this volume.

30. Winchevsky, *Rodkinson*, 56, 59. See also Winchevsky, *Gezamelte Verk*, 9:160–61, 275–76. Yosef Klausner summarized Winchevsky's description of Rodkinson as "the work of a craftsman," but added that "even so, for better or worse, he is not always true to the facts as we know them," citing the critiques of Y. H. Levin and Kamionsky (Klausner, *Historiyah*, 6:310).

31. We will expand on this episode below. For an overview, see Ley, "Der Wiener Antisemitismus-Streit," 143–67; Hellwing, *Der konfessionelle Antisemitismus*, 143–48, 160–83.

32. Rodkinson, *Barkai* 1, 40.

33. Ibid., 51–52. See also Rodkinson, *Tekhunat Ruah ha-Israeli*, 24; Rodkinson, *History of the Talmud*, 2:19.

34. So it appears in the essays by Joseph Dan, *He-Hasidut ha-Frumkinianit*, 261–74; Dan, "A Bow to Frumkinian Hasidism," 175–93; Dan, *Jewish Mysticism*, 87–109. A similar tone is heard from Gedalyah Nigal in *Sippurei Rodkinson*. For a slight more balanced treatment, see Heller, "He Should be Called Sama'el," 77–92; Heller, *Further Studies in the Making of the Early Hebrew Book*, 195–215.

35. Deinard, *Kehilat Amerika*, 1:2, 5–9, 65–66; Deinard, *Or ha-Me'ir*, 6; Deinard, *Devir Efraim*, 3–5, 11. On Deinard's role in expanding Jewish collections in leading American libraries, see Schapiro, "Ephraim Deinard," 152–54; Berkowitz, *Ephraim Deinard*, 13–45; Berkowitz, "Ephraim Deinard: Bibliophile and Bookman," 137–52; Berkowitz, "Solzberger-Deinard Relationship," 229–39; Druck, "Nedidat Sefarim," 3; Newman, "Solomon Roubin and Ephraim Deinard," 355–64; Grossman and Ahlborn, *Judaica at the Smithsonian*, 69–80; Weinstein, "First Deinard Collection, 31–48; Kabakoff, *Shocharim ve-Ne'emanim*, 23–24, 36–38, 51–54 (including a letter from Deinard in which he writes, "I am very pleased that I merited to spread our literature in our land [America], something which no one else attempted or could have done"). Deinard was in contact with Yosef Hazanovitch regarding transferring books to Jerusalem (Kabakoff, *Shocharim ve-Ne'emanim*, 32–33). Sometime close to 1928 he attempted unsuccessfully to sell his personal collection to the National Library of Jerusalem; the books were ultimately sold to the library at Harvard University; Deinard to Schwadron (Manuscript); Marx, "Jewish Libraries in America," 78–82.

36. Malachi, "Orkhim Ivrim be-Amerikah," 844. On the importance of this type of work, see Shmeruk, *Sifrut Yiddish*, 212; Faierstein, "Hasidism: The Last Decade in Research," 118.

1. The Life and Works of Michael Levi Rodkinson

1. Surprisingly, Rodkinson wrote at one point that he completed his fiftieth year on 1887, in which case his date of birth must be moved up to 1837 (Rodkinson,

Barkai 1, 51–52). Nevertheless, we can believe the statements he published close to his death, which also included statements by his son, noting the year as 1845. See also Kressel, *Leksikon*, vol. 2, col. 838.

2. For the history of this episode, see Jacobs, *Seeker of Unity*, 11–26; Elior, *Torat ha-Elohut*, 3–21; Elior, Ha-*Mahloket*, 266–86; Etkes, *Ba'al ha-Tanya*, 81–84, 414–36. Deinard ridiculed Rabbi Aharon ha-Levi because of his connection to Rodkinson and saw him as crazed (Deinard, *Mashgei Ivrim*, 3–4; Deinard, *Alatah*, 85; Deinard, *Zmir Aritsim ha-Rishon*, 4; Deinard, *Sefer ha-Kundas*, 69; Deinard, "Alei Hemed, Hor ha-Har," 2–3; Deinard, *Zikhronot Bat Ami*, 2:11–13). He even possessed a satire in manuscript titled "Rehavam ve-Yerovam," describing the dispute over the leadership of Habad after the death of Rabbi Shneur Zalman.

3. See, for example, Rodkinson, *History of the Talmud*, 1:137–38. Elsewhere he expressed a desire to write a biography of his grandfather (Rodkinson, *Toldot Amudei ha-Habad*, opening). When the first volume of *The Jewish Encyclopedia* was published with its entry on Rabbi Aharon of Starosselje, Rodkinson was furious that the author erred in a number of matters and, what's more, did not mention that Rodkinson was his grandson (Rodkinson, "As to Rabbi Aron Ben Maishe Halevi," 257). In a copy of the book *Avodat ha-Levi* (Warsaw, 1866) owned by Isaiah Tishby, we find a dedication in Rodkinson's own hand to his son (from 1882), pointing out that he was the grandson of the author. He would later present his grandfather's teachings as pure philosophy (see chapter 3 in this volume).

4. On Beck see Kressel, *Kitvei Israel Dov Frumkin*, 13–114; Kressel, *Leksikon*, vol. 2, cols. 654–55; Bartal, "Al Demuta ha-Rav Adatit," 121–22. The journal *Ha-Havatselet* was founded in 1863 and Frumkin began to contribute to it in 1870. The connection between the brothers was preserved in some form or another; they wrote in each other's publications and maintained a correspondence between them.

5. Rodkinson, *Toldot Amudei Ha-Habad*, xii, in a note.

6. Rodkinson, *Urim ve-Tumim*. Published in the printing house of Eliyahu Eigel and Yosef Haas. See Cohen, *Defus Tshernovits*, 275–77; Ben Gurion, *Rishmei Kuntresim*, 437–38.

7. Zalmina Vitepsker, *Ma'aseh Nifla'ah*. See Rapoport-Albert, *Hagiography*, 156; and chapter 2 in this volume.

8. This literature has been collected by Nigal in *Sippurei Rodkinson*. See chapter 2 in this volume.

9. Chajes, *Hitragshut ha-Nefesh*. On the author see Assaf, *Untold Tales*, 156–57. The book was reprinted in 1896 as part of Chajes's commentary on the prayer book: Chajes, *Ikvei Shalom*. When this edition arrived in America and Rodkinson came across it, he was furious that his name had been removed from it (Rodkinson, *History of the Talmud*, 2:19).

10. Berdyczewski, *Tsiyun*, 45.

11. Tsazmir, *Luhot ha-Eidut.* The book was accompanied by approbations given to Tsazmir by Yosef Shaul ha-Levi Natanson and Shlomoh Kluger.

12. Rodkinson, *Urim ve-Tumim* (1864). The pamphlet was reprinted a number of times in the second half of the nineteenth century, in Hebrew and in Yiddish, but it seems that Rodkinson was not involved in these editions.

13. On the title page it was written that the book was published in Lemberg in 1856 in the printing house of Kugel (Mondshine, *Torat Habad*, 84–85). This date has already been noted as perplexing (Heller, "He Should be Called Sama'el," 79, 90), but undoubtedly the numbers were reversed and should read 1865, since the printing house of Kugel began its activities only in 1861 (Friedberg, *Toldot ha-Defus ha-Ivri be-Poloniyah*, 86); an identical edition of the *Tanya* was printed by Drucker alone, in the same place and at the same printing house, in 1864 (Mondshine, *Torat Habad*, 102–3).

14. Israel Dov Ber of Vilednik, *She'erit Israel.* The book includes a preface on the importance of a headstone. He consulted with Rabbi Aharon of Chernobil and Rabbi David of Tolna. We will elaborate on other editions below. Deinard would later ridicule Rabbi Israel, apparently in the wake of Rodkinson's publishing of his book (Deinard, *Alatah/Am To'ei Levav*, 85).

15. Despite Rodkinson's claim in his introduction to *She'erit Israel* that he had not included approbations, since such a book had no need for them, he did include the approbation of Rabbi Yosef Shaul ha-Levi Natanson, which was at times decried as a forgery. On the problematic nature of this approbation and the speculation that it was forged, see Weisberg, *Gaon ve-Shivro*, 100–102; Mondshine, "Introduction," 42, 100. A critique of such speculations can be found in Reichersberg, *Divrei Sefer*, 7. Rodkinson later referred to the charge of forgery in his book in German, when he accused Yosef Kohen-Tsedek (whom he dubbed *Kohen On*, "the priest of On") of first making the charge (Rodkinson, *Der Schulchan Aruch*, viii).

16. Friedberg, *Toldot ha-Defus ha-Ivri*, 135.

17. Israel of Bahafoli, *Ateret Tiferet Israel.* The contents of the book were put in writing by a Habad Hasid by the name of Rabbi Meir of Lithuania, and printed by Avraham ha-Kohen and Shmuel Zeiliger. Rodkinson was mentioned in the approbation of Rabbi Aharon of Chernobil, who included at its head a "sales contract" made between him and Zeiliger in Odessa; the statement is signed "the publisher."

18. Emden, *Iggeret Bikoret.* Rodkinson also composed an introduction to the work (Refael, "Kitvei Rabbi Ya'akov Emden" 245–46).

19. Heinrich Felix Paulizky, *Marpe la-Am.* The name of the printer is omitted; see Rodkinson, *History of the Talmud*, 2:19. On the book, see Zalkin, "Scientific Literature and Cultural Transformation," 256–57.

20. Israel Dov Ber of Vilednik, *She'erit Israel* (1868).

21. Dik, *Der Purim Shpigel; Kuperman, Vigderil ben Vigderil*; Rodkinson, *History of the Talmud*, 2:19. Here too it is possible that he published similar books that did not bear his name.

22. *She'alot u-Teshuvot Rabbi Joseph ibn Migash.* The year is delineated by a phrase with the numerical value of 630, equivalent to 1870.

23. Rodkinson wrote an introduction on the nature of the composition (fols. 2a–b).

24. Gottlober, "Rusland," 313. On his journey, see Goldberg's Introduction to *Zikhronot u-Masa'ot*, 12–3, 40–42, 45.

25. Zederbaum, "Bi-Gevurah ve-Lo be-Sheti," 465–66. Additional facts appear in the author's complementary essay, "Mi-Kol Melamedai Hiskalti," 77–80. His statements were picked up by Kohen-Tsedek, who reprinted Zederbaum's essay in his books (*Sfat Emet*, 5–8; *Ohalei Shem*, 81–82). Deinard noted that Rodkinson "boasted" that he had sat in prison seventeen years! (Deinard, *Kehilat Amerika*, 2:137; Deinard, *Tselem ba-Heikhal*, 152, 155); he even knew enough to recount many "facts" from that unknown period with colorful flourishes (Deinard, *Mashgei Ivrim*, 8–9). From here it was a short step to other exaggerations that were later absorbed into scholarly literature, such as the statement that he had been in jail seventeen times (Berkowitz, *Deinard*, 92). We should not discount the speculation that Rodkinson had lost his shirt in the market in St. Petersburg, as befell many others (and which was given eloquent literary expression by Perets Smolenskin and Sholem Aleichem). The information on Rodkinson found in the contemporary Russian press is still in need of additional research.

26. Rodkinson, *Me-Az Yatsa Matok*, 1–4; Rodkinson, *Matsat-Mitsvah*, 29–32.

27. Winchevsky wrote that he changed his name in order to evade military service, while others tell that the name change was related to his financial difficulties.

28. On Rodkinson's Hasidic activities and their context, see chapter 3 in this volume.

29. On the journal and its contributors, see the long article by Zitron, "Reshimot le-Toldot ha-Itonut ha-Ivrit: Ha-Kol"; Rabinowitz, "Kakh Kotvim Historiyah Etslenu," 1022–23, 1041–42. See also Klausner, *Historiyah*, 6:310–13, 337–49, 396–97; Gilboa, *Leksikon*, cols. 258–64; Poll, *Jüdische Presse*, 105–6; Tsamriyon, *Die hebräische Presse*, 272–76; Kouts, "'Gavoah' ve-'Namukh' bi-Kefifah Ahat," 26–32; Kouts, *Ma'arikhim u-Mikhtavei Itim*, 42–54.

30. We can assume that Rodkinson was moved to publish a new paper in the wake of a meeting he had with Aleksander Zederbaum, at which they spoke of cooperating. Zederbaum agreed to Rodkinson's suggestion that he become a writer for *Ha-Kol*, but later retracted, a decision that caused much friction between them over the years (Zederbaum, "Mi-Kol Melamedai Hiskalti," 77–78).

31. On the beginnings of the Jewish press at that time, see Klausner, *Historiyah*, 4:111–28; Zinberg, *Toldot*, 7:17–58; Kressel, *Guide to the Hebrew Press*, i–viii; Gilboa, *Leksikon*, cols. 25–32; Bartal, *Me-"Umah" le-"Leom,"* 136–41; Kouts, *La naissance de la presse hébraïque moderne*; Sofer, *Eyn Lepalpel! Iton "Ha-Tsefirah."*

32. Rodkinson, "Divrei Shalom ve-Emet," 1–3. Deinard would later tell that he tried to prevent the printing of the *Aleh le-Mivhan* by revealing his "iniquities" to the authorities (Deinard, *Mashgei Ivrim*, 10–11).

33. Frumkin, *Ha-Kol*, 77; Rodkinson, "Ha-Kol Omar Kera," 31–32.

34. In its first year (1876) *Ha-Kol* had one special edition and forty-eight regular issues; in its second (1877), fifteen; in its third (1878), one hundred; in its fourth (1879), seventy-two; in its fifth (1880), forty-eight; in all, 284 issues were printed. The journal was occasionally relaunched in Vienna and in a few cities across America (in its sixth and seventh years), as we will see below.

35. Rodkinson also wished to enlist Judah Leib Gordon (Rodkinson to Judah Leib Gordon (Manuscript), December 5, 1886).

36. Extremely valuable details on *Ha-Kol* appear in Winchevsky's memoirs, *Gezamelte Verk*, 9:155–67, 289–97. On his connections to Rodkinson, see Marmer, "Moris Vintshevski, Zein Leben, Virken un Shafn," 43–51, 57–65; Malachi, "Morris Vintshevski," 287–88, 317–18; Klausner, *Historiyah*, 6:307–50. On the assistants, see Lofman, "Itonai Yehudi be-Shalosh Yevashot," 138–42; Sokolow, *Ketavim*, 3:25–28; Zitron, "Reshimot le-Toldot ha-Itonut ha-Ivrit: Ha-Kol," 357, 458–59, 537–38, 639, 818–19; Rabinowitz, "Kakh Kotvim," 1022–23, 1041–42.

37. Malachi, *Massot ve-Reshimot*, 159.

38. As late as 1874 Perets Smolenskin had harsh words for the writers who were multiplying like flies "and journal publishers sprouting up like wild grass, ignorant men who do not understand how to write a single sentence properly, who mangle our language with their obscene spirit; we look upon them all with disgust, and are repulsed when we see who they are who would be counted among our fellows" (Smolenskin, *Ha-Tsefirah*, 591–92). Paperna had similar words for the papers of Kohen-Tsedek (*Ketavim*, 27–29, 50).

39. Kouts, *Ma'arikhim*, 44.

40. Lachover, *Toldot ha-Sifrut*, 2:292–93. See similar statements in Klausner, *Historiyah*, 6:310.

41. Zitron, "Ha-Kol," 538; Rabinowitz, "Kakh Kotvim," 1022–23, 1041–42; Karol, *Ha-Emet*, 42–43.

42. Rabinowitz, "Kakh Kotvim," 1022. Later Rabinowitz, who served as the acting editor, recounts how Rodkinson reordered the essays and even emended their content—a fact that infuriated him and caused his departure. He described his time in Koenigsberg and his contacts with Lieberman and others in an autobiography

published, partially, in 1929 (Rabinowitz, *Otobiyografiyah* (Manuscript); Kressel, "Be-Reishit ha-Sotsiyalizm," 6–15; Katzenelson, "Eliyahu Volf Rabinovits," 1).

43. "Regarding Herr Rodkinson's request to enlist many subscribers for his journal titled *Ha-Kol*, it has been decided to answer him that this journal is not in accord with the goals of the Society" (Rosenthal, *Hevrat Marbei Haskalah*, 1:139). On the Society's support of Hebrew journalism, see *Hevrat Dorshei Haskalah, Me-Heshbon*, 102.

44. For example Rodkinson, Letter to Judah Leib Gordon (Manuscript), December 5, 1876; March 22, 1878.

45. Deinard's phrase; Deinard to Judah Leib Gordon (Manuscript), 1878.

46. Zitron, "Reshimot le-Toldot ha-Itonut ha-Ivrit: Ha-Kol," 418. One of the paper's agents got into an argument with Rodkinson and published an anonymous essay against him: Bush, "Mikhtavei Sofrim"; Rodkinson, "Mikhtavei Sofrim"; Bush, "Mikhtavei Sofrim. Kenigsberg (Hitnatslut)". On this episode and parodies of the Zohar composed by Rodkinson in ridicule against the same man, see Malachi, "Le-Toldot ha-Levanon," 115.

47. Zitron, "Reshimot le-Toldot ha-Itonut ha-Ivrit: Ha-Kol," 418, 460; Lilienblum, *Igrot M. L. Lilienblum le-Y. Y. Gordon*, 161. From here sprouted Deinard's story that Rodkinson wished to found a Hasidic paper to respond to their persecutors (Deinard, *Masghei Ivrim*, 9–10).

48. On *Ha-Kol la-Am* and its various manifestations, see Zitron, *Geshikhte*, 1:89–116; Winchevski, *Gezamelte Verk*, 10:9–11; Poll, *Jüdische Presse*, 118–20; Shmeruk, *Sifrut Yiddish*, 289–90. Its contributors included Gavriel Ravitch and Mordekhai Plongian. This paper is awaiting its own comprehensive study. Despite this, there is extensive research on *Kol Mevaser* and the beginnings of the Yiddish press (see Zinberg, *Kultur Historishe Shtudies*, 159–89; Zinberg, *Toldot Sifrut Israel*, 7:127–46; Zitron, *Geshikhte*, 5–74; Malachi, *Kol Mevaser*, 49–121; Shmeruk, *Sifrut Yiddish*, 261–93; Orbach, *New Voices of Russian Jewry*, 108–23, 155–81, 204–6; Werses, "*Hakitsah Ami*," 321–50). For Deinard's criticisms, see *Mashgei Ivrim*, 45–46.

49. Abramovitch, "Tsu Unzere Yuden," 153–54. See Zitron, *Geshikhte*, 1:102–5; Zitron, "Reshimot le-Toldot ha-Itonut ha-Ivrit: Ha-Kol," 418–19; Karol, "Ha-Emet," 17.

50. Winchevsky, "Pirkei Zikhronot," 82–83; Winchevsky, *Gezamelte Verk*, 9:191–321; Winchevsky,"Zikhronot al Asefat Hakhamim," 21–25; Gilboa, *Leksikon*, cols. 270–72; Tsamriyon, *Die hebräische Presse*, vol. 1:270–72; Eisenstadt, *Perakim*, 177–80.

51. Rodkinson, "Et Asher Nadarti Eshalem," 77; also in an announcement in *Ha-Kol* 2, no. 1.

52. Rodkinson, "Ha-Asefah Tiftah," 1–2.

53. Rodkinson, Letter to Buber (Manuscript), n.d. Courtesy of the National Library of Israel, Jerusalem. From the letter it seems that Buber had advised Rodkinson to translate the Zohar into Hebrew, and this was Rodkinson's response: "It is true that Aramaic is not unfamiliar to me, and I will hasten to write it in Hebrew," but "all the same, I could not follow his advice, for I have not the time; would that I did; it seems that my hard work and money was all for naught, for, according to many, all of the sanctity of the Zohar is in its Aramaic language."

54. See Rodkinson's note in *Asefat Hakhamim* 5 (1878), 69.

55. Winchevsky, "Asefat Hakhamim," 21. See also Winchevsky, "Rodkinson," 57.

56. Lilienblum, *Ketavim Otobiografi'im*, 2:167; Winchevsky, *Gezamelte Verk*, 9:261–62, 278–85; Klausner, *Historiyah*, 4:244–51; Karol, *Ha-Emet*, 35–36; Friedlander, *Be-Mistarei ha-Satirah*, 3:147–215.

57. Warhaft, "Tsiyon la-Nefesh"; see Deinard's response in Deinard, "Hashkafah Kelalit"; Deinard, "Igeret el ha-Mo"l." Leibowitz would later use Warhaft's words in his own disputes with Deinard (Leibowitz, *Tene Bikurim*, 7; Leibowitz, *Deinard u-Sefarav*, 5–7).

58. Kohen-Tsedek, *Ohalei Shem*, 82; Deinard, *Masa be-Eiropa*, 9; Deinard, *Mashgei Ivrim*, 11; Deinard, *Zikhronot*, 2:34. For additional parodies of the name see Winchevsky, "Rodkinson," 55. When in 1892 Deinard assembled a price list for booksellers, he inflated the price of *Asefat Hakhamim*, along with Zweifel's *Ha-Sanegor*, to limit sales (Leibowitz, *Mishpato Yiten la-Or*, 12–13; Leibowitz, *Deinard u-Sefarav*, 17–18). According to his own testimony, he was driven to do so by the criticism of him those publications contained.

59. Zitron, "Reshimot le-Toldot ha-Itonut ha-Ivrit: Ha-Mabit," 60–61; Klausner, *Historiyah*, 5:133. A colorful portrait of the personal side of that dispute can be found in Zitron's memoirs, *Nofekh*, 351–55.

60. Zederbaum, "Bi-Gevurah ve-Lo be-Sheti," 465–66.

61. For example, he called Zilberman, the editor of *Ha-Magid*, "Bar Kaspa" (Son of Silver). On this type of wordplay, see Zitron, "Reshimot le-Toldot ha-Itonut ha-Ivrit: Ha-Kol," 961–63; Winchevsky, "Rodkinson," 55.

62. Zitron, "Reshimot le-Toldot ha-Itonut ha-Ivrit: Ha-Kol," 417; Provest, "Ha-Itonut ha-Ivrit," 248–51.

63 . Kaminer, "Ets Erez ve-Ezov," 4–5, 45–46, 59–65. See Katzenelson, "Meshorer Leumi," 62. Nahum Leib Samuel Novoplansky (Nahal ha-Bashan) also mocked Zederbaum, on the pages of *Ha-Kol*: Novoplansky, "Davar be-Ito," 15–18. In the margins of this essay, Rodkinson accused Zederbaum of libel.

64. Friedberg, "Shilumim la-Riv"; Friedberg, "Davar el ha-Korim." On Friedberg, who would later write *Zikhronot le-Veit David*, see Zogorodski, "R. Avraham Shalom Friedberg," 301–5; Ravnitsky, *Dor u-Sofrav*, 170–74.

65. Zederbaum's comments are cited in Friedberg, "Davar el ha-Korim," 390.

66. Friedberg, "Zikhronot," 239. See also Malachi, *Igrot Sofrim*, 32–33.

67. Berkowitz, "Mi-Ma'arekhet ha-Emet," 7.

68. Lilienblum, "Shishah Mikhtavim," 381; Winchevsky, *Gezamelte Verk*, 10:11.

69. Lilienblum, *Kol Kitvei Mosheh Leib Lilienblum*, 1:140–67, 168–92. His comments were published, with additions and rebuttals, in future editions of *Ha-Kol* between the months of Tevet and Shevat 5639 (1879). Rodkinson even translated the essay into Russia and attempted to publish it, appealing in vain to Judah Leib Gordon and "The Society for the Promotion of Culture among the Jews of Russia"; Rodkinson to Judah Leib Gordon (Manuscript), March 22, 1878. Deinard mocked both Rodkinson and Lilienblum, who put hope in the rabbinical assembly of 1879 (Deinard, *Masa be-Eiropa*, 104–5).

70. In one of the issues of *Ha-Mabit* from 1878 Smolenskin wrote, "I acknowledged from the start that *Ha-Mabit* would not address matters of faith (Smolenskin, "El ha-Korim," 32; Deinard, "Al Ha-Mabit," 230–32).

71. Lilienblum, *Igrot*, 161; Lilienblum, *Ketavim Otobiyografi'im*, 2:174.

72. In the wake of this essay followed a controversy into which Rodkinson stepped as well, to heatedly defend Lilienblum's opinions; Rodkinson continued to develop ideas of religious reform even if his was a very different approach than Lilienblum's. See Klausner, *Historiyah*, 4:232–43; Zitron, "Ha-Kol," 639.

73. Rivkind, *Leket Igrot*, 353; the letter was written at some point in 1878. Regarding the move by writers to *Ha-Kol*, Perets Smolenskin wrote in the margins of one of Deinard's essays in *Ha-Shahar*, "I do admit (though I'm embarrassed to do so), that others whom I admired in my heart were drawn by the owner of *Ha-Kol*, for it is already acknowledged that many Jewish writers are not spoiled, and they will accept any place that is offered to them" (Deinard, "Igeret el ha-Mol," 336).

74. Zederbaum, "Ma'aneh Rakh," 596–97.

75. Gottlober, "Mikhtav Galui," 850. Gottlober would later become a contributor to *Ha-Kol* himself.

76. Three editions were published, with contributions from Yosef Brill, Mordecai Plongian, Tsvi Cherchevsky, Yosef Leib Sossnitz, Judah Leib Gordon, Yitshak Eizik Etkin, and David Sidorsky. These editions contained the continuations of Lilienblum's *Mishnat Elisha ben Abuyah* under the title *Mishnat Yishuv Olam*. See Gilboa, *Leksikon*, cols. 285–86.

77. Rodkinson, "Me'asef le-Khol ha-Mahanot," 1–5. See also one of his essays in *Ha-Kol*, Rodkinson, "Me-Az Yatsa Matok," 1039–42, 1051–54, 1060.

78. The essay was published there, and Rodkinson clearly did not write it ("Elim ve-Elilim," 41–51, 68–70).

79. Brill, "Midrash Sofrim," 1:85, 141, 197–98, 563, 622; 2:181–82.

80. Mezah, "Sefer Hadash," 4; Mezah, *Tefah Meguleh*. Mezah sought to publish an expanded version of the composition in 1889 and to do so turned to Judah Leib Gordon, who was at that time embroiled in a dispute with Zederbaum, asking him to add "whatever you wish about this worthless scoundrel." Gordon wrote in the margins of the letter, "Such a request does not merit a response, but only to be left to rot" (Mezah to Judah Leib Gordon (Manuscript), Courtesy of the National Library of Israel, Jerusalem). According to Apel (*Be-Tokh Reishit ha-Tehiyah*, 144), the pamphlet was actually written by David Frishman with Mezah listed as the author. The work in fact includes the work of Frishman and poems by Gordon. See Malachi, *Igrot Frishman*, 47, 49, 72. On disputes involving Zederbaum, see Malachi, *Igrot Frishman*, 140–45; Breinin, *Zikhronot*, 3–4, 23–24; Frishman, *Ketavim*, 4:66, 70.

81. Winchevsky, "Rodkinson," 58–59.

82. Winchevsky, "Erets Rusyah ve-Ha-Kol," 25–27. See also Winchevsky, *Gezamelte Verk*, 9:11; Malachi, *Massot ve-Reshimot*, 163–64; Klausner, *Historiyah*, 6:317.

83. Lifshitz, *Zikhron Ya'akov*, 2:184. On Lifshitz see Bartal, "Zikhron Ya'akov," 409–14.

84. On Feinberg's support, see Deinard, *Tselem ba-Heikhal*, 155. Rodkinson continued to enjoy the support of this banker.

85. Winchevsky, *Gezamelte Verk*, 9, 325–45; 10, 29–32. See Marmer, "Moris Vintshevski," 63, 6607; Lofman, "Itonai Yehudi," 138–42.

86. Kohen-Tsedek, *Mikha'el ha-Nehepakh le-Sama'el*; Kohen-Tsedek, *Sfat Emet*. For additional explanation of Kohen-Tsedek's motives (related to the activities of Naftali ha-Levi), see Winchevsky, "*Rodkinson*," 59–60; Winchevksy, *Gezamelte Verk*, 10:308–13.

87. Kohen-Tsedek, *Sefer Musar Haskel*. See the critiques in *Ha-Kol*: Winchevsky, "Sefer Musar Haskel"; Rodkinson, "Me-Az Yatsa Matok," 5–9, 1067–76.

88. Kohen-Tsedek to Fuenn (Manuscript), Courtesy of the National Library of Israel, Jerusalem. Kohen-Tsedek would later respond fiercely to his critics, claiming that *Sefer Musar Haskel* was well received and "all the journals I've published for our fellow Jews, in their respective languages and lands, testify to his good name" (Kohen-Tsedek, *Or Hadash*, introduction, 11–12, and in the body of the text, 7–8, 11).

89. Zederbaum, "*Binah bi-Sefarim*," 95–96.

90. Rodkinson, "Davar Ehad," 1–2; see also Rodkinson, "Me-Az Yatsa Matok," 1–3; Rodkinson, *Matsat-Mitsvah*, 12–13, 21–22, 29–32; Rodkinson, *Barkai*, 1:49–50. A similar picture appears in other accounts: see Ben Hillel ha-Kohen, *Olami*, 1:95, 122; Zitron, "Ha-Kol," 962–63.

91. Zederbaum, "Mi-Kesem Le-Kazav," 430. See also Zederbaum, "Ha-Rotseh Leshaker," 411–13; Zederbaum, "Bi-Kehal Yehudei Rusyah," 520. Deinard would later respond to these and similar comments by Zederbaum with sarcasm; see Deinard, *Sefer ha-Ployderzak* (Gilboa, "Ha-Ployderzak," 118–19); Deinard described *Ha-Kol* and *Ha-Melits* as members of the antinational "Black Chamber" (Deinard, *Divrei ha-Yamim*, 2:16–18).

92. Berenfeld, *Zikhronot*, 193; Berenfeld, "David Gordon," 378–79; Rodkinson, "Me-Har ha-Melekh," 717–19. This event led to violence between Berenfeld's father and Rodkinson; see Berenfeld, "Lemberg," 414.

93. Rodkinson's described his move as one "from the king's city (Koenigsberg) to the city of the monarchy (Berlin)" ("Me-Har ha-Melekh," 717–19).

94. *Ha-Medabar le-Israel* printed twelve issues between 1881 and 1882. The first issue was published on 22 Elul, 5641 (1881). See Zitron, "Ha-Kol," 1002; Tsamriyon, *Die hebräische Presse*, 1:276; Provest, "Itonut," 248–51; Lin, *Die hebräische Presse*, 77; Gilboa, *Leksikon*, 291–92.

95. Rodkinson, *Ha-Hozeh*, subtitled, "That which I envision I shall tell to the House of Israel, among all that occurs in the worlds of politics, Judaism, literature, and science." Twenty-two issues were published in 1882, sixteen in Berlin and the rest in Hamburg. The German name of the paper was *Der Zeher: Wochenschrift für Handel, Politik, und Literature im Hebräischer Sprache*. See Zitron, "Ha-Kol," 1002; Gilboa, *Leksikon*, cols. 295–96.

96. Deinard repeated these charges in a number of essays in both the press and in his later books: *Masa be-Eiropa*, 162; "Odessa," 580–81; *Mashgei Ivrim*, 12; *Tselem ba-Heikhal*, 155–56; *Zikhronot*, 2:35; "Mizreh ha-Reshet," 6; "He'arat ha-Mo''L," 4; Rodkinson's response can be found in Rodkinson, *Barkai*, 1:39–40. On the relationship between Delitzsch and Rodkinson, which included the exchange of letters, see Rodkinson, *Pentateuch, Its Languages*, 28; Rodkinson, *Even Sapir*, 27–28.

97. Kohen-Tsedek, *Ohalei Shem*, 82.

98. Rodkinson, Letters to Lazarus (Manuscript), May 4, 1881. Courtesy of the National Library of Israel, Jerusalem. The letter was written on the letterhead of the organization *Verein zur Erhaltung und Vertzeitung der Hebräischen Sprache (Association for the Preservation and Representation of the Hebrew Language).*

99. Rodkinson to Shteinshneider (Manuscript), n.d. The letter includes an attempt by Rodkinson to earn his daughter admission into the Berlin Jewish School for Girls, headed by Steinschneider.

100. Rodkinson, "Demamah ve-Kol Eshma," 3–4; Rodkinson, "Mah Anu," 7–8. Contributors to the paper during its time in Hamburg included Winchevsky, Shlomoh Rubin, and Aharon Yehuda Leib Horowitz (Ayala"h). Deinard attributed the break in the paper's production and its move to Hamburg to the fact that, while

in Berlin, Rodkinson's "true" face had been revealed by Herman Strock (Deinard, *Tselem ba-Heikhal*, 155–56; Berkowitz, "Deinard," 91).

101. Rodkinson, "Demamah ve-Kol Eshma," 5–6.

102. Rodkinson, "Hizayon Ma'atsiv," 14; Rodkinson, "El Mol Ha-Magid." Zitron explained this propaganda of Rodkinson's and stressed the financial benefit of Rodkinson's propaganda (Zitron, "Ha-Kol," 1002; Zitron, *Toldot Hibat Tsiyon*, 110–11). On the reflection of this controversy in the Hebrew press, see Salmon, "Gordon," 161–62; Geffen, "Whither to Palestine or to America?" 179–200. See also Frishman's ridicule of the entire controversy in his *Ketavim*, 4:44–45, 54–55.

103. Tsamriyon, *Die hebräische Presse*, 1:274–75.

104. Rodkinson, *Tefilah le-Mosheh*, 29, 97.

105. Deinard, *Masa be-Eiropa*, 162. See also Deinard, *Kitot be-Israel*, 8; Deinard, *Mashgei Ivrim*, 12; Deinard, *Zikhronot*, 2:35.

106. Berkowitz, "Deinard," 14, 92. See also Kohen-Tsedek, *Sfat Emet*, 21–22, 38.

107. Rabinowitz, *Sefer ha-Zikaron*, 72–73.

108. Rodkinson, *Matsat-Mitsvah*, subtitled "Blood Libels! What have our rabbis done? What have our Maskilim done? How Israel will be saved." The addresses provided for sales of the book were Rodkinson's home in London and the house of H. D. Lippe in Vienna.

109. There is a wide-ranging body of literature on this sentence and on the rise of modern antisemitism, including Bartal, *Me-"Umah" le-"Leom,"* 172–202; Handler, *Blood Libel*; Katz, *Sinat Israel*, 258–64, 356–58; Nathan, *Der Prozess von Tisza-Eszlàr*; Fischer, "Anti-Semitism in Hungary," 106–55, 255–59. For a current bibliography, see the comparative studies by Kieval, "Middleman Minorities and Blood," 208–33; Kieval, "The Importance of Place," 135–65; Kieval, *Languages of Community*, 181–97.

110. Rodkinson, *Matsat-Mitsvah*, 3. The charge was based on the Talmudic saying, "Let the one who suffers inspect his deeds" (T. B. Berachot, 5a).

111. Rodkinson, *Matsat-Mitsvah*, 5–10. Rodkinson referred also to the controversy over the leniency regarding eating legumes on Passover, which had been forbidden for various extralegal reasons.

112. Rodkinson, *Matsat-Mitsvah*, 10–11. He published similar statements in *Ha-Kol*; see Zitron, "Ha-Kol," 459–60.

113. Rodkinson, *Matsat-Mitsvah*, 12–13. Some recoiled from this statement, especially given that the question of religious reform was not central to their work (see more on this below).

114. Rodkinson, *Matsat-Mitsvah*, 14.

115. Ibid., 16–17.

116. Ibid., 17–19, 21.

117. Ibid., 26.

118. His arguments were printed in *Ha-Melits* in 1868 and 1869 under the title *Orhot ha-Talmud* (Lilienblum, *Kol Kitvei*, 1:7–52). Rodkinson printed Lilienblum's later words on the topic in *Even Sapir* (1886). On Lilienblum's fight for religious reform, see Katzenelson, "Ha-Milhamah ha-Sifrutit," 76–110; Klausner, *Historiyah*, 4:198–206, 211–17; Zinberg, *Toldot*, 7:147–64; Orbach, *New Voices*, 134–45; Breiman, *Pulmus ha-Tikunim*; Breiman, "Introduction," 74–77; Breiman, *Ha-Pulmus*; Shaked, "Introduction," 12–13, 32–34; Bartal, *Me-"Umah" le-"Leom,"* 153–57.

119. Rodkinson's work also bore certain parallels to that of Judah Leib Gordon. For a summary of Gordon's position, see Katzenelson, "Ha-Milhamah ha-Sifrutit," 140–62; Stanislawski, *For Whom Do I Toil?*; Feiner, "Yehudah Leib Gordon ke-Anti-Klerikal," 211–29; Friedlander, *Bein Halakhah le-Haskalah*; 181–322. On the controversy over the relevance of religious reforms in 1881–1882, see Karniel, "Bein Yehudah Leib Gordon le-Sokolov," 327–30.

120. Levin, "Mikhtav," 97–98. See Rodkinson's statements in *Matsat-Mitsvah*, 12–13.

121. Levin to Smolenskin (Manuscript), Courtesy of the National Library of Israel, Jerusalem.

122. Rabinowitz and Levin, "Mi-Zeh Ehad umi-Zeh Ehad," 163–65; Druyanov, *Ketavim*, 2:102–8. The complete version of Rabinowitz's statements remain in manuscript; (Rabinowitz to Judah Leib Levin (Manuscript). Rodkinson responded in *Even ha-Roshah*, 38–39. For a harsh critique of this essay, if from a very particular point of view, see Frishman's claim that the new nationalism was a "new Sabbatianism" (Malachi, *Igrot Frishman*, 35).

123. Gordon, "Besorat Sefarim: Matsat-Mitsvah ve-Alilat ha-Dam," 31. On Gordon's opinions regarding the Haskalah, reforms, and antisemitism, see Salmon, "Gordon," 157–61.

124. Deinard, *Or ha-Me'ir*, 77; Deinard, *Mashgei Ivrim*, 12; Deinard, *Zikhronot*, 2:35; Deinard, *Tselem ba-Heikhal*, 156; Deinard, *Divrei ha-Yamim*, 2:17–18, 63; Kohen-Tsedek, *Sfat Emet*, 80, 85–91, 95; Kohen-Tsedek, *Ohalei Shem*, 86–89.

125. Smolenskin, *Matsat-Mitsvah*, 299–300. Smolenskin's comments stem from his own understanding of the source of modern antisemitism and the proper responses to it; see Breiman, *Ha-Pulmus*, 5–15. Nevertheless, Smolenskin prevented the publication of a denunciation (Sirotkin, *Mefarsemin et ha-Hanafim*).

126. Aharon Yehuda Leib Horowitz (Ayala"h) had earlier written in praise of immigration to America as being as favorable to moving to the Land of Israel. In the 1870s he spent time in America and was one of the founders of the paper *Ha-Tsofeh le-Veit Israel*, along with Tsvi Hirsch Berstein. Descriptions of his travels, along with information for travelers, can be found in his memoirs (Horowitz, *"Rumaniyah*

ve-Amerikah"; Horowitz, "Mi-Zikhronotai"). See Gartner, "Rumania and America," 67–92; Malachi, "AYaLa"H," 210–17; Klausner, "*Shneurson,*" 104–5; Klausner, "*Hibat Tsiyon,*" 22–25, 60; Kressel, *Leksikon*, vol. 1, cols. 580–81.

127. Horowitz, "Hamburg," 20–21.

128. Rodkinson, *Tefilah le-Mosheh*. The German subtitle was *Ursprung und Entwickelung des Phulacterein-Ritus bei den Juden* (Origin and Evolution of the Phylactery-Rite among the Jews). The book was dedicated to Shlomoh Feinberg of Koenigsberg in thanks for his financial help and for securing Rodkinson's release from jail. In the same city and year Deinard printed his book *Masa ba-Erets ha-Kedem*. See Ha-Kohen, "Ha-Defus ha-Ivri be-Hungariyah," 243–44.

129. These include letters from Moritz Lazarus of Berlin (Rodkinson, *Tefilah le-Mosheh*, ix–x), Shlomoh Rubin of Vienna ((Rodkinson, *Tefilah le-Mosheh*, x–xi), Israel Mikhel Rabinowitz of Paris (translator of the Talmud into French; (Rodkinson, *Tefilah le-Mosheh*, xii–xiii) and others, all responding to the ideas raised in this book and *Matsat-Mitsvah*. Throughout the book, Rodkinson relies on an essay by Yehoshuah Heschel Schorr published in *He-Haluts* (Schorr, "Tefillin"; Schorr, *Ma'amarim*, 191–221). But Rodkinson went farther than Schorr, and his claims were much more extreme than his. In general, his positions were exceptional among the Maskilic writers. See, e.g., Reifman, "Mahloket Hakhamim be-Tefillin," 389–90. On Rodkinson's book in the context of Haskalah literature, see Cohn, *Tangled Up in Text*, 3–4, 117.

130. Rodkinson, *Tefilah le-Mosheh*, 15.

131. Ibid., 5.

132. Ibid., 16.

133. Ibid., 35, 39–41, 43, 45–46.

134. Ibid., xii. His response was to statements by Gordon in *Ha-Magid* and Ayala"h in *Ha-Tsefirah*.

135. Ibid., xii–xiii.

136. Ibid., xiii. Heaimed his remarks at, among others, Kohen-Tsedek, who was then residing in London. Further on, Rodkinson complains that he was intentionally being ignored by many journals, and that his book would soon appear in German as well.

137. Ibid., 47.

138. Deinard, *Mashgei Ivrim*, 12; Deinard, *Zikhronot*, 2:35; Deinard, *Tselem ba-Heikhal*, 156. A scathing critique appeared in *Kol Mahzikei ha-Dat*, emphasizing the reformist tendencies of the book that could only end in the annulment of the commandments (Ish Lapidot, "Al ha-Tefillin," 3–4, 6–7).

139. Kohen-Tsedek, *Ohalei shem*, 73–74, 81–95; Kohen-Tsedek, *Ha-Torah veha-Mitsvah*, 47–48, 86–89. The second section of the latter book (57–112) is

dedicated to a critique of the Halachic work *Shnei ha-Mattot* by Naftali ha-Levi, published in Vienna in 1883 at the printing house where Smolenskin worked. Kohen-Tsedek mocked this author who sought to be a religious leader to the Jews, describing him as "a Darwinist turned Halachic authority," and his books as "Darwinism painted in the images of our holy Torah" and "the ideals of *He-Haluts* [Schor's radical journal] in the language of the *Shulhan Arukh*." He used similar language to describe his cooperation with Rodkinson in *Ha-Kol*, despite the latter's critique of ha-Levi's earlier book, *Toldot Adam*. See Nelachovsky, *Ketavim*, 43, 46–48; Ha-Levi to Rubin, 55–56.

140. Slutsky, *Toldot ha-Itonut*, 291–92; Slutsky, "Kritikus," 48–49. Deinard pounced on Dubnow's comments with his sword drawn; see Deinard, *Masa be-Eiropa*, 130.

141. Dubnow, *Sefer ha-Hayyim*, 147.

142. Rodkinson, *Tefilah le-Mosheh*, inside dust cover (lacking in most copies). See Rodkinson, *Tefilah le-Mosheh*, xi, note 4; Rodkinson, *Even ha-Roshah*, 6, 15 (the latter includes the unpublished introduction to the book).

143. Rodkinson, *Matsat-Mitsvah*, vi, 26; Rodkinson, *Tefilah le-Mosheh*, xii, 143.

144. Kohen-Tsedek, *Ha-Torah veha-Mitsvah*, 87.

145. Kohen-Tsedek, 87–88. See also Kohen-Tsedek, 7, 60, 98.

146. Yaakov Hayyim ha-Levi Korn, *Kisalon*; Rodkinson, *Matsat-Mitsvah*, 31. In *Tefilah le-Mosheh* (92) he wrote that the work "is not yet complete, for my essay *He-Halom veha-Agunah* is missing from it. If I found even a little relief, I will once again publish it with the permission of the author in a special edition, as well as translate it into a modern language." See Kohen-Tsedek's response to the critique in Korn's publication (Kohen-Tsedek, *Or Hadash*, 11–12).

147. Rodkinson to Heller (Manuscript), December 19, 1884, Courtesy of the National Library of Israel, Jerusalem. Among other things, he requested financial aid, writing in the third person, "You gave strength to poverty (to Herr Smolenskin); please be a cover for the poor Rodkinson. This is the third day that the latter has lain in his bed, with an illness of the head. . . . His wife has held out her hands from London, asking for bread for my children, who seek shelter from the pounding rain." Heller lent his aid on various occasions to Perets Smolenskin (see Breinin, *Smolenskin*, 41–42, 161–62).

148. Rodkinson, *Matsat-Mitsvah*. On the reviews in the German press, see Bloch, *Zikhronot*, 1:113.

149. Rodkinson, *Even ha-Roshah*. Rodkinson listed his London residence as the address for book purchases.

150. Rodkinson, *Even ha-Roshah*, 21–22.

151. Ibid., 23–24.

152. Ibid., i–iii. The plan of *Even ha-Shulhan* was also mentioned in another of Rodkinson's books, *Levaker Mishpat*, 27n18. According to the wording there, this section was meant to include a fierce critique of the *Shulhan Arukh*'s enslavement of the Jews and the damage it inflicted on their religious lives.

153. Rodkinson, *Levaker Mishpat*. On these events, see Hartston, *Sensationalizing the Jewish Question*, 208–11.

154. Rodkinson, *Levaker Mishpat*, 1.

155. Ibid., 13.

156. Ibid., 25, 30, 32. At the end of the work (51–52) Rodkinson added a long note on Jesus and Christianity.

157. Ibid., 27.

158. Ibid., 28–29.

159. Ibid., 12, 14. Rodkinson was not the only one who laughed at the author of *Lev ha-Ivri*, and even his great opponent Ephraim Deinard published a scathing critique mocking the "Hebrew youth" and his book, which Deinard described as full of "juvenilia and falsehoods" fit for "the company of clowns" (Deinard, *Shibolim Bodedot*, 49–57).

160. Kohen-Tsedek, *Ha-Torah veha-Mitsvah*, 87.

161. Slutsky, *Kritikus*, 48–49.

162. Rodkinson to Frumkin (Manuscript); Rodkinson, *History of the Talmud*, vol. 1, 82. See also Gottheil, *The Life of Gustav Gottheil*, 322. Some would later disparage the relationship between the two (Friedkin, "Sehok Tsadik Tamim," 3).

163. For example, Smolenskin, "Matsat-Mitsvah"; Deinard, *Zikhronot*, vol. 2, 35–36; Kohen-Tsedek, *Ohalei Shem*, 82, 85, 96. Ish Horowitz also made allusions (*Me-Ayin le-Ayin,* 203n1).

164. Zweifel, "Al ha-Temurah," 43–44; Cherikover, *Yehudim be-Itot Mahapekhah*, 280–83, 305. Rodkinson himself had harsh words for the missionaries in one of his books (*Igeret ha-Talmud*, 10).

165. Rodkinson, *Der Schulchan Aruch und seinen Beziehungen zu den Juden und Nichtjuden* (The *Shulhan Arukh* and Its Relationship to Jews and Non-Jews). On the book see Hartston, *Sensationalizing the Jewish Question*, 207–11. The book was translated from Hebrew by David Loëwy, who two years earlier had written a book against Rohling (Loëwy, *Rohling*) and owned a printing house in which the books of Samuel Joseph Bloch were printed. See Fuchs, *Nefutsot Yehudah*, 200–201.

166. Rodkinson, *Der Schulchan Aruch*, vii.

167. Rodkinson to Frumkin (Manuscript). These letters from 1884–1885 are part of the multiyear correspondence, not all of which remains intact. In one of the letters Rodkinson recounts the doings of his children at length.

168. The rumor of Rodkinson's desire to relaunch *Ha-Kol* reached the ears of Deinard, who wrote at the start of 1886: "Indeed his voice (*Ha-Kol*) has not been heard since his pact with the missionaries in Germany and Britain, but who knows if he will open his mouth to bark again, since his friends and supporters are still alive, and it is told that he seeks to open his voice [*kolo*] in Vienna" (Deinard, *Masa be-Eiropa*, 9).

169. Elkushi, *Esrim Igrot*, 48. It seems that Rodkinson sought to do there what he had done in Berlin by publishing *Ha-Medaber le-Israel*, that is, to publish a paper in which "No one would know that he is involved."

170. Frishman, *Kantor*, 39–53. *Ha-Yom* was first published in 1886. See Tal, *Kantor*, 172–74.

171. Rodkinson to Buber (Manuscript), March 7, 1885, April 24, 1885.

172. Rodkinson to Heller (Manuscript), December 19, 1884.

173. Rodkinson, "Kol Ya'akov," 15.

174. Rodkinson, "Hazot Ha-Kol," 1–8. This was *Ha-Kol*'s sixth year, and it continued in continuous numeration from issue 258 to issue 307. Its contributors included Aaron Jellinek, Eliezer Zweifel, Lilienblum, Salomon Mandelkern, Shlomoh Rubin, Gottlober, Frank, and Reuven Asher Braudes. See Gilboa, *Leksikon*, cols. 263–64; Kouts, *"Ma'arikhim,"* 54.

175. Rodkinson, "Hoda'ah ve-Hoda'ah," 17–18; Rodkinson, "Kol Anot," 142; Jellinek, "Oytseikhnugen Eines Anhengers Fon Ya'akov Frank," 40–42, 59–62. See chapter 3 in this volume.

176. For example, Rodkinson, *Ha-Talmud veha-Shulhan Arukh*.

177. Rodkinson, *Even Sapir*; . See the advertisement for the upcoming book in Rodkinson, *Igeret Petuhah*, 2.

178. Lilienblum, "He'arot al Sefer Tefilah le-Mosheh," in Rodkinson, *Even Sapir*, 11–18; Krochmal, "He'arot," in Rodkinson, *Even Sapir*, 19–35 (see the second part of his 1885 book *Iyun Tefilah*, 26–37). The critique of Krochmal's book included criticism of Rodkinson's *tefillin* (Sokolow, *Sdeh Tsofim*, 315–18; see *Historiyah*, vol. 4, 78–104; Shelly, *Mehkar ha-Mikra*, 102–5). They also leveled many and varied criticisms against Krochmal for his scholarship and the religious reforms he proposed (Krochmal, *Agudat Ma'amarim*, 1; Krochmal to Rubin, 56 (in which he lambasts those who saw him as a Spinozist)).

179. Lilienblum, "He'arot al Sefer Tefilah le-Mosheh," in Rodkinson, *Even Sapir*, 17–18. On Lilienblum's change of paths, see Breiman, *Ha-Pulmus bein Lilienblum le-vein Ahad Ha'am*.

180. Rodkinson, *Even Sapir*, 17, note 50.

181. Rodkinson, *Even Sapir*, 46–59.

182. Rodkinson, *Ha-Talmud veha-Shulhan Arukh*, 10–12, 141–44, 155–57. Rodkinson fiercely attacked Justus in a number of articles in *Ha-Kol*, recounting

his iniquitous life story at length (Rodkinson, *Im Hatimat ha-Gilyon*, 112). These attacks were particularly important a few months later, when attempts were made to paint Rodkinson in the image of Justus.

183. Rodkinson, "Hazut Ha-Kol: Ha-Sifrut ha-Talmudit," 225–35; Rodkinson, "Hazut Ha-Kol: Im Atem Mekablim," 258–67; Rodkinson, "Hazut Ha-Kol. Kankan Yashan Male Hadash," 273–75. Two of these were reworked and published in special editions (Rodkinson, *Igeret Petuhah*,; Rodkinson, *Igeret ha-Talmud*). See Deinard, *Sifrat Israel*, vol. 2, 30; Rodkinson, *Kehilat Amerika*, vol. 2, 44.

184. Rodkinson, *Igeret Petuhah*, 1–7.

185. Rodkinson, *Igeret ha-Talmud*, 8.

186. Ish Shalom, *Davar al Odot ha-Talmud*; Benedict, *Ish Shalom*, 271–73. The pamphlet was dedicated to Isaac Hirsch Weiss. Rodkinson claimed that he received the publication from Weiss, who was his close associate. During that time, Weiss and Ish Shalom published editions of *Beit Talmud*, which was devoted to philological and historical analyses and which kept its distance from controversy over the Talmud (see for example the comments in the first edition, Vienna, 1880, 3–4).

187. Rodkinson, *Igeret ha-Talmud*, 3–7.

188. Ibid., 3.

189. Ibid., 5.

190. Ibid., 9.

191. Rodkinson, *Igeret Petuhah*, 14–15; Rodkinson, *Igeret ha-Talmud*, 8. According to his testimony, he gained widespread support upon the release of this publication, including from a number of rabbis and scholars (among them Ish Shalom and Moritz Lazarus) (Rodkinson, *Igeret ha-Talmud*, 3, 13–14). He planned on publishing the fifty letters he received in a special edition; while this plan was never accomplished, a number of the letters were included at the beginning of the Talmud volumes he published later in America.

192. Rodkinson, *Igeret Petuhah*, 7. Elsewhere he claimed that he had received a written threat containing, among other things, the following words: "You desire to shorten the Talmud and to lengthen your days, and I desire the Talmud be lengthened and your days shortened" (Rodkinson, *Igeret ha-Talmud*, 13).

193. Rodkinson, *Igeret Petuhah*, 15. In the second issue he even described the work schedule, and claimed that the project could be completed within three years (*Igeret ha-Talmud*, 11–13).

194. Ish Shalom, *Divrei Sofrim*, 244–45.

195. Ha-GeMaR"A, "Ha-Kol Kol Eisav," 1–2. The author may have been Mosheh Aryeh Leib Harmelin, the publisher of *Ha-Holets* and an active contributor to it. The paper's editor, who sensed the personal and sarcastic tone of the article, added a marginal note disclaiming all responsibility for such articles. See

also the fierce critique in other issues of *Kol Mahzikei ha-Dat* deriding "the barking" Rodkinson and his plans to abridge the Talmud ("R.," "Mikhtav Lelamed," 4; Blumberg, "Mikhtav Oz," 6).

196. Rodkinson, *Masekhet Nezikin*, 86–87. The remainder of the satirical tractate parodied socialism.

197. On Bloch, see Bloch, *Yosef Shmuel Blokh*, 85–91; Toury, "Josef Samuel Bloch," 41–63; Grunwald, *Vienna*, 438–47; Wistrich, *Jews of Vienna*, 277–309; Weitzmann, "Politics of the Viennese Jewish Community, 1890–1914," 127–30; Feldman (R. Binyamin), *Kenesset Hakhamim*, 13–15; Sadan, *Avnei Gevul*, 75–83.

198. Rohling, *Der Talmudjude, Zur Beherzigung für Juden und Christen aller Stände*. See Hellwing, *Der konfessionelle Antisemitismus*, 171–83. On the influence of the book in Austria, see Wistrich, "Georg von Schoenerer," 675–88; Wistrich, *Jews of Vienna*, 223–34; Kieval, "Importance of Place," 142.

199. Berkley, *Vienna and Its Jews*, 77–80; Grunwald, *Vienna*, 430–37; Wistrich, *Jews of Vienna*, 277, 281–85, 296; Tietze, *Die Juden Wiens*, 243–45; Katz, *Sinat Israel*, 190–91, 269–70; Pulzer, *Rise of Political Anti-Semitism*, 49–52; Pulzer, *Eine Geschichte des österreichischen Antisemitusmus*, 84–89, 157–58; Rozenblit, *Jews of Vienna*, 155–56; Rozensaft, "Jews and Antisemites," 62–63. For studies mentioning Rodkinson, see Hellwing, *Der konfessionelle Antisemitismus*, 143–48, 160–83; Ley, "Der Wiener Antisemitismus-Streit," 147–63; Hartston, *Sensationalizing the Jewish Question*, 189–218.

200. Bloch, *Erinnerungen aus meinem Leben*, 1:145–85; Bloch, *Zikhronot*, 1:121–50. The second part of the memoirs is dedicated to a detailing of the court ruling on the blood libel spread by Paulus Meir. The third section was never published. Bloch continued to spar with Rohling in future books (Bloch, *Israel und die Völker*).

201. See contemporary descriptions of him in Bloch, *Zikhronot*, 1:84–94; Rodkinson, *History of the Talmud*, 1:110–12; Lipa, "Et Sofrim," 11–12; Gordon, "Dr. Yustus," 106; Ehrenpreis, "Barukh she-Petaranu," 4–5; Stengler, "Divrei Emet ve-Ahavah," 12–20 (on Justus's treatment of the Kabbalah); Bloch, *Ve-Da Mah she-Tashiv*, 64–66, 57–76, 102–5; Zitron, *Me-Ahorei ha-Pargod*, 2:118–33. For surveys in scholarly literature, see Hellwing, *Der konfessionelle Antisemitismus*, 137–39; Hartston, *Sensationalizing the Jewish Question*, 204–7. Rohling's letters to Justus were published in the Hebrew press as well (Zederbaum, "Mikhtavim," 534–36; Slonimsky, "Lifnim min ha-Kela'im," 144–45). Some accounts tell that he ultimately converted to Islam, while others mention that he traveled to Rome to present his German translation of the *Shulhan Arukh* and the Talmud to the Pope. In 1895 he published a special edition on the Kabbalah, which also included ridicule of Rohling (Justus, *Die Kabbala*). This unstable and colorful figure awaits dedicated research.

202. Bloch, *Zikhronot*, 1:113–15.

203. Deinard, *Tselem ba-Heikhal*, 141–43. In many places he recounted the biography of this Lichtenstein-Hirschenson, author of *Derekh ha-Kodesh: yevuar yesodei dat ha-ivrit lefi yesodei hokhmat ha-emet* (1872), *Sheva Hakhamot sheba-Talmud u-Midrash* (1883), and *Toldot Yeshua ha-Mashiah* (1883). See Deinard, *Tselem ba-Heikhal*, 141–43; Deinard, *Zikhronot*, 2:133–38; Deinard, "Mitsvah Lefarsem et ha-Rama'im," 112; Deinard, Odessa," 580–81; Deinard, *Masa Karim*, 29; Berkowitz, *Deinard*, 86–89. In several places it seems that Lichtenstein-Hirschenson was deeply influenced by Habad teachings and that he was involved with the son of Israel of Rhizin (see Zitron, *Me-Ahorei ha-Pargod*, 2:113–17 (on 113 it is written that Rodkinson wrote against Lichtenstein-Hirschenson); Assaf, *Hetsits ve-Nifga*, 75–76; 411).

204. Bloch, *Zikhronot*, 1:114–15. See also Bloch's letters to Deinard (Manuscript), 1880, 1883, Deinard Archive, JTS Library.

205. Bloch, *Zikhronot*, 1:114.

206. Ibid., 1:115.

207. Ibid., 1:116. His comments were directed at his opponents in the elections and especially the community leader Emmanuel Baumgarten, who gave Rodkinson financial aid (Bloch, *Zikhronot*, 60, 109, 114, 156–58; Wistrich, *Jews of Vienna*, 283).

208. Rodkinson, "Hadashot Belulot," 105–6, 173; Rodkinson, "Et Livhor ve-Et Lerahek Bahur," 161–64; Rodkinson, "Ke-Tseiti et ha-Ir," 177–78, 185–86.

209. Rodkinson, *Barkai*, 1:21–25.

210. Rodkinson, *History of the Talmud*, 1:106–9, 126. See Hartston, *Sensationalizing the Jewish Question*, 193–94, 205. Rodkinson was in contact with both men.

211. Bloch, "Brimann and R."; "Bloch to Lemberg"; Jellinek, "Third Conspirator." See also Rodkinson, *Barkai*, 1:5–20. Bloch claimed that the essays had such an impact that, even without Rodkinson being named in them, "his name passed from mouth to mouth. Everyone distanced themselves from him; families whose homes he used to frequent requested him not to visit again, and when he greeted them, they did not return the greeting; only one man stayed loyal to him, without a hint of vacillation, to prison and beyond, and that was Emmanuel Baumgarten, the leading citizen of the Viennese Jewish community" (Bloch, *Zikhronot*, 116–19). On the response of the Hebrew press, see Zederbaum, "Huts le-Artsenu," 1447–48; Ben Yehudah, "Brimann," 45.

212. Sadan, *Avnei Gevul*, 81.

213. Rodkinson, *Milhemet ha-Shalom*, 3–7; Rodkinson, *Eleh ha-Mishpatim*, 113–17; Rodkinson, *Ha-Talmud veha-Shulhan Arukh*, 141–43, 155–57; Rodkinson, *Levaker Mishpat*.

214. Bloch also claimed that Herzl depended on antisemitic arguments. According to Chaim Bloch, who possessed material from Yosef Shmuel Bloch's estate, the third volume of Bloch's memoirs contained attacks on Herzl. Edited versions of these unpublished chapters were cited in Chaim Bloch's book, *Mi Natan le-Mesisah*, 3–6. Slightly later, an essay was published in English that cited selections from the latter book (Bloch, *Hertsl*, 154–64). On Yosef Shmuel Bloch's relationship to Herzl, see Wistrich, *Jews of Vienna*, 305–9, 469–71; Wistrich, *Ha-Tsiyonut u-Mitnagdeihah*, 178–81.

215. Deinard, *Mashgei Ivrim*, 12; *Tselem ba-Heikhal*, 155. Deinard's cutting words were later printed almost in full. When in 1888 he published his book *Adir*, containing a poem on Rohling and Brimann (13–23), he made no mention of Rodkinson. Nevertheless, his later and more extreme statements were accepted by most of the scholars who heard them, such as Eisenstein (*Otsar Zikhronotai*, 109); Berkowits (*Deinard*); and Ley (*Der Wiener Antisemitismus-Streit*, 161–63).

216. Rodkinson to the Editor (Manuscript); Rodkinson, *Barkai*, 1:17–18.

217. Rodkinson, "Teshuvah me-Ahavah," 369–79.

218. See the announcement to this effect at the end of Rodkinson's *Barkai*, vol. 2 (unpaginated). At one point he noted two pamphlets, "*Ma'amar ha-Ishut*" and "*Ahavat Adam*," published in Vienna in 1886 (Rodkinson, *History of the Talmud*, 2:19 (referring to the essays as being published serially in *Ha-Kol* throughout 1885); and at another he said that the latter pamphlet was published in German as *Menschen Liebe* (Rodkinson, *Tekhunat Ruah ha-Israeli*, 32–33).

219. Rodkinson to Fuenn (Manuscript), Courtesy of the National Library of Israel, Jerusalem.

220. Fuenn, "Leharhik Lazut Sefatayim," 108.

221. Jellinek, *Denial*. The comments were quickly published in Hebrew as well (Gordon, "Yustus ha-Sheini," 422; Gordon, "Be'ad Rodkinson," 30; Ben Yehudah, "Mi-Huts la-Arets," 56–57). Similar comments were made by Chaim Bloch, who met Rohling in his old age (Bloch, "Bikur Etsel Rohling," 642–44, 662–64; Bloch, *Ve-De Mah she-Tashiv*, 64–66, 57–76, 102–5). Inter alia, he told that he saw in Rohling's home Maskilic writings from such authors as Isaac Baer Levinsohn, Zweifel, Rodkinson, and Schorr. Regarding Rodkinson, he wrote, "I asked him (Rohling) about his relationship with Rodkinson, who had been accused by Dr. Bloch, Sokolow, and Ephraim Deinard of supplying material to Rohling. He answered me, 'I never met him. I remember that Brimann had brought me his book *Matsat-Mitsvah ve-Alilat Dam* and said that the author too knew the whole truth, but the Jews supported him and he had written the book. More than that I neither know nor remember'" (Bloch, 68). Chaim Bloch, too, wrote apologetic literature (Bloch, *Blut und Eros*), and printed a sort of "Encyclopedia of Apologetics"—"A Letter in Response to the Libels against Israel" (Bloch, *Heikhal le-Divrei Hazal*, 39–110).

222. Werber, "Hadashot be-Israel," 143. See also Bloch, *Zikhronot*, 1:119–20.

223. Rodkinson, *Programs*, 94–5; Rodkinson, *Igeret Petuhah*, 2. He had originally called it *Kol ha-Et*.

224. Rodkinson, *Barkai*, vol. 1. The name was excerpted from the motto of the publication: *Barkai, Schutschrift des M. L. Rodkinssohn gegendi lügenhaft-verläumderischen Angrifte Des Reichsraths Abgeordneten Dr. Bloch*. See Kantor, "Shulhan ha-Sifrut," 3; Toury, "Josef Samuel Bloch und die Jüdische Identität," 51–52, 63. On financial support by Baumgarten (who also supported *Ha-Shahar*), Bloch wrote, "There is no reason to believe that he knew the contents of the book for which he collected money from fellow Jews" (Bloch, *Zikhronot*, 1:121). When Deinard listed the books in Meir Zoltzberg's library, and found there some of Rodkinson's works, he wrote about *Barkai*, "*Barkai*, containing slander against the Rabbi Dr. Bloch, printer of the weekly *Ostereichische Wochenschrift* and leading scholar in Vienna" (Deinard, *Or ha-Me'ir*, 64; Berkowitz, "Or ha-Me'ir," 58).

225. Rodkinson, *Barkai*, 1:21–23.

226. Ibid., 1:23, 25.

227. Ibid., 1:26–27, 36–39.

228. Ibid., 1:35–36, 43–44; Jellinek, "Ya'akov Frank," 40–42, 59–62; Rodkinson, "Kol Anot," 143. See chapter 3 in this volume.

229. Rodkinson, *Barkai*, 1:40, 42.

230. Ibid., 1:6–20.

231. Ibid., 1:48–49, 51–53.

232. Gordon, "Barkai," 38; Gordon, "Od ha-Pa'am," 64; Ben Yehudah, "Rodkinson u-Blokh," 80.

233. Gordon, "Harav et Riveinu," 34–35. Nevertheless, he had no doubts that Aharon Brimann (Justus) had provided the Kabbalistic sources to Rohling for the blood libel.

234. Anonymous, "Hadashot bi-Gevul Israel," 7–8.

235. Rodkinson, *Wahrheit gegen Lüge*. A handful of copies remain from this special edition, one of which is held by Goethe University in Frankfurt.

236. Rodkinson, *Barkai*, vol. 2. The German title also changed: *Barkai (Morgenblitze): Sammlung für Wissenshaft Bildung und Leben*. See Gilboa, *Leksikon*, col. 320; Provest, "Ha-Itonut ha-Ivrit," 252–53. Meir Kahn Bistrits and Mosheh Dov Goldman were among the contributors.

237. Kopp, *Zur Judenfrage nach den Akten des Prozesses Rohling-Bloch*; Rodkinson, "Besorat Sefarim," *Barkai*, 2:41–45. A summary of the book was translated and published in the same year in *Ha-Yom* by Ze'ev Schorr (Malachi, *Igrot Sofrim*, 90). Rodkinson would later praise Kopp (Rodkinson, *History of the Talmud*, 1:112–15). On Kopp and his legal activities, see Bloch, *Zikhronot*,

1:71–75, 82, 103; "Ad Ergi'ah Lashon Sheker," 3; Hartston, *Sensationalizing the Jewish Question*, 200–203.

238. Rodkinson, "Besorat Sofrim," *Barkai*, 2:43.

239. Rodkinson, "Besorat Sofrim," 44–45.

240. Rodkinson, "He'arah bi-Devar ha-Ot R. she-Nimtsa be-Mikhtav Rohling," *Barkai*, 2:46–48. A similar conclusion appears in the letters of Justus published in *Ha-Tsefirah* (Slonimsky, "Lifnim Min ha-Kela'im," 144–45). A number of years earlier Jellinek had written critically of Rohling, but Bloch came out against him as having abandoned the open struggle against antisemitism (Bloch, *Zikhronot*, 1:54, 59, 60). See also Zederbaum, "Devarim be-Itam," 581–82; Wistrich, *Jews of Vienna*, 238–69, 277; Rosenmann, *Dr. Adolf Jellinek*, 151–70.

241. Rodkinson to Brill (Manuscript).

242. Rodkinson, "Tekhunat ha-Ruah ha-Israeli," 1–16; Rodkinson, "Al Devar Sifreinu," 119–21, 127–28; Bloch, *Zikhronot*, 1:120–21. Meir Kahn Bistrits, a contributor to the publication, attacked the essay, which he claimed to be full of "blasphemy against the holy fathers" (Bistrits, *Bi'ur Tit ha-Yaven*, xvii–xviii).

243. Ben Yehudah, "Rodkinson u-Blokh," 80.

244. Bloch, *Zikhronot*, 21. According to Bloch, this was the wording of the notice from the Viennese police.

245. See the descriptions in the Hebrew press: Gordon, "Tsadik Nitpas be-Avon ha-Dor," 94; Werber, "Vien," 191; Zederbaum, "Ma'asar," 547–48.

246. Rodkinson, *Barkai*, vol. 2, 47–48.

247. Zederbaum, "Ma'asim be-Khol Yom," 813; Bloch, *Zikhronot*, 112. In Bloch's later works dealing with the Rohling affair (as in other contemporary summaries), Rodkinson is not mentioned at all. See, e.g., Bloch, *Israel und die Völker* (a summary of the affair that includes translated excerpts from the Talmud, the *Zohar*, and the *Shulhan Arukh*); Zweifel, *Zer Nitsahon* (a hymn to Bloch); *Kvod Hakhamim* (poems and letters in praise of Bloch).

248. See Deinard, *Mashgei Ivrim*, 14; Deinard, *Kehilat Amerika*, 1:9. Deinard arrived in New York on October 6, 1888, via Liverpool, with his wife, four children, and eleven trunks of books and manuscripts (Weinstein, "First Deinard Collection," 32, 44). Elsewhere Deinard explained that "it was never in my heart to settle in that land" (i.e., America), which was in his eyes "a graveyard" for the nationalist idea; rather, he aspired to settle in Zion (Palestine) (Deinard, *Divrei ha-Yamim*, 2:57–62).

249. Deinard, *Tselem ba-Heikhal*, 156–57, 171.

250. Deinard, "Mezureh ha-Reshet," 6 (Rodkinson is referred to here by the letter "R."). On this essay, see also Malachowsky, *Ketavim*, 2:61; Deinard, *Mashgei Ivrim*, 13.

251. Deinard, "Divrei ha-Mol," 1. See also Deinard, "Hor ha-Har," 2–3.

252. Deinard, "Espor Kol Atsmotav," 1–4. See also Deinard, "Eleh Toldot Sama'el," 2–3.

253. Anonymous, "Sinat Hinam," 43.

254. The episode is frequently mentioned in Deinard's book, *Mashgei Ivrim*, 12–13.

255. Kabakoff , "Me-Igrotav shel Ze'ev Shor," 311. Schorr dubbed all of his opponents "apostates" and "missionaries."

256. Deinard, "Al ha-Pisgah," 7. Deinard even republished a number of articles from *Ha-Pisgah* in *Ha-Leumi* 17 (1889). See, for example, Melinkof, "Mikhtav," 6; Schorr, "Mikhtav," 4; Miller, "Mikhtav," 4; Sobel, "Tsa'ar Ba'alei Hayim," 6.

257. Contributors included: Shalom Yosef Zilberstein, Gershon Miller, Minkowsky, Avraham ha-Kohen, and Gershon Rozenzweig. See Gilboa, *Leksikon*, col. 264; Malachi, "Le-Toldot ha-Itonut," 117–22; Malachi, "Shivim ve-Hamesh Shanah," 665–67; Brody, "Hebrew Periodical Press in America," 137–38; Brody-Zeldner, "Itonim Ivri'im be-Amerikah," 221; Kabakoff, *Halutsei ha-Sifrut*, 136, 215; Malachowsky, *Ketavim*, 2:61. Deinard was angered by Malachi's above-mentioned essay and dubbed its author "some licentious youth from the Holy Land" because he praised Rodkinson (Deinard, *Mashgei Ivrim*, 13; Deinard, *Zikhronot*, 2:26; Deinard, *Tselem ba-Heikhal*, 157; Kohen-Tsedek, *Ohalei Shem*, 82). According to Eisenstein, people welcomed Rodkinson when he arrived only because "his iniquitous deeds in Europe had not yet been made known." He himself had welcomed Rodkinson "by mistake" (*Otsar Zikhronotai*, 109).

258. Rodkinson, *Tekhunat Ruah ha-Israeli*, preface, 3. On the failure of Hebrew life in America in the 1890s, see Malachi, "Toldot ha-Tenuah ha-Ivrit be-Amerikah," 212–36.

259. Rodkinson, *Tekhunat Ruah ha-Israeli*, 26, 30. Deinard attacked the book upon its appearance and tied it to missionaries (Deinard, *Sifrat Israel*, 2:100–101; Deinard, *Kehilat Amerika*, 2:137; Deinard, *Mashgei Ivrim*, 13–14; Deinard, *Zikhronot*, 2:36; Friedkin, "Sehok Tsadik Tamim," 2. Leibowitz praised Deinard for his "mighty fight against M. L. Rodkinson's *Tekhunat Ruah ha-Israeli* . . . which renders impure everyone who sees it" (*Hokhmat Yehudah*, 52); elsewhere, he added, "The traitor to his people Michael Levi Rodkinson came here (. . .) and in his abhorrent *Tekhunat Am ha-Israeli* wrote that Abraham our Father purposely traded Sarah our Mother. He has certainly read Voltaire" (Leibowitz, *Deinard u-Sefarav*, 14). See Rodkinson, "Al Davar Sifrenu," 119–21, 127–28.

260. Rodkinson, *Tekhunat Ruah ha-Israeli*, iv, 32–33; Dik, *Die Shehne Helene*. Rodkinson had a complex relationship with Smolenskin, and they traded insults over the years. See Rodkinson, "Smolenskin," 65.

261. Rodkinson, *Ha-Sanegor*; Frumkin, "Ha-Sanegor," 77. See Malachi, "Ha-Sanegor"; Gilboa, *Leksikon*, cols. 355–56; Deinard, *Sifrat Israel*, 2:71; Deinard,

Kehilat Amerika, 2:99; Brody, "Hebrew Periodical Press in America," 138. Contributors to the paper included Naftali Herts Imber, Aleksander Kohut, Mordekhai ben Hillel ha-Kohen, Aharon Rudin, Tsvi Gershoni, Yehezkel Yehudah, Mosheh Yafeh, Avraham ha-Kohen, and Y. D. Eisenstein. Nehemiah Shmuel Leibowitz wrote fierce articles against this paper (Kahana, *Hokhmat Yehudah*, 52–53).

262. Malachi, "Ha-Sanegor," 219. See, e.g., Deinard, *Mashgei Ivrim*, 4, 6–7; Deinard, *Zikhronot*, 2:28–29, 36; Deinard, *Tselem ba-Heikhal*, 154. Similar things were rumored about Deinard; for example, see Leibowitz, *Deinard u-Sefarav*, 21.

263. See Yitshak Rabinowitz's comments to Judah Leib Levin on Rodkinson's second attempt at the paper (Kabakoff, *Shoharim ve-Ne'emanim*, 89). See Fuch's comments on Rodkinson and the "sages" who accompanied him ("Bo'u Heshbon," 306).

264. Malachi, "Ha-Sanegor," 219–20.

265. Deinard, *Sefer ha-Ploiderzak*; Deinard, *Or ha-Me'ir*, 83; Deinard, *Kehilat Amerika*, 2:664. Deinard satirized the editors elsewhere as well (Deinard, *Mistarei Neu York*, 4–7, 9–10; *Sefer ha-Kundas*, 2, 120–21, 171–75).

266. Deinard, *Sefer ha-Ploiderzak*, 29–32. A number of the book's coded names have been deciphered (Malachi, "Amerikah vi-Yerushalayim," 667; Gilboa, "Ha-Ploiderzek," 116–21; Gilboa, *Leksikon*, cols. 442–44; Reisin (*Dapim*, 377–78; Berkowitz, "Deinard's (Or Mayer) Catalogue," 66; Leibowitz, *Mikhtavim*, 45–46; Leibowitz, *Mishpato Yiten le-Or*, 18–20; Leibowitz, *Deinard u-Sefarav*, 9–10, 20 (according to his testimony, Deinard printed the pamphlet in order "to take revenge on the periodicals that had exposed his face and revealed his sins to all").

267. Malachi, *Masot u-Reshimot*, 181. See also, Malachi, *Igrot Sofrim*, 84–86; Leibowitz, *Tene Bikurim*, 20–25. For surveys of the Hebrew press in America during those years, see Persky, "Itonut Ivrit," 1–8; Miklishensky, *Toldot ha-Sifrut ha-Ivrit be-Amerikah*, 16–17; Malachi, "Min Ha-Tsofeh ba-Erets he-Hadashah ad Ha-Doar," 114–16; Malachi, "Orkhim Ivrim be-Amerikah," 843–45; Malachi, "Shivim ve-Hamesh Shanah," 665–67; Kabakoff, *Mekorot*, 224–31; Kabakoff, *Shocharim ve-Ne'emanim*, 27–30, 39–42. On the competition and controversies between the Yiddish papers in America, see Goldberg, *Getsel Zelikovitz*, 125–33.

268. Fuchs, "Bo'u Heshbon," 306.

269. Schwartzberg, *Tikatev Zot la-Dor Aharon*, 7, 9, 20. On Schwartzberg see Kabakoff, *Shocharim ve-Ne'emanim*, 138–47.

270. Rodkinson, *History of Amulets, Charms and Talismans*.

271. Rodkinson, *History of Amulets, Charms and Talismans*, ii–vii. Compare his earlier statements (Rodkinson, *Tefilah le-Mosheh*, 6–7, 22, 28–29, 57, 86 (on amulets)). Rubin made similar comments (*Avnei Milu'im*, 12–13).

272. Rodkinson, *History of Amulets, Charms and Talismans*, vii. Rodkinson told of having an additional book ready to be published that would serve as a

supplement to the earlier one, titled *The History of Tephilah, Tzitith and Mezuzah*, but it was never published (Rodkinson, *History of Amulets, Charms and Talismans*, 93).

273. Rodkinson, "Karaites"; Rodkinson, *History of the Talmud*, 1:25–33, 36–42, 138–60.

274. Rodkinson, *The Pentateuch, Its Languages and its Characters: A Treatise upon the Original Language and the Early Translations of the Pentateuch into Greek and Aramaic*. These topics were treated in Rodkinson's earlier books (*Tefilah le-Mosheh*, 52–53, 105).

275. Rodkinson, *The Pentateuch, Its Languages and Its Characters*, v.

276. Rodkinson to Lazarus (Manuscript), 1895.

277. The essay was also published as a special edition (Rodkinson, *Ha-Hotsa'ah ha-Hadashah*). See Deinard's sarcastic notes (*Sifrat Israel*, 2:70–71; Deinard, *Kehilat Amerika*, 2:97).

278. Rodkinson, "Od al Targum ha-Talmud," 4.

279. Rodkinson, *Masekhet Rosh ha-Shanah*; Rodkinson, *Masekhet Kidushin*. A twenty-six-page introduction was added to *Masekhet Rosh ha-Shanah* that spoke of the nature of the work and approbations. The English edition had a slightly different title page: *Tractate Rosh Hashana of the New Edition of the Original Babylonian Talmud*. See Deinard, *Sifrat Israel*, 2:101–2; Deinard, *Kehilat Amerika*, 2:138.

280. In 1895 he wrote the following: "Please take kind notice of the bearer, Mr. Rodkinson, who has undertaken a piece of literary work never before dreamt of by any literateur; he has the whole Talmud translated into English, the first volume of which is out already. He wants you to subscribe for the library, and I can best recommend him"; Wise to Rodkinson (Manuscript). See also Wise, "On Rodkinson," 4–5; Wise, "New Talmud," 4–5. Elsewhere he stated that there was no need to dig through his past, and that he was only a "poor old Jew" whose sole desire was scientific research; Wise to Shulman (Manuscript).

281. Rodkinson, *Masekhet Rosh ha-Shanah,* Hebrew section, i–xix.

282. Rodkinson, *Masekhet Rosh ha-Shanah,* xix–xxii; English section, v–xi.

283. Rodkinson to Buber (Manuscript), March 24, 1895; May 22, 1895; November 7, 1897. Buber sought to subscribe only to the Hebrew version of the Talmud.

284. Rodkinson, *Prospectus* (1896). Rodkinson's nephew, Avraham Frumkin, also participated in the work of translation, but did not particularly value the nature of the project or its quality (Frumkin, *Friling fun Idishen Sotzyializm*, 178–79).

285. Rodkinson, *Tractate Shabbat, New Edition of the Babylonian Talmud: English Translation, Original Text Edited, Formulated, and Punctuated by Michael L. Rodkinson, Revised and Corrected by the Rev. Dr. Isaac M. Wise.*

286. Rodkinson, *Prospectus* (1898). See also *History of the Talmud*, 2:12–18. The name of the society is displayed on a number of Rodkinson's letters to Shlomoh Buber (Manuscript), 1897.

287. Norbert M. Rodkinson, "Rodkinson's Self defense," 4; Wise, "In Defense of M. L. Rodkinson," 4. Some of the slurs were printed in Deinard's publications, including some aimed at Jellinek (see, e.g., Asaf ha-Mazkir, "Ba-Kol mi-Kol Kol," 6).

288. Friedkin, "Sehok Tsadik Tamim," 3; Malachowsky, "Ruah Sheker ve-Shikhor," 3–4.

289. For example, the poet Tsvi Gershoni wrote that, due to financial pressure, he translated forty folios from Tractate Shabbat, and that after he finished Rodkinson revised his text without showing him the results, causing him to withdraw from the translation (Kabakoff, "Tsvi Gershoni le-Or ve-Igrotav," 355; Kabakoff, *Halutsei ha-Sifrut*, 105; Rodkinson, "A Few Words in Reply to Rev. Dr. K. Kohler's Criticism," 346).

290. Haikin, *Yiddishe Bletter*, 318. See also Malachi, "Orkhim," 844; Sokolow, "*Feuilleton*," 97.

291. Rabinowitz, "Besorat Sefarim," 4; Rabinowitz, "Be-Huts le-Artsenu," 4–5.

292. For a sample of the critique, see Epstein, "*Makor Barukh,*" 804; Deinard, *Mashgei Ivrim*, 14; Deinard, *Zikhronot*, 2:37; Deinard, *Kehilat Amerika*, 2:72; Deinard, *Sifrat Israel*, 2:52; Malachi, "Orkhim," 844. On the fierce opposition to reform by Hebrew and Yiddish writers, see Kabakoff, *Shocharim ve-Ne'emanim*, 344–52; Kabakoff, "Hebrew Sources of American Jewish History," 222–24; Kabakoff, "Role of Wolf Schur as Hebraist and Zionist," 433–39, 453–54; Goldberg, *Getsel Zelikovitz,* 337–38. An extreme example can be found in Schorr, *Netsah Israel*, 240–57; Deinard, *Sefer ha-Kundas*, 149–57.

293. Eisenstein, *Bikoret Rosh ha-Shanah*, 17–20, 33–40; Eisenstein, *Bikoret Shabbat*, 25–50; Eisenstein, *Ma'amarei Bikoret* (previously published in *Ner ha-Ma'aravi* and again in *Yalkut Amerika*, under Deinard's editorship); Eisenstein, *Otsar Zikhronotai*, 109, 285–301. A portion was reprinted in an essay in *Ha-Tsefirah* (Reisin, "Kitsur ha-Talmud," 370, 374–75). See also Rodkinson's response ("Ha-Hotsa'ah he-Hadashah," i–vi).

294. Leibowitz, *Eikhah Rabati*, 10–12. Previously printed with changes in *Ha-Magid* in 1895. Compare Sobel, "Igeret Petuhah"; Sobel, "Ziyufei Rodkinzon," 4–5.

295. Leibowitz to Buber (Manuscript), Courtesy of the Nationsl Library of Israel, Jerusalem. In another letter Leibowitz wrote about the state of Jewish studies in America: "They have already ceased to say that there is no God on earth and that there is no point in researching and reading the books of the ancients. The

Holy One, blessed be He, wanted to bring the total destruction of Judaism and so opened to it the gates of America."

296. Leibowitz, *Al Davar ha-Talmud*, 33–35; Deinard, *Or ha-Me'ir*, 96; Felsenthal, *Bernhard Felsenthal Teacher in Israel*, 240–41; Kabakoff, *Halutsei ha-Sifrut*, 101–2. Meir Ish Shalom described his relationship with Rodkinson and his reticence regarding his recent work in an unpublished letter; Ish Shalom to Leibowitz (Manuscript).

297. Rubin, *Bikoret*, 107–9. For another instance of Rubin's anger toward Rodkinson, see Schorr, *Mikhtav*, 4.

298. Kohler, "New Talmud Translation by Rodkinson and Wise," 272–74.

299. Rodkinson, "A Few Words in Reply to Rev. Dr. K. Kohler's Criticism," 345–46; Kohler, "Brief Rejoinder to Rodkinson and Wise," 457; Temkin, *Isaac Mayer Wise*, 303.

300. Rodkinson, *History of the Talmud*, 2:102–3.

301. Goldschmidt began the project in 1897 and completed it in 1935. According to his testimony, his translation served as a response to the erroneous claims of August Rohling. See Goldschmidt, "Targum ha-Talmud," 309–30. For his criticism of Rodkinson and his translation (primarily regarding the inexplicable omissions and general inaccuracy), as well as the correspondence between the two from 1907, see Goldschmidt, 327–28.

302. For studies on the translation see Kabakoff, *Halutsei ha-Sifrut*, 101–2; Gries, *Book in the Jewish World*; Goldman, *Hebrew Printing in America*, 1:503–6; Mintz, "Words, Meaning and Spirit," 123–25; Mintz, "Talmud in Translation," 125–27; Mintz and Goldstein, *Printing the Talmud*, 314–15; Heller, "He Should be Called Sama'el," 86–89; Heller, *Further Studies in the Making of the Early Hebrew Book*, 217–50.

303. Rodkinson, *Talmud Bavli: New Edition of the Babylonian Talmud. Original Text Edited, Corrected, Formulated and Translated by Michael L. Rodkinson.*

304. Rodkinson, *History of the Talmud* (printed on high-quality paper by the New Talmud Publishing Company). Sections from this *History* had been previously published in the English press (Rodkinson, "Reuchlin and Pfefferkorn"). Another edition, with certain details omitted, was published in Boston in 1918 under the title *The Babylonian Talmud*, in twenty volumes, in addition to the two-volume introduction (printed on low-quality paper with minor changes by The Talmud Society). In 2003 the entire translation was uploaded to the Internet (http://www.sacred-texts.com/jud/talmud.htm).

305. Rodkinson, *Prospectus* (1904). The portrait and documents within were printed in the first volume of *History*. Complaints over the prize that Rodkinson received in Paris are found in an essay by the translator of the Talmud into German (Goldschmidt, "Targum ha-Talmud," 327).

306. Rodkinson to Dubzhevitz (Manuscript) 1898, 1899. According to Rodkinson family records, he was married three times. His third wife was a good number of years younger than him. One of his sons was Rudolph Marks (Max), an actor in the Yiddish theater (Heller, "He Should be Called Sama'el," 82; Koegel, *Music in German Immigrant Theater*, 340, 527; Kabakoff, *Master of Hope*, 171).

307. Rodkinson to Sossnitz (Manuscript), 1900.

308. Rodkinson to Buber (Manuscript), 1897.

309. Rodkinson, *Pentateuch, Its Languages and Its Characters*, 30.

310. Sokolow, "Fuilleton," 97.

311. Rodkinson, *History of the Talmud*, 2:19. Elsewhere he described *Yovel* as a sort of novel (Rodkinson, *Tekhunat Ruah ha-Israeli*, 3).

312. Winchevsky, "Rodkinson," 56, 59.

313. Eisenstein, *Otsar Zikhronotai*, 109.

314. "Sekirah," 120; "Hazkarat Neshamot," 18.

315. Rodkinson, "Smolenskin," 165.

2. The Beginnings of Hasidic Hagiography

1. Dan, *Ha-Sippur he-Hasidi*, 189–95. As we will see, Rabbi Nahman of Bratslav's *Sippurei Ma'asiyot* was a different sort of book.

2. Piekarz, *Hasidut Breslev*, 106–7, 128–31; Gries, *Book in the Jewish World*, 37–40; *Ha-Besht*, 414; Dan, *Ha-Novelah he-Hasidit*, 7–15.

3. Nigal, *Mehkarim be-Hasidut*, 2:311–21, 349–64. A striking example is the writings of Rabbi Yitshak Yehiel Yehudah Safrin (see Nigal, *Melaktei Ha-Sippur he-Hasidi*, 13–18; Dan, *Ha-Sippur he-Hasidi*, 190–91, 194).

4. For a fuller treatment of this phenomenon, see Meir, *Imagined Hasidism*.

5. Dan, *Ha-Sippur he-Hasidi*, 190, 194–95. See also Elshtein, "Bo'u Litkon," 450–54; Mondshine, *Shivhei ha-Besht*, 56.

6. Shmeruk, *Sifrut Yiddish*, 211.

7. Gries, "Ha-Omnam Meitav ha-Sippur Kazavu?," 87.

8. Dubnow, *Toldot he-Hasidut*, 41–42. See Bartal, "Be-Vuah Me'uvetet," 15.

9. Mondshine, *Shivhei ha-Besht*, 55–57; Lieberman, *Ohel Rahel*, 3:6; Assaf, *Regal Way*, 42–43.

10. Meir, *Gilgulav shel Megaleh Sod*, 24, 34, 56.

11. Kurzweil, *Be-Ma'avak al Erkhei ha-Yahadut*, 68–85; Feiner, "Be-Emunah Bilvad," 99–101; Feingold, "Ha-Sefer veha-Sifrut," 85–100; Kohen, "Ha-Tekhnikah ha-Lamdanit," 145–59, 152–53; Parush, *Nashim Korot*, 101–39; Werses, "*Hakitsah Ami*," 88–98.

12. Meir, *Imagined Hasidism*, first and fifth chapters.

13. Friedberg, *Toldot ha-Defus ha-Ivri*, 112–14, 162–63; Kohen, "Defus Tshernovits," 315–16.

14. Gries, "Ha-Omnam Meitav ha-Sippur Kazavu?," 88–90; Gries, *Book in the Jewish World*, 117–19; Friedberg, *Ha-Defus ha-Ivri be-Levov*, cols. 545–47.

15. Some of his books were later collected in a new edition (Bodek, *Sippurim Hasidi'im*; Nigal, *Sippurim Hasidi'im mi-Lemberg*, 157–465; Bodek, *Nifla'ot ha-Emet*; Bodek, "Seder ha-Dorot he-Hadash," 1:1–192). See on him Nigal, *Mehkarei Ma'arav u-Mizrah*, 225–32; Nigal, *Melaktei ha-Sipur he-Hasidi*, 30–52; Handler, *Ha-Sipur he-Hasidi*; Wunder, *Me'orei Galitsiyah*, vol. 1, cols. 416–19.

16. On Walden, see Nigal, *Ha-Siporet he-Hasidi*, 36–37; Zederbaum, *Keter Kehunah*, 105–6; Eisenstadt, *Dor Rabanav ve-Sofrav*, 3:13–14; Sherberk, *Zikhronot ha-Motsi le-Or Shlomoh Sherberk*, 153; Rubinstein, "He'arot," 140–50.

17. Walden, Letter (Manuscript); Deinard to Kahana (Manuscript), 1901.

18. Nigal, *Mehkarei Ma'arav u-Mizrah*, 232–34.

19. Katina, *Rahamei Av*. See Cohen, "Arba'ah Sefarim Anonimi'im u-Mehabreihem," 136; Cohen, "Ha-Defus ha-Ivri be-Tshernovits," 332, no. 174; Jacobs, *Their Heads in Heaven*, 121–31.

20. A first attempt was made by Gedalyah Nigal, *Ha-Siporet he-Hasidit*, in the appendix (in the second edition, 308–13; this list is also missing from the English translation of the book). See also Elstein, "Bo'u Litkon," 459–535.

21. Rosenfeld was the first to attribute *Kehal Hasidim* to Rodkinson (*Ha-Tsofeh le-Veit Ya'akov*, 48). Deinard continued the attribution (*Herev Hadah*, 5; Deinard, *Kitot be-Israel*, 8; Deinard, *Mashgei Ivrim*, 4–6, 16; Deinard, *Zikhronot*, 2:28–29, 38–39; Deinard, *Tselem ba-Heikhal*, 153; Deinard, *Zmir Aritsim ha-Sheni*, xvii; Frumkin, *In Frinling Idishen Sotsiyalizm*, 168). From there it entered academic scholarship (Berkowitz, "Deinard," 90; Dan, *Ha-Sippur he-Hasidi*, 198–204; Assaf, *Untold Tales*, 141. Even in 1867 there were those who knew that Walden was the author (Zederbaum, *Keter Kehunah*, 105; Lippe, *Bibliographisches Lexicon*, 516). Walden collected others' work in his book without credit (Nigal, *Mehkarei Ma'arav u-Mizrah*, 203–35). Ish Horowitz apparently meant Rodkinson when he wrote, "It is known that the book *Kehal Hasidim* was written by a man of intrigue and deception, who at the end of his life converted—and so too the book *Sipurei Tsadikim*" (*Me-Ayin ule-Ayin*, 203, no. 1). Deinard erroneously attributed *Seder ha-Dorot he-Hadash* to Rodkinson (Deinard, *Kitot be-Israel*, 8); and Dov Sadan attributed *Sippurim Nora'im* (Munkatsch 1894) to Rodkinson, claiming that he was hidden behind the name Kaidener (*Bein She'ilah le-Kinyan*, 91).

22. Dinur, *Be-Mifneh ha-Dorot*, 89–92.

23. Habermann, *Sha'arei Habad*, 293.

24. Deinard to Kahana (Manuscript), 1901.

25. Gries, *Book in the Jewish World*, 35–38; Rapoport-Albert, "Ha-Tenuah he-Hasidit," 245–46 and n. 126; Rapoport-Albert, "Hagiography," 144, 156. Much research has been dedicated to Habad historiography by Ada Rapoport-Albert, Israel Bartal, Zeev Gries, David Assaf, Rachel Elior, and others.

26. Gries, *Book in the Jewish World*, 35–40. Gries elaborates elsewhere (Gries, "Ha-Reka ha-Yehudi," 46–56; Gries, "Ha-Omnam Meitav ha-Sippur Kazavu?," 85–94). See also Habermann, *Ketav, Lashon, ve-Sefer*, 256–57; Yasif, "Mehkar ha-Folklor," 18–20; Assaf, *Regal Way*, 42; Mondshine, *Shivhei ha-Besht*, 56–57.

27. Elishevits, "Ha-Tsenzurah," 69.

28. Assaf, *Regal Way*, 42; Gertner, "Reishitah shel Ketivah Historit Ortodoksit be-Mizrah Eiropah," 293–336.

29. Gertner, "Reishitah shel Ketivah Historit," 333; on Walden, ibid., 302, 319–20; on Bodek, ibid., 303.

30. One of many examples is the printing of the writings of Rabbi Mosheh Elyakim Beriah, the son of Rabbi Israel of Kozhnitz. See Nigal, *Mehkarim be-Hasidut*, vol. 1, 287–307.

31. Gedalyah Nigal omitted the homiletic portions from his reedited collections of Hasidic tales, leaving the impression that the stories always stood apart from the homilies, when in fact he had created new books.

32. Katina, *Korban he-Ani*, 57b–58b; this section is missing from the 1872 edition. Katina also wrote the hagiographic collection *Rahamei Av*.

33. On Wolf, see Sokolow, *Sefer Zikharon*, 37; Kressel, *Leksikon*, vol. 1, col. 695.

34. See, e.g., "Hitnatslut ha-Motsi la-Or," in Emden, *Sfat Emet* (Lvov, 1877). The first books to be printed were *Torat ha-Kenaot* and *Mitpahat Sefarim* (Lvov, 1870). See Ettinger, "Pulmus Ya'abets," 346.

35. Rapoport-Albert, "Hagiography," 156.

36. Zweifel noted this fact (*Shalom al Israel*, vol. 2, 26; vol. 3, Sefer Rishon, 17). See Feiner, "Ha-Mifneh be-Ha'arakhat he-Hasidut," 373. Nevertheless, signs of a positive approach to Hasidism can be identified in expressions of solidarity or apologetics, as in the writings of Polish Jews in the 1860s (Wodziński, "Neither Hated, nor Solidarity," 120–37).

37. Ruderman to Judah Leib Gordon (Manuscript), 1874.

38. Linetski, *Dos poylishe yingl*. First published in *Kol Mevaser* (1867) and in many editions until the Holocaust; it has also been translated into English (*The Polish Lad*). On the author, his work, and its influence, see Riminik, "Tsu der Geshickte," 181–98; Schalit, "Der Tsenzur-Ekzempliar," 13–20; Miron, *A Traveler Disguised*, 5–6, 241–48; Goldberg, "Yiddish Satire." On the work in the context of the anti-Hasidic trend of *Kol Mevaser*, see Orbach, *New Voices of Russian Jewry*, 118, 156–58, 169, 170, 205.

39. Kovner, *Ha-Sifrut ha-Ivrit*, 130.

40. Werses, *Megamot ve-Tsurot*, 91–109. There is no complete picture of anti-Hasidic satire in the second half of the nineteenth century. See Davidson, *Parody in Jewish Literature*. We also learn of the interest in Hasidism in this period among Maskilim by the coverage in the Hebrew press of the pursuit of Bratslav Hasidim by other Hasidic communities (Assaf, "Adayin Lo Nishkat ha-Riv," 465–506; Meir, "Goral ha-Tzadikim," 283–313).

41. Rodkinson, *Urim ve-Tumim*.

42. Chajes, *Hitragshut ha-Nefesh*. On the author see Assaf, *Untold Tales*, 156–57.

43. The title page lists that the book was printed in Lemberg in 1856 in the printing house of Kugel, a detail corroborated in bibliographic studies (Mondshine, *Torat Habad*, 84–85). The numbers were doubtlessly reversed and should read 1865.

44. Israel Dov Ber of Vilednick, *She'erit Israel*. The second edition was published in Zhitomir in 1868, and the third in Koenigsberg in 1877. Rodkinson removed his name from later editions.

45. Rodkinson, *Urim ve-Tumim* (1865). The work was published a number of times in the second half of the nineteenth century, in Hebrew and Yiddish, but it seems that Rodkinson had no part in these editions.

46. Rodkinson, *Shivhei ha-Rav*. On the various editions, see Habermann, *Sha'arei Habad*, 352–54, 364; Nigal, *Mehkarei Ma'arav u-Mizrah*, 207, 219–21.

47. Nigal, *Mehkarei Ma'arav u-Mizrah*, 212–19; Nigal, *Sippurei Rodkinson*, 15–97. Rodkinson's name is alluded to by his initials at the end of the introduction (Habermann, "Hashlamot," 361). Brief references to the book were made by Zederbaum (*Keter Kehunah*, 97), which seem to indicate that he did not know the identity of the author, or at least thought it unimportant at the time.

48. Nigal, *Mehkarei Ma'arav u-Mizrah*, 221–24; Nigal, *Sipurei Rodkinson*, 99–138. Nigal published the later books without significant changes, in Nigal, *Sipurim Hasidi'im mi-Lemberg*, 21–155.

49. Rodkinson, *Shivhei ha-Rav*, 1.

50. *Shivhei ha-Besht* (Rubinstein), 23–26. On the similarity to the frame of Boccaccio's *Decameron*, see Gries, *Book in the Jewish World*, 105. A similar story appears in a later Bratslav tradition (Hazan, *Avnaneyah Barzel*, 29, no. 30): "After the Baal Shem Tov's passing, his disciples gathered together and each one told what he knew; the gathering was at the home of Rabbi Gedalyah, who knew all the tales of the Baal Shem Tov, may the memory of the righteous be for a blessing, and there was another who also knew stories, and that is how *Shivhei ha-Besht* was made. And it seems that Rabbi Gedalyah of Linits made *Shivhei ha-Besht*"; compare Natan of Nemirov, *Sihot ha-Ran*, 93, no. 138; Reiner, "Shivhei ha-Besht," 149.

51. This became a central target of critique for many Maskilim. Such criticism was made even during the "years of silence" in Hasidic hagiography; see,

e.g., Levinsohn and Perl, *Divrei Tsadikim*, 16. The critique found symbolic expression in the reference to the stories as being told "behind the oven" of the study hall, where the idlers and gossipers would gather to pass the time by trading tales.

52. Rodkinson, *Shivhei ha-Rav*, 1.

53. Rodkinson, *Eidat Tsadikim*, 17, 81.

54. Rodkinson, *Shivhei ha-Rav*, 1.

55. Zalmina Vitepsker, *Ma'aseh Nifla'ah*. The book was reprinted by Mondshine, *Kerem Habad* 4, no. 2 (1992): 247–65. On the book, see Habermann, *Sha'arei Habad*, 323–24, nos. 119–20; Habermann, *Torat ha-Rav*, 167; Cohen, "Ha-Defus ha-Ivri be-Tshernovits," 325, no. 141, 329–30, no. 161; Shmeruk, *Sifrut Yiddish*, 212–13; Nigal, *Mehkarei Ma'arav u-Mizrah*, 220; Rapoport-Albert, "Hagiography," 156.

56. Zalmina Vitepsker, *Ma'aseh Nifla'ah*, 2.

57. Rodkinson, *Sippurei Tsadikim*, 100.

58. Rodkinson, *Eidat Tsadikim*, 15.

59. Rodkinson, *Eidat Tsadikim*, 43. On the book see Teller, "Masoret Slutsk," 15–38.

60. Shmeruk noted as much (*Sifrut Yiddish*, 209–13).

61. Walden, *Shem ha-Gedolim he-Hadash*, "Rabbeinu ha-Besht," 38a. R. Aharon Roth's critique can be found in *Shomer Emunim*, 26b. Some found a hint of heresy in this book regarding another matter (Tefilinsky, *Imrei Sefer*, 468).

62. Mondshine, *Shivhei ha-Besht*, 52–54; Sefer *Ma'aseh ha-Shem*, vol. 3, 843–44; Tefilinsky, *Imrei Sefer*, 449–50.

63. Rodkinson, *Shivhei ha-Rav*, vol. 3; Rodkinson, *Eidat Tsadikim*, 17. Compare Bodek's comments in *Sippurim Hasidi'im*, 9, 69, 190–91.

64. Heilman (*Beit Rabbi*, 4) mentions *Shivhei ha-Rav* as a book printed "from various rumors with no basis in fact," and built on "shaky foundations." At the time that he criticized *Shivhei ha-Rav* and *Toldot Amudei ha-Habad*, he noted only Rodkinson's incorrect sources and did not address "his heresy" as some others did. Later (5) he attacked Zweifel specifically for being a Maskil. See Shmeruk, *Sifrut Yiddish*, 212–13.

65. See Habermann, "Hashlamot," 361.

66. Rodkinson, *Shivhei ha-Rav*, at the start of the book. The acrostic was omitted from most of the later editions of the book, perhaps because it was the only place in the book hinting at the name of the author.

67. Rodkinson, *Eidat Tsadikim*, 16.

68. Ibid., 17. The phrase "False Haskalah" used by Rodkinson here is also derived from the Haskalah, even though the use here is more inclusive (Feiner, "Ha-Ma'avak be-Haskalah ha-Mezuyefet," 3–23).

69. Rodkinson, *Shivhei ha-Rav*, 2. This matter is especially prominent in the satires of Josef Perl, who imitated the "language of the Hasidim" and intentionally used incorrect Hebrew derived directly from Yiddish expressions and translations from it, for the purpose of mocking the pidgin of the Hasidim in comparison to the "pure speech" of the Maskilim (Perl, *Ma'asiyot ve-Igrot*, 42–48; Werses, "Mi-Lashon el Lashon," 81–83).

70. Introduction to *Mifalot Tsadikim*, in Bodek, *Sippurim Hasidi'im*, 70. See also Bodek, *Ma'aseh Tsadikim im Divrei Tsadikim*, 3: "Stories like these are worthwhile for every soul, small and great alike, wise and foolish alike . . . and men great in wisdom and service will also find it of great benefit." On being copied from Rodkinson's writings, see Bodek, *Sippurim Hasidi'im*, 9, 14.

71. Rodkinson, *Eidat Tsadikim*, 17.

72. Ibid., 100.

73. See Dan, *Ha-Sippur he-Hasidi*, 200–202; Nigal, *Mehkarei Ma'arav u-Mizrah*, 205–6.

74. Meaning the second edition of Krochmal's *Moreh Nevukhei ha-Zman*, printed by Mikhel Volf with an introduction by Meir Letteris in Lvov, 1863 (Krochmal, *Moreh Nevukhei ha-Zeman*).

75. "He-Haluts" seems to refer to the journal published by Yehoshua Heshel Schorr. The first issue was published in Lemberg in 1851. The writing of this introduction was soon followed by the publishing of the fifth (Breslau, 1860), sixth (Breslau, 1862), and seventh (Frankfurt, 1865) issues. In 1866 the first issue was republished. A. L. Harmelin anonymously published the critical book *Ha-Holets* in Lvov, 1862. It is hard to imagine Walden attacking this book, which itself aimed its attacks at Schorr. See Gilboa, *Leksikon*, cols. 105–8, 428–29; Cohen, "Yehoshua Heshil Shor veha-Haskalah ha-Radikalit," 70–71, 89–91, 112.

76. Erter, *Ha-Tsofeh le-Veit Israel*. The second edition, with additions, was published in Vienna in 1864.

77. Finilish, *Darkah Shel ha-Torah* (Vienna, 1861).

78. Perhaps the intent is Dik's work *Masekhet Aniyut* (Berlin, 1848).

79. "Compiler's Introduction," Walden, *Kehal Hasidim*.

80. Zederbaum, *Keter Kehunah*, 105–6.

81. Rodkinson, *Shivhei ha-Rav*, 1–2; Rodkinson, *Eidat Tsadikim*, 15–16; Rodkinson, *Sippurei Tsadikim*, 100.

82. Piekarz, *Ha-Hanhagah ha-Hasidit*, 15–59; Piekarz, *Hasidut Breslev*, 190–98; Piekarz, "Natan mi-Nemirov," 217–19. It is most reasonable to see this as a response to the Haskalah. On the undermining of the concept of "faith in the sages" (in the Hasidic sense) among the Maskilim, especially in the writings of Josef Perl and Yehoshua Heshel Schorr, see Friedlander, "Irur Ma'amadah shel 'Emunat Hakhamim,'" 363–75; Friedlander, *Bein Halakhah le-Haskalah*, 138–77.

83. Gries, *Book in the Jewish World*, 119–20.

84. Rodkinson, *Shivhei ha-Rav*, 1–2.

85. Nigal, *Mehkarei Ma'arav u-Mizrah*, 205–6; Bodek, *Sippurim Hasidi'im*, 24–25, 142–43.

86. Rodkinson, *Sippurei Tsadikim*, 101. See the implementation of this trend in ibid., 121.

87. Ibid., 17. Take for example the end of the first story (Rodkinson, *Eidat Tsadikim*, 20): "From this story everyone can learn an ethical lesson about how to be careful to live by the work of his hands and to keep and delight in the Sabbath without workaday thoughts, and to happily accept everything that befalls him as being for the best. By this he will merit righteous and pious children, who will hasten our salvation and the redemption of our souls, amen." See more in Rodkinson, *Eidat Tsadikim*, 24, 35, 39, 42, 60, 66. Such examples are missing from *Shivhei ha-Rav*.

88. Nigal, *Mehkarei Ma'arav u-Mizrah*, 206. See for example the stories collected by Bodek in *Nifla'ot ha-Emet*, 197–248.

89. Rodkinson, *Eidat Tsadikim*, 72–78; Nigal, *Mehkarei Ma'arav u-Mizrah*, 217–18.

90. Hasidic works published in our times also make use of traditions brought in Rodkinson's early books. Some make a point of omitting his name; see for example Landau, *Ha-Rabbi R. Elimelekh mi-Lizensk*, 210; Parush, *Or Yekarot*, vol. 1, 42. Others mention his name but ignore his affinity with the Haskalah; for example, Horowitz (*Torat Ha-Magid*, vol. 2, 69–72) refers to the author as "The rabbi and Hasid Michael Frumkin."

91. Hazan, *Kokhvei Or*, 35–36. The books referred to are Rodkinson's *Eidat Tsadikim*, Walden's *Kehal Hasidim*, Bodek's *Pe'er mi-Kedoshim*, and *Shivhei ha-Tsadikim* (perhaps the intent was Bodek's *Ma'aseh Tsadikim* or Mendel Zitron's *Shivhei Tsadikim*, which was published afterward in Warsaw, in 1883).

92. Hazan, *Kokhvei Or*, 36n3.

93. On the unique nature of Bratslav hagiography, see Piekarz, *Hasidut Breslev*, 128–31; Dan, *Jewish Mysticism*, vol. 4, 127–28; Dan, *Ha-Sippur he-Hasidi*, 183–85; Weiss, *Studies*, 255–57.

94. Shmaryahu ben Rabbi Levi Yitshak Schneerson, "Devarim Ahadim," in Teitelbaum, *Ha-Rav mi-Liadi*, 1:ix.

95. Slonimski, "Malshinai be-Seter," 77–78. The comments were printed in *Ha-Shahar he-Hadash* under the editorship of Mosheh Orenstein. At the start of the essay the editor noted that since Smolenskin's *Ha-Shahar* had ceased publication, criticism of the Hasidim had ceased as well, and in its absence the Hasidim were multiplying. He claimed it was his goal to address this distortion with *Ha-Shahar he-Hadash* and with a book left in manuscript, titled *Ha-Tsofeh he-Hadash*

le-Veit Israel. See Assaf, "Mevaser Hadashot be-Kehal Kadosh Sadagora," 117–24; Assaf, *Regal Way*, 45n101.

96. Bloch, *Mikhtavim Mekori'im* (1920), 84, at the top of the list of hagiographic collections. The book includes writings from the Herson *genizah* (a repository of discarded scrolls). Aside from this collection, he wrote a number of books on Hasidism in German and Hebrew, in which he accepted Simon Dubnow's essential premise of the decline of the generations in Hasidism. Nevertheless, he would later stress his Hasidic lineage, his relations with various Hasidic rebbes, and the importance of Hasidism in the generation after the Holocaust. His archive, preserved by YIVO in New York, is a rich store of materials on the history of later Hasidism.

97. See, e.g., Bloch, *Aus Mirjams Brunnen.*

98. On the copying of Rodkinson's stories into Hasidic collections and the influence of his stories on Hebrew literature, see Nigal, *Hasidic Tale*, 37, 44, 50; Nigal, *Melaktei ha-Sippur he-Hasidi*, 25, 28–29; Werses, *Ha-Hasidut*, 236–37, 242, 245–47, 249.

99. E.g., in the writings of S. I. Ish Horowitz, Rav Tsair, Ephraim Deinard, Shimon Berenfeld, Mordekhai David Brandstetter, and even Chaim Nahman Bialik in a number of his letters. For a fuller treatment see Ross, *Masoret Ahuvah u-Senuah.* The opposition of Hasidim to the neo-Romantic literature, as to stories with no clear Hasidic source, has already been treated in academic scholarship; see, e.g., the words of the Munkatsher Rebbe in Shapira, *Divrei Torah*, vol. 2, 261–64, 280–83; Assaf, *Regal Way*, 41–43; Ross, "Teguvah Hasidit," 237–76.

100. Dan, *Ha-Sipur he-Hasidi*, 195, 204, 211–12; Handler, *Ha-Sippur he-Hasidi*, 2–3; Ben Amos, *Ha-Sifrut ha-Amamit ha-Yehudit*, 79. See also Gries, *Book in the Jewish World*, 123–24.

101. Elior, *Freedom on the Tablets*, 38; Bar Yosef, "Ha-Rehabilitatsiyah Shel ha-Mistikah," 218–19.

102. E.g., Krauss, "Milhemet Tsarfat Rusiyah," 31–33; Krauss, "Be-Ikvot Pesak Din shel Ma'alah," 29–31. Krauss cites the words of Pesah Ruderman (discussed below) without mentioning his name, and questions Rodkinson's connection to Hasidism even in the earlier period. Such rhetoric, which adopts claims of certain Maskilim in order to disparage others, is widespread in the apologetic writings of the Habad school until our day.

103. Zederbaum, *Keter Kehunah*, 77–79; Gordon, "Aharit Simhat Tugah," *Ketavim*, 23.

104. On his esteem for Habad, see Zweifel, *Shalom al Israel*, vol. 1, first section, 44, 47–48; vol. 1, second section, 51–60; vol. 3, first book, 44–45; vol. 3, second book, 36–37, 49; vol. 4, 6, 73, 115–16; Zweifel, *Sanegor*, 73–74, 104. Zweifel visited the court of Menahem Mendel Schneurson and eulogized him in *Ha-Magid*

(Zweifel, *Ha-Tsadik Avad*). To the poem he appended lengthy notes, including some with apologetic explanations of his connections to Habad. The book was later reprinted without these notes (Zweifel, *Tushiah*, Part Two: *Shirim*, 34–38). See Feiner, "Ha-Mifneh be-Ha'arakhat he-Hasidut," 339–40, 345.

105. Zweifel, *Shalom al Israel*, vol. 1, second section, 105–7; vol. 2, 20–2, 128; vol. 3, first book, 9–10, 40; vol. 3, second book, 29, 64. In the final volume (127–35) Zweifel offered his advice to those Hasidic rebbes who had the power to reform Hasidism and to bring peace between the parties. Some claimed that his comments regarding the decline of Hasidism in the first volume (second section) were added only in the wake of the dispute (Ish Horowitz, "Le-Toldot Tsveifel," 347–48).

106. Zweifel, *Shalom al Israel*, vol. 1, second section, 105. See also vol. 3, second book, 133. Elsewhere Zweifel placed in the mouth of a Hasid the following words on the praise tales "spread by word of mouth that were and are being printed": "Every nation and tongue has such tales as these that make it unique. And if you think to distance yourself from such story collections and ban them, since their exaggerations exceed the bounds of credibility, you must object not only to the praises of the Baal Shem Tov and his disciples, but also to the exaggerated praises of many Kabbalists, which their disciples, and sometimes they themselves, could not refrain from telling, and which reason cannot accept. I have brought here examples for you to see; consider them all, and then you can judge all of them together, not only these about the Baal Shem Tov and his company" (Zweifel, *Shalom al Israel*, vol. 2, 68). These words also appear in the essay "Keisam ve-Korah," presented as written in a Hasid's letter (Zweifel, *Shalom al Israel*, vol. 1, 62–125).

107. Zweifel, *Shalom al Israel*, vol. 1, 126.

108. Ibid., vol. 1, 21. These comments refer to "wonder tales from the elder Hasidim about the Baal Shem Tov and his disciples," without making mention of any specific book.

109. E.g., Zweifel's use of citations from *Shivhei ha-Besht* (Zweifel, *Shalom al Israel*, vol. 1, first section, 50). Elsewhere he wrote that *Shivhei ha-Besht* is a book "full of fabrications, nonsense, and madness, yet . . . some of the stories in it can be counted as true . . . for so we find that the non-Jewish sages too write down folk tales and popular sayings and find something of value in them" (Zweifel, *Shalom al Israel*, vol. 3, first book, 37). Zweifel criticized Simon Dubnow's early essays on Hasidism that were published in *Voskhod* for using *Shivhei ha-Besht* as a historical source (Ish Horowitz, *He-Hasidut veha-Haskalah*, 35 in the notes). He is to be believed when he writes that "as much as Zweifel strove to be an advocate for Hasidism, he refused to accept a single line of *Shivhei ha-Besht* and other such books as historical material." See Feiner, "Ha-Mifneh be-Ha'arakhat he-Hasidut," 339.

110. Zweifel, *Shalom al Israel*, vol. 3, second book, 64–72.

111. Gottlober, "Rusland," 313. On this trip to St. Petersburg see Goldberg, "Mavo," 12–13, 40–42, 45.

112. Zederbaum, "Bi-Gevurah ve-Lo be-Sheti," 466.

113. Ruderman, "Hashkafah Kelalit." Rodkinson is intended here, as noted by Mondshine (*Shivhei ha-Besht*, 53).

114. Weisberg, *Gaon ve-Shivro*, 14–15. The comment was made in 1883.

115. Halperin, *Kevod Hakhamim*, 16a.

116. In the discussion of the relationship of the Baal Shem Tov to the book *Hemdat Yamim*, David Kahana referred to this statement in *Kehal Hasidim* without mentioning the name of the author and without passing any judgment on him; see Kahana, *Even ha-To'im*, 81–82. In the second edition of the book, the source was correctly listed as *Shivhei ha-Besht* (Kahana, *Toldot ha-Mekubalim*, 1:149).

117. Halperin, *Kevod Hakhamim*, 15a.

118. Hayim Vital, *Eits Hayim*. See Meir, *Rehovot ha-Nahar*, 131–32.

119. Deinard, *Tselem ba-Heikhal*, 153. See also Deinard, *Zmir Aritsim ha-Sheni*, xvi–xix, where he presents *Shivhei ha-Besht* as "a vile and filthy book, full of nonsense like no other . . . , even its author laughs heartily at the Hasidim who believe it," and attacks Graetz for using hagiographic sources in his historical studies.

120. Deinard, *Tselem ba-Heikhal*, 153–54. See also Deinard, *Am To'ei Levav*, 85.

121. Deinard, *Mashgei Ivrim*, 4–5.

122. Deinard, *Zmir Aritsim ha-Sheni*, xxii.

123. Deinard, *Herev Hadah*, 9.

124. Friedkin, "Sehok Tsadik Tamim," 2–3.

3. Images of Hasidism

1. Gottlober, "Rusland," 313.

2. Friedberg, *Toldot ha-Defus ha-Ivri be-Poloniyah*, 135.

3. According to his opponents, he was expelled from St. Petersburg due to failure to pay his debts (Zederbaum, "Bi-Gevurah ve-Lo be-Sheti," 465–66). See chapter 1 in this volume.

4. Rodkinson, "Divrei Shalom ve-Emet," 1–3; Zitron, "Reshimot le-Toldot ha-Itonut ha-Ivrit: Ha-Kol," 338. Kahana later faced similar attacks by one of the Kabbalists of Jerusalem (Halperin, *Kevod Hakhamim*, 11b–21b).

5. On Rodkinson's papers, see Zitron, "Ha-Kol"; Zitron, *Geschichte*, 89–116; Tsamriyon, *Die hebräische Presse in Europa*, 270–72; Eisenstadt, *Perakim be-Toldot Tenuat ha-Poalim ha-Yehudit*, 1:177–80; Gilboa, *Leksikon*, cols. 270–72; and for greater detail, see chapter 1 in this volume.

6. Rodkinson, *Sippurei Tsadikim me-Arba'ah Meitivei Lekhet.*

7. Rodkinson, *Siftei Kedoshim me-Arba'ah Meitivei Lekhet.*

8. Nigal, *Mehkarei Ma'arav u-Mizrah*, 222, no. 44.

9. Kohen-Tsedek, *Sfat Emet*, 43–44, 51–64.

10. Ibid., 1. See also Dan, *Ha-Sippur he-Hasidi*, 190.

11. Rodkinson, "Me-Az Yatsa Matok," 8.

12. Rodkinson, *Sippurei Tsadikim meha-Hut ha-Meshulash* (1896).

13. See Wunder, *Me'orei Galitsiyah*, vol. 5, cols. 394–95; Nigal, *Melaktei ha-Sippur he-Hasidi*, 176–86. As Nigal has shown, Shenkel included Rodkinson's earlier stories in the new collections.

14. Rodkinson, *Sippurei Tsadikim meha-Hut ha-Meshulash*, 48.

15. Ibid., Introduction, quoting Jeremiah 4:22.

16. E.g., *Shivhei ha-Rav*, Lemberg 1885, Munkatsh 1895; *Eidat Tsadikim*, Pressburg 1870, Lublin 1900.

17. Sokolow, "Sifrut Israel," 35; there Sokolow stresses the importance of research and criticism of books addressed to, in his words, "the masses" of traditional society.

18. A fine example of such infringement can be found in the outcry by Miller, the author of the Hasidic hagiographic work *Besorot Tovot*, which he claimed was stolen and printed under another name. This author presented his hagiographic works as a counterpoint to the publishing in journals of tales in Yiddish (Miller, *Besorot Tovot*, "Moda'ah").

19. Israel Dov Ber of Vilednik, *She'erit Israel* (1877). The book was printed at the printing house of L. Frange in Koenigsberg. Rodkinson himself acknowledged in one of his later books that he was the one who brought this edition to press.

20. Friedberg, "Shilumim la-Riv," 264. Weisberg also mocked this edition, "revealing" that Rodkinson was the editor (Weisberg, *Gaon ve-Shivro*, 28, 33, 99–100). Throughout this satire, the author mocked those he dubbed "half-Maskilim and half-Hasidim," and it seems that, once again, his target was Rodkinson (Weisberg, *Gaon ve-Shivro*, 24, 78).

21. Rodkinson, *Toldot Amudei he-Habad*, 41n36; Elior, *Torat ha-Elohut*, 15n59. The reference is to the book Sefer *Sha'arei ha-Avodah*, first published in Shklov in 1821. See also Habermann, *Sha'arei Habad*, nos. 278–79. This book earned Zweifel's esteem as well (*Heshbono shel Olam*, 44).

22. Zweifel also cited statements by Senior Sachs in *Ha-Tehiyah* (Zweifel, *Shalom al Israel*, vol. 3, second book, 49). Compare Gottlober, *Orot me-Ofel*, 16.

23. See Rodkinson, *Even ha-Roshah*, 30–31.

24. Rodkinson, *Or Israel.* On the title page Rodkinson listed himself as the editor of *Ha-Kol* and *Kol la-Am*.

25. Rodkinson, *Toldot Amudei he-Habad.*

26. "Petah ha-Toldah," in Rodkinson, *Or Israel*, xxx–xxxii.

27. On the remainder of the work see Rodkinson, *Tefilah le-Mosheh*, 90, no. 2.

28. In the words of the subtitle: "*Toldot Amudei he-Habad*, being the fourth part of the book *Toldot Ba'alei Shem Tov*." It seems that the earlier parts were never written, and Rodkinson skipped straight to the fourth volume.

29. From the title page of *Toldot Amudei he-Habad*.

30. See the fuller treatment in Feiner, *Haskalah ve-Historiyah*; Gertner, "Reishitah shel Ketivah Historit Ortodoksit," 293–336.

31. Zederbaum, *Keter Kehunah*; 74–153 are dedicated to Hasidism.

32. Zweifel, *Shalom al Israel*, vols. 1–4 (the last volume does not deal with Hasidism). On the book and its editions, see Feiner, "Ha-Mifneh be-Ha'arakhat he-Hasidut," 336–79; Feiner, *Haskalah ve-Historiyah*, 416–30; Wiederkehr-Pollack, *Eliezer Zvi Zweifel and the Intellectual Defense of Hasidism*; Wiederkehr-Pollack, "Eliezer Zvi Hacohen Zweifel: Fogotten Father of Modern Scholarship on Hasidism," 87–115; Rapoport-Albert, "She'alot u-Teshuvot," 71–122.

33. Prozer, *Igrot*, 29.

34. Gottlober, *Toldot ha-Kabbalah veha-Hasidut*. On the book, see Prozer, *Igrot*, 47, 51; Lapidos, "Yehudah Leib Gordon al ha-Sifrut ha-Ivrit Bat Zemano," 295–98; Goldberg, "Introduction to *Zikhronot u-Masa'ot,* by Avraham Ber Gottlober," 12, 21, 35–36; Werses, *Haskalah ve-Shabta'ut*, 169–74; Feiner, "Ha-Mifneh be-Ha'arakhat he-Hasidut," 337, 374–76.

35. Gottlober, "Kol Kore," 396.

36. Ruderman, "Hashkafah Kelalit," 86–104. Ruderman, who came from a Habad family, wrote a number of short works deriding Hasidism (Ruderman, "Tseror Mikhtavim Me'et Mi she-Hayah Hasid," 124–35, 180–87, 311–19; Ruderman, *Ha-Dibbuk*).

37. *Ha-Shahar* printed entire stories of Kahana's: "Even ha-To'im," "Even Negef," and "Even Ofel." These and others were edited and collected in the book *Toldot ha-Mekubalim* (1813–1814), which was reprinted a number of times. See Werses, *Haskalah ve-Shabta'ut*, 174–79. On books and essays of his, both published and unpublished, see Ish mi-Beit Ga"D, *Eleh Shemot*, 27–28; Kristianpoller, *Die Hebräische Publizistik in Wien*, 3:31–32.

38. Many Maskilim mocked those who expressed fear of the book due to its outer design, for example Levinsohn and Perl (*Divrei Tsadikim*, 9). Their comments were frequently repeated in Hebrew literary works influenced by the satires, e.g., Gordon's "Shnei Yamim ve-Laylah" (*Ketavim*, 3) and "Ha-Avot veha-Banim" (*Ketavim,* 2–3).

39. See, e.g., Deinard, *Zikhronot*, 1:39, 42; Krauss, "Be-Ikvot Pesak Din."

40. Rodkinson, *Or Israel*, vi–x.

41. Ibid., 1–3.

42. Rodkinson, *Toldot Amudei he-Habad*, 1–6.

43. Ibid., 96–112. On 112 he wrote that the remainder would come in future books. As noted, these were never published.

44. Karlinsky, *Historiyah she-Keneged*, 111–13. See also Karlinsky, "Dawn of Hasidic-Haredi Historiography."

45. Many examples of a similar nature have been collected by Werses (*Haskalah ve-Shabta'ut*, 99–124, 140–43, 248–52). See also Meir, "Toldot ha-Meta'ate'a ha-Nifla," 463–74).

46. Werses, *Haskalah ve-Shabta'ut*, 167–69; compare his comments on Zweifel (Werses, *Haskalah ve-Shabta'ut*, 139–40).

47. Zweifel, *Shalom al Israel*, 2:12–13.

48. Rodkinson, *Or Israel*, xii–xiii.

49. Ibid., 144.

50. See Scholem, *Studies*, 422–23; Werses, *Haskalah ve-Shabta'ut*, 152–53, 169; Rapoport-Albert, "Devar Mah," 12–13.

51. Jellinek, "Oytseikhnugen Eines Anhengers Fon Ya'akov Frank," 40–42, 59–62.

52. Rodkinson, *Barkai*, 1:36.

53. Ibid., 38–39; Rodkinson, *Barkai*, "Kol Anot," 143.

54. For an opposing view, see Werses's comment (*Haskalah u-Shabta'ut*, 153): "There is a reasonable basis to assume that the negative responses of the paper's readers was due not only to the language of the manuscript but also to its intellectual content and to the favorable and objective tone taken toward the movement by the editor in his introduction."

55. Rodkinson, *Or Israel*, xi, xii.

56. Ibid., xiii, xvi–xvii, xxxvi, 53n21, 69n23, 70n24, 72n25, 73n26, 87n29, 94, 96, 99, and more; Rodkinson, *Toldot Amudei he-Habad*, 12 (in the note), 14, 23, 26n21, 35n32, 80n56, among many others.

57. Rodkinson, *Or Israel*, xii.

58. Ibid., 103n36. See a fuller treatment in Meir and Werses, *Reishit Hokhmah*, 42–43.

59. Rodkinson, *Or Israel*, xii. See also Rodkinson, *Or Israel*, 25.

60. Ibid., (n. 10); 13 (in the note). Ruderman ("Hashkafah Kelalit," 92n9) wrote: "According to the Habad Hasidim, some Mitnaged or heretic invented the tales in *Shivhei ha-Besht* to mock the Baal Shem Tov with lies and worthless words." See Mondshine's comments (*Shivhei ha-Besht*, 52–53). Weisberg also mentioned the claim in 1883 (*Gaon ve-Shivro*, 14): "What more do you need to know—their heresy extends even to what they say about the holy book *Shivhei ha-Besht*, that some joker of a Mitnaged wrote those stories to have a good laugh"; and Deinard (*Kitot be-Israel*, 5) wrote, "Even today we don't know if some joker

was its author who wanted to make fun of the Hasidim, as some Hasidic fools believe today, or if in truth it was some awful fool who believed them all himself, and wished to bring good upon his people by giving his foolish tales legs." Ish Horowitz (*He-Hasidut veha-Haskalah*, 49n1) wrote, "Even *Shivhei ha-Besht* itself—the first and most important source of Hasidic legends—is accounted by many to be a fraud and secretly the work of an anonymous Mitnaged (Pesach Ruderman, *Ha-Shahar* 6:92), even though in my opinion it cannot be true."

61. Deinard made the charge that an avaricious fraud wrote *Shivhei ha-Besht* and that the Baal Shem Tov himself never existed; see Deinard, *Alatah*, 1–44; Deinard, *Tselem ba-Heikhal*, 153–54; Deinard, *Kitot be-Israel*, 4–6. On the idea that the Magid of Mezritsh "invented" the Baal Shem Tov, see Deinard, *Ha-Ya'ar be-Ein Dov*, 139; Deinard, *Zmir Aritsim ha-Sheni*, viii–x.

62. Rodkinson, *Or Israel*, 13, 25n14. See Rubinstein, "Sippurei Hitgalut," 157–86.

63. *Shivhei ha-Besht* (Rubinstein), 17–19, 41–45, 59, 326–28, 330; Perl, *Megaleh Temirin*, 1b; Zederbaum, *Keter Kehunah*, 88–90; Orenstein, *Ish Hamudot*, 18. See Bartal, "Bavuah Me'uvetet," 15; Mondshine, *Shivhei ha-Besht*, 52–58; Etkes, "Magia u-Ba'alei Shem," 40–41.

64. Krochmal, *Ha-Ketav veha-Mikhtav*, 5–10. In this introduction Krochmal claimed that he was a descendant of the Baal Shem Tov. On the book and its context, see Shelley, *Mehkar ha-Mikra*, 103–4; Nadler, "Besht a Spinozist," 359–89. His relationship to Spinoza was nevertheless complex: he claimed (Krochmal, *Even ha-Roshah*, 68) that he was not "among the followers, heaven forbid, of Spinoza and his opinions; praise to God, his philosophy already seems to me old and rusty."

65. Rodkinson, *Or Israel*, 14–15n10. Rodkinson mentioned the ridicule of this book by the Maskilim, and agreed that no one could be called "Adam" in Jewish history. He fulfilled his duty by referring to the figure as "*Adam ha-gadol*," ending his words with the phrase "such is enough for one who understands."

66. Rodkinson, *Or Israel*, 13. On this solution see Rosman, "Makor Histori," 188–92.

67. On this meeting see Rodkinson, *Or Israel*, 8n8. Rodkinson noted that Walden told him that he had a first edition of *Shivhei ha-Besht* with the approbation of the author of *Me'ir Netivim*, but he did not manage to see it because he was forced to leave Warsaw. See also Refael, "Shivhei ha-Besht," 364.

68. Rodkinson, *Or Israel*, xi.

69. Ibid., xi (note 9).

70. Ibid., xi–xii (note 9).

71. Rodkinson, *Toldot Amudei ha-Habad*, 9–10n11, 30–31n26.

72. Rodkinson, *Or Israel*, 8n8, 33n17; 36n29, where he speaks of "a fabricated story" that Walden inserted into his book and which "should be erased so

that no disgrace come upon us"; 43n59, on some "untrue" matter in the book. Nevertheless, at times he cites *Shem ha-Gedolim he-Hadash*, apparently favorably (40n43, 41nn50–51, 42n55).

73. Rodkinson, *Or Israel*, 13 (in the note); he says here that "it is impossible to understand what is written in them." He even definitively identified Walden as the author of *Kehal Hasidim* and noted that he copied the stories of Menahem Mendel Bodek (Rodkinson, *Or Israel*, 36n29). See similar statements in Rodkinson, *Or Israel*, 102n35. Elsewhere he noted that the author of *Kehal Hasidim* copied from his book *Sippurei Tsadikim* (and did not deny that he himself had written hagiographies) (Rodkinson, *Or Israel*, 39n41).

74. Rodkinson, *Or Israel*, 36 (note 29); see also Rodkinson, *Or Israel*, 46 (note 18) and 93 (note 32). Elsewhere he unequivocally dismisses Bodek's book *Seder ha-Dorot he-Hadash* (Rodkinson, *Or Israel*, 13–102, note 35).

75. Rodkinson, *Toldot Amudei ha-Habad*, 11–12, 36, 43, 94; Rodkinson, *Toldot Amudei ha-Habad*, *Or Israel*, 39, note 41.

76. Rodkinson, *Or Israel*, 43–44 (note 60). Rodkinson aimed his barbs at two books bearing Rabbi Pinhas's name: (a) Israel of Kozhnitz's *Sefer Ner Israel* (Vilna, 1922), about which he cited the remark by Rabbi Eizik of Komarna that the teachings ascribed to Rabbi Pinhas and collected at the end of the book were in fact never uttered by him; and (b) *Sefer Midrash Pinhas*, about which he wrote, "This year too, the Warsaw printer RaNDa"Z renewed the printing of *Midrash Pinhas*, adding even more forgeries to it . . . and all the while laughing to himself at the chance to deceive the critic and the Hasidim who would pay full price, for the name R. Pinhas Koretser is so dear to them."

77. E.g., Rodkinson, *Or Israel*, 93, 137; Rodkinson, *Toldot Amudei ha-Habad*, 12, 44.

78. Rodkinson, *Or Israel*, 27, note 16; Rodkinson, *Toldot Amudei ha-Habad*, 8 (in the note), 19–20, note 17. On another of Rodkinson's attacks on Ruderman, see Kohen-Tsedek, *Sfat Emet*, 62.

79. Rodkinson, *Or Israel*, 117. See also Rodkinson, *Or Israel*, 127–28, 136; Rodkinson, *Toldot Amudei ha-Habad*, 7, 18–19, note 16 (where he argues with David Kahana over the observance of the commandments by the Hasidim), 42.

80. See his fierce critique of Graetz (Rodkinson, *Toldot Amudei ha-Habad*, 8).

81. Rodkinson, *Shivhei ha-Rav*, first story. His reference to *Matsref ha-Avodah* is found in Rodkinson, *Toldot Amudei ha-Habad*, 38. On the problematic nature of this book, which was first printed in Koenigsberg in 1858, see Lamm, *Torah Lishmah*, 208–18; Mondshine, *Matsref ha-Avodah*, 165–75; Eliach, *Avi ha-Yeshivot*, 2:609–21; Etkes, *Yahid be-Doro*, 124–30. See statements against the change in name and the book as a whole in Zweifel, *Shalom al Israel*, vol. 1 (first section), 31; vol. 2, 56–60; Deinard, *Kitot be-Israel*, 8–9.

82. Rodkinson, *Toldot Amudei ha-Habad*, 3–6, in the pages of which is brought a long citation from Samuel Joseph Fuenn regarding "the three shepherds" from *Kriah Ne'emanah* (1860). See also Rodkinson, *Toldot Amudei ha-Habad*, 19–20.

83. Compare the opposite statement by Deinard, *Alatah*, 57–58. On this matter see Etkes, "*Yahid be-Doro,*" 151–60. On the image of the Vilna Gaon among the Maskilim, see Werses, "*Hakitsah Ami,*" 25–66. See also Stern, *The Genius: Elijah of Vilna and the Making of Modern Judaism.*

84. E.g., Zimriyon, *Shivhei Tsadikim.* See Nigal, *Mehkarim be-Hasidut*, 2:420–24; Nigal, *Mehkarei Ma'arav u-Mizrah*, 293–97.

85. On the author and his book, see Feiner, *Haskalah ve-Historiyah*, 305–7; Etkes, "Yahid be-Doro," 48–52; Stampfer, "On the Creation and the Perpetuation of the Image of the Gaon of Vilna," 53–54, 60–61; Katzman, "Li-Demut ha-Gaon R. Yehoshua Heshil Levin," 742–82.

86. Deinard, *Herev le-Hashem ule-Israel*, 101 (in the note); Deinard, *Alatah*, 55–58. On the reading of *Aliyot Eliyahu* as a book of wonder tales, see Katz, *Zikhronot*, 16.

87. See the fuller treatment in Katzman, "Li-Demut ha-Gaon," 703–12.

88. Mapu, *Mikhtavim*, 22.

89. On Zweifel and his treatments of "The Three Shepherds," see Zweifel, *Shalom al Israel* (Rubinstein), vol. 1, 65–66; Dinur, *Be-Mifneh ha-Dorot*, 24, no. 15; Feiner, "Ha-Mifneh," 351, 358, 363–65. In the 1880s Yitshak Kaminer presented a similar picture in his poetry, counting the three movements (and not their founders) positively, while still criticizing the negative elements in each (Kaminer, *Shirim*, 25–28, 29–37, 216–29). For a romantic picture of Kaminer, see Ravnitsky, *Dor u-Sofrav*, 143–59.

90. Menasheh of Ilya, *Pesher Davar.* See Barzilay, "Acceptance or Rejection," 1–20; Barzilay, "*Menasseh of Ilya*"; Kosman, "Sefer Pesher Davar le-Rabbi Menasheh mi-Ilya," 191–228; Zweifel, *Shalom al Israel* (Rubinstein), vol. 1, 44; Werses, "Hakitsah Ami," 48–49. Deinard described Menasheh of Ilya as a "madman" (Deinard, *Sifrat Israel*, vol. 1, 50).

91. Rodkinson, *Or Israel*, xv–xvi.

92. Rodkinson, *Toldot Amudei ha-Habad*, 12 (in the note).

93. Deinard, *Herev Hadah*, 5.

94. Kohen-Tsedek, *Ohalei Shem*, 81–82. See also Kohen-Tsedek, *Ohalei Shem*, 73–74, 84.

95. Deinard, *Kitot be-Israel*, 8. See also Deinard, *Mashgei Ivrim*, 12; Deinard, *Tselem ba-Heikhal*, 156.

96. E.g., Heilman, *Beit Rabi*, 4–5; Mondshine, "She'erit Israel," 41; Plotzky, "Ha-Kli Hemdah u-Fulmuso Neged Mezuyyafei ha-'Historiya,'" 682–85. The

bulk of Plotzky's criticism is directed at Rodkinson's *Toldot Ba'alei ha-Shem* and the tradition regarding the connection between Hasidism and the author of *Or ha-Hayim*.

97. Plotzky hinted that Rodkinson was responsible for forging the Herson collection ("Ha-Kli Hemdah u-Fulmuso Neged Mezuyyafei ha-'Historiya,'" 682–85). To Rodkinson was also ascribed the polemical book *Yalkut ha-Ro'im* (1869), dealing with the Zanz-Sadigora dispute; there is no basis to such speculation. See Kressel, "Yalkut ha-Ro'im," 111.

98. Deinard, *Mashgei Ivrim*, 7, 15–16; Deinard, *Zikhronot*, vol. 2, 39, 42. In these books he even claimed that Rodkinson was not the author of his own books but that others had ghostwritten them for him, "since he himself did not even know how to hold a pen in his hand, and so, until his dying day, all of his books were written by others, just like most of the Hasidic rebbes." A similar claim would later be made by Mendel Piekarz, who described Arthur Green's book on Rabbi Nahman of Bratslav as an attempt to present "a *tsadik* for members of the New World" (see Piekarz, *Hasidut Breslev*, 219–46).

99. Deinard, *Mashgei Ivrim*, 7.

100. Zweifel, *Shalom al Israel*, vol. 2, 22–23. See Ish Horowitz, "Le-Toldot Tsveifel," 347–48; Prozer, *Igrot*, 56; Paperna, *Ketavim*, 207–8.

101. Deinard brings an anti-Hasidic anecdote from Zweifel on Aharon of Karlin in the spirit of *Megaleh Temirin*, and repeated it in a number of his works: Deinard, *Tselem ba-Heikhal*, 149–51; Deinard, *Mashgei Ivrim*, 7–8, 15–16; Deinard, *Zikhronot*, vol. 2, 30; Deinard, *Herev Hadah*, 4–5, 11–12; Deinard, *Miflagot be-Israel*, 39. Deinard wrote these words long after the release of *Shalom al Israel*, and they did not preclude him from using Zweifel's approbation when it came time to publish his book *Masa Krim* in 1878.

102. Zweifel too faced harsh attacks on his writings, but they were recognizably different from those Rodkinson faced; see Ish Horowitz, "*Le-Toldot Tsveifel*," 347–48; Feiner, "Ha-Mifneh."

103. Kohen-Tsedek, *Mikha'el ha-Nehepakh le-Sama'el/ Sfat Emet*. See also Kohen-Tsedek, *Ohalei Shem*, 73–74, 85, 90–91; Kohen-Tsedek, *Ha-Torah veha-Mitsvah*, 86–89. These statements also fed the denunciation of Rodkinson sent to Smolenskin's *Ha-Shahar* but never published (Sirotkin, "Mefarsemin et ha-Hanafim" [Manuscript]).

104. Friedberg, "Shilumim la-Riv," 264. This charge appeared in another article, Simonowitz, "Mikhtav Galui," 404.

105. Friedberg, "Shilumim la-Riv," 288. The *tahash* was an unknown animal named in the Bible as providing the skins for the Tabernacle; the rabbinic tradition described them as having multi-colored, evershifting skintone.

106. Ruderman, "Hashkafah Kelalit."

107. Smolenskin, "Toldot Ba'alei Shem," 31–32.

108. Rodkinson himself wrote a satire against his opponents and published parodies in the language of the Zohar in *Ha-Kol*; see Kohen-Tsedek's angry response in *Sfat Emet*, 1–2, and an analysis of one "Zoharic" fragment by Malachi in *Mi-Neged Tireh*, 67–68, note 130; see also Davidson, *Parody in Jewish Literature*, 239.

109. Brandstetter, "Mi-Hayil el Hayil," 163. See also Rosenfeld, *Ha-Tsofeh le-Veit Ya'akov*, 48 (in the notes); "Me'ora'ot Nora'ot de-Irenu." The anonymous author of the last composition aimed his darts at Rodkinson but also at Deinard; see Davidson, *Parody in Jewish Literature*, 210.

110. Dubnow, *Toldot he-Hasidut*, 403.

111. Dubnow, "Igrot el Horodetski," 218 (from June 17, 1909); Dubnow, "Igrot," 128.

112. Rodkinson's nephew, Avraham Frumkin, who since the end of the nineteenth century was connected to socialist and anarchist groups in London and New York, published a small book on the Baal Shem Tov with a Romantic bent, presented as a "folk tale" (Frumkin, *Ha-Besht).* The author listed his sources at the end of the book: Graetz's books, Avraham Kahana's book on the Baal Shem Tov, *Ma'aseh Tsadikim*, *Divrei Tsadikim*, *Seder ha-Dorot he-Hadash*, and *Shivhei ha-Besht*. He does not name a single book by his relative, even though the book was published within Rodkinson's lifetime and in close proximity to his residence. Neither did he know which books had been written by Rodkinson, and erroneously ascribed to him the book *Kehal Hasidim*; see Frumkin, *In Friling fun Idishen Sotsiyalizm*, 168. Deinard mentioned this book in his criticism of socialists with affinities for Hasidism (Deinard, *Tsiyon Ba'ad Mi*, 118).

113. Rodkinson, "Me-Az Yatsa Matok," 1–3, 5–9. Here he responded in detail to criticism of him in Kohen-Tsedek's book *Mikha'el ha-Nehepakh le-Sama'el*.

114. Rodkinson, *Tefilah le-Mosheh*, 90, no. 2.

115. For a description of the latter-named books and the turns in Rodkinson's life, see chapter 1 in this volume.

116. Lilienblum, *Kehal Refa'im*; Lilienblum, *Kol Kitvei Mosheh Leib Lilienblum*, vol. 2, 413–69. At the end of the book, which drew heavily on Isaac Baer Levinsohn's *Emek Refa'im*, he appended notes in the style of those Josef Perl included in *Megaleh Temirin*, giving the following warning above them: "I will write my notes, to show that the dream of my poem is not a dream in vain, and that it does not contain idle words and that all of its words are built on golden foundations, that is, the books of the great men of Israel, whose (turbid) waters we drink until today" (Lilienblum, 462). On this work, see Klausner, *Historiyah*, vol. 4, 217–24.

117. Rodkinson, *Even ha-Roshah*, 5.

118. Rodkinson, *Tefilah le-Mosheh*, 33.

119. Ibid., 33–34 and others. On this division within Haskalah literature, see Meir, *Megaleh Sod*, 43–45.

120. Rodkinson, *Tefilah le-Mosheh*, 14.

121. Ibid., 14, no. 12.

122. Rodkinson, *Tefilah le-Mosheh,* 34, no. 3.

123. Rodkinson also had harsh words for R. Hanokh Heinikh of Radzin, known as "Ba'al ha-Tekhelet," the grandson of Rabbi Mordekhai Yosef of Izbitsa, and the tractates he composed from his own knowledge (Rodkinson, *Tefilah le-Mosheh,* 21, no. 5; 121–23; no. 2).

124. Rodkinson, *Tefilah le-Mosheh,* xi. For a biography of Shlomoh Rubin, ses Graber, "Toldot Shlomoh Rubin," 144–47; Stern, *Salomon Rubin: Sein Leben und seine Schriften*; Jackont, *Shlomoh Rubin.* On his relationship with Hasidism, see Rubin, *Igeret*, 99–100; Horodecky, *Ha-Hasidut veha-Hasidim*, vol. 3, 103–5; vol. 4, 110–15; Teller, "Keta'ei Zikhronot," 81; Assaf, *Regal Way*, 143–45.

125. Rodkinson, *Tefilah le-Mosheh*, 150–51.

126. Ibid., 90.

127. Rodkinson, *Even ha-Roshah*, 30–31.

128. In a series of books appended to *Ha-Shahar* between 1874 and 1876, Rubin addressed the connection between the Kabbalah and Christianity, writing in one place tjat "the Kabbalists should be considered complete Christians" (Rubin, *Menahem ha-Bavli Hu Mani ha-Parsi*, 48–50); and "let not the reader be astounded when I mention 'the Kabbalists and the Christians' in the same breath, for in truth they are twins from conception and from birth . . . and there is no difference between them except in their deeds . . . the Kabbalists of recent days, from the days of R. Isaac Luria to Shabbetai Tsvi and the Frankists and the Zoharists and the Hasidic *tsadikim*, have become more abhorrent, and they are like the Christian masses in the crudeness of their faith" (Rubin, *Sod ha-Sefirot*, 23–25). Elsewhere, in describing the "secret societies," he wrote that the Frankists combined the Kabbalah with Christianity (Rubin, *Razei Olam*, 33–36). Rabbi Mosheh Rozenson, "the Kabbalist Maskil," came out fiercely against Rubin's comments, defending the Kabbalah in a number of essays and books and attempting to bring Judaism and Christianity together (Rozenson, *Divrei Shalom o Mishpat ha-Kabbalah*, vol. 2, 76–79; Rozenson, *Mashol Timshol*, 78). On Rozenson see Schalit, "Mosheh Rozenson, Zeine Hiburim, Tsavah un Matsevah," 113–23; Steinschneider, *Ir Vilna*, vol. 2, 179–81; Appel, *Be-Tokh Reishit ha-Tehiyah*, 560–64; Katz, *Zikhronot*, 39–43; and see his daughter's book, Havah Skomorowska, *Der Emes Vegn Mosheh Rozenson*. Surprisingly, Deinard was close to "the new Kabbalist"; see for example Deinard, *Igrot Sofrim* (Manuscript), 18–25.

129. Deinard made such claims at the start of the twentieth century as part of his scathing polemical stance in attacking Rodkinson; see for example Deinard, *Ha-Ya'ar be-Ein Dov*, 211–12. There were certainly some Hebrew writers during those years who attempted to integrate Kabbalah and Christianity, for example in the letters of Yehiel Tsvi Lichtenstein-Hirschenson, especially *Derekh ha-Kodesh* (1872). See Sobel, "Toldot Spinoza ve-Shitato," 16. Such comments frequently appeared in book reviews from 1888 in the missionary journal *Edut le-Israel* ("Bikoret Sefarim," 31–32, 95–96). I will address elsewhere, and at greater length, the relationship of Jewish converts to Christianity in the second half of the nineteenth century to Kabbalah and Hasidism.

130. Rodkinson, *Even ha-Roshah*, vol. 1, 31.

131. Indeed, Rabbi Tsvi Hirsch of Zidichov had already claimed that the Habad Kabbalistic system was incorrect due to its reliance on philosophy and "rational analysis" (*hakirah*), but it is unusual to find the charge being reversed and used against other Kabbalists. For Rabbi Tsvi Hirsch of Zidichov's comments on Habad, see Loewenthal, *Communicating the Infinite*, 172–73; Haran, "Heirut be-Tokh Emunah," 330–31. Rabbi Meir Shalom of Kalushin would later express a similar opinion; see Yellin, *Sefer Derekh Tsadikim*, 10b–11a.

132. See a fuller treatment in Meir, *Imagined Hasidism*, fifth chapter.

133. Deinard, *Miflagot be-Israel*, 40.

134. See, e.g., Rodkinson, *History of Amulets.*

135. Rodkinson, *Talmud Bavli*; Rodkinson, *History of the Talmud*. See the fuller treatment in chapter 1 in this volume.

Epilogue

1. In a similar spirit did Shmuel Josef Agnon in turn write about Rodkinson; see Agnon, *Me-Atsmi el Atsmi*, 260–61.

2. In this context it is worth mentioning the favorable views of Tsvi Hirsch Segal toward Hasidism. Segal taught Talmud in a rabbinical seminary in Zhitomir and was a close associate of Zweifel; a small portion of his writings were published under the title *Likutei Tsvi;* few details about his life and relation to Hasidism are reported by Paperna, *Kol ha-Ketavim*, 214–22. On Zweifel's influence on the public impression of Hasidism see Feiner, "Ha-Mifneh," 374–79. See also the views of Reuven Asher Braudes (*Ha-Dat veha-Hayyim*, 2:26–41), who, along with Menasheh of Ilya, saw the Ba'al Shem Tov as a religious reformer, in contrast with Elijah Gaon of Vilna. On his Rodkinson's complicated relationship with Hasidism, see Weinfeld, "Ish Hasid," 237–44. It is to be stressed that his favorable view of Hasidism frequently appeared only in his writings on the Ba'al Shem Tov and early

Hasidism, and did not apply to Hasidism as a living movement in the second half of the nineteenth century. See the brief satire by Hisda bar Hisda, published in *Ha-Shahar*, that was critical of those who viewed Hasidism through a Romantic lens or saw the Ba'al Shem Tov as a "reformer" ("Milah de-Metika ke-Duvsha," 383–90). See also Deinard, *Herev Hadah*, 9–11.

Glossary

Baalei Shem—traveling folk healers who used esoteric knowledge, especially the use of divine names (hence the term *baalei shem*, lit., "masters of the name [of God]"), to effect healings, bring on healthy births, and protect the people from the Evil Eye.

Bloch-Rohling Affair—an episode in the 1890s, begun when Joseph S. Bloch accused August Rohling in print of forging Talmudic texts in his anti-Semitic writing; Rohling in turn sued him for libel, withdrawing the suit at the last moment.

Brimann, Aron Israel (Dr. Justus)—a Jew who converted to Christianity and published the anti-Semitic book *Der Judenspiegel* in 1883; he worked with August Rohling, a German Catholic theologian and anti-Semitic polemicist.

Frankist Movement—an antinomian messianic movement, primarily in mid-eighteenth-century Poland, led by Jakob Frank; it was viewed by its opponents as a continuation of the Sabbatian heresy and as an amalgamation of Judaism and Christianity.

Habad Hasidism—an exceedingly intellectual branch of the Hasidic movement begun in White Russia in the late eighteenth and early nineteenth centuries by Rabbi Shneur Zalman of Liady.

Hasidism—a pietistic revival movement among Eastern European Jews that began in the mid-eighteenth century; inspired by Israel ben Eliezer (1700–1760), referred to as the Baal Shem Tov, and led by his disciples, it exposed the masses to many elements of the Kabbalah that had previously been reserved for the educated elite.

Haskalah—an intellectual and social movement of the late eighteenth and nineteenth centuries that had elements of both the European Enlightenment and Romanticism. Its adherents, known as Maskilim, held a wide range of ideologies, from Orthodox rabbis seeking moderate reform to more radical Reform thinkers and secular nationalists. One of the movement's primary activities was writing and publishing new forms of Jewish literature and media, especially in Hebrew.

Israel Baal Shem Tov—Israel ben Eliezer (Podolia, 1700–1760), known as the Baal Shem Tov; the inspiration for and purported leader of the pietistic revivalist movement known as Hasidism. He was seen variously by members of Eastern European society as a wonder-working healer, a semimessianic spiritual leader, and an ignorant fraud.

Jellinek, Adolf (Aaron)—an Austrian rabbi of the Reform movement who also dedicated his energies to academic scholarship and combatting anti-Semitism.

Kabbalah—a body of esoteric knowledge and practices that emerged in medieval Spain, with roots in ancient Judaism; it entered the public realm in the seventeenth and eighteenth centuries due to the rise of the printed book, the Sabbatian movement, and the Hasidic movement.

Matsah Shemurah—unleavened bread used for the Passover holiday, which was "guarded" from the grinding process on to make sure it did not come into contact with moisture and thus to ensure its unleavened state.

Mitnaged—an Orthodox opponent of the Hasidic movement. The figurehead of the Mitnagdim was the famous rabbi Elijah Gaon of Vilna. Mitnagdim accused Hasidism of continuing the antinomian and populist tendencies of the Sabbatian movement.

Sabbatianism—a messianic movement centering around the figure of Shabbetai Tsvi (1626–1676), who proclaimed himself the messiah and inspired a large part of Jewish society to throw off the bonds of Jewish law and immigrate to the Holy Land in anticipation of the coming Redemption. Long after Shabbetai Tsvi's death, secret factions of the movement persisted within Jewish society.

Shneur Zalman of Liady—the founder of the Habad branch of Hasidism in White Russia in the late seventeenth and early eighteenth centuries; his thought presented traditional Kabbalistic concepts in exceedingly intellectualized form.

Tefillin—phylacteries worn by Jewish men during the morning prayer service (and by some especially pious men all day long) on their arms and heads, in keeping with such biblical verses as Deuteronomy 6:8.

Tiszaeslár Affair—a trial in 1883 in which Franz Delitzsch defended Judaism against accusations made by August Rohling.

Tsadik—lit., "a righteous man" in Hebrew; in the eighteenth and nineteenth centuries it had the specific connotation of a Hasidic spiritual leader, who was likely known for not only his ethical achievements but also his spiritual and charismatic ones, which may have included miracle-working.

Wissenschaft des Judentums—"Science of Judaism," a movement begun by Leopold Zunz (1794–1886), a German academic who coined the term to refer to the study of Jewish religion, history, and culture using the tools of modern critical scholarship.

Bibliography

Abramovich, Shalom Yaakov. "Tsu Unzere Yuden!" *Ha-Kol La-Am* 39 (1877): 153–54.

Agnon, Shmuel Josef. *Me-Atsmi el Atsmi*. Jerusalem and Tel Aviv: Schocken, 1976.

———. *Sefer Sofer ve-Sippur: Sippurim al Sofrim ve-al Sefarim*. Jerusalem and Tel Aviv: Schocken, 1978.

Aharon of Starosselje. *Avodat he-Levi*. Warsaw: n.p., 1866.

Amen [pseud.]. "Ba'al ha-Mevaser (Demut Ikonin shel Rabbi Yosef Kohen-Tsedek)." *Ha-Tsefirah* 14 (1904), lit. supp.: 86–88.

Appel, Yehudah. *Be-Tokh Reishit ha-Tehiyah: Zikhronot u-Khetavim mi-Yemei "Hovavei Tsiyon" be-Rusiyah*. Tel Aviv: Guttenberg, 1936.

Assaf, David. "Adayin Lo Nishkat ha-Riv Hinam: Ha-Ma'avak Neged Hasidut Breslav." *Zion* 59 (1994): 465–506.

———. *Hatsits ve-Nifga: Anatomiyah shel Mahloket Hasidit*. Haifa: Haifa University Press, 2012.

———. "Me-Oyev le-Ohev: Darko shel Rabbi Akiva Shalom Hiyyut mi-Toltshin me-Hitnagdut le-Hasidut." In *Mi-Vilnah le-Yerushalayim: Mehkarim be-Toldoteihem uve-Tarbtam shel Yehudei Mizrah Eiropah Mugashim le-Professor Shmuel Werses*, ed. David Assaf, Israel Bartal, Avner Holtzman, Hava Turnienski, Shmuel Feiner, and Yehudah Friedlander. Jerusalem: Magnes, 2002, 46–47.

———. "Mevaser Hadashot be-Kehal Kadosh Sadigora: Satirah Anti-Hasidit Lo Noda'at." *Kesher* 17 (1995): 117–24.

———. *The Regal Way: The Life and Times of Rabbi Israel of Ruzhin*. Trans. David Louvish. Stanford: Stanford University Press, 2002.

———. *Untold Tales of the Hasidim: Crisis and Discontent in the History of Hasidism*. Trans. Dena Ordan. Waltham, MA: Brandeis University Press, 2010.

Assaf ha-Mazkir. "Ba-Kol mi-Kol Kol." *Ha-Leumi* 14 (1889): 6.

Bader, Gershom. *Medinah ve-Hakhameihah*. New York: Appel, 1934.

Bar Yosef, Hamutal. "Ha-Rehabilitatsiyah shel ha-Mistikah ha-Yehudit." In *Sefer Zikaron le-Gershom Shalom (Mehkarei Yerushalayim be-Mahshevet Israel 20)*, ed. Joseph Dan. Jerusalem: Hebrew University Press, 2007, 207–50.

Bartal, Israel. "Al Demuta ha-Rav Adatit shel ha-Hevrah ha-Yehudit bi-Yerushalayim." *Pe'amim* 57 (1994): 114–24.

———. "Bein Haskalah Radikalit le-Sotsiyalizm Yehudi." In *Ha-Dat veha-Hayyim: Tenuat ha-Haskalah ha-Yehudit be-Mizrah Eiropah*, ed. Emmanuel Etkes. Jerusalem: Zalman Shazar Center, 1993, 328–35.

———. *Me-"Umah" le-"Leom": Yehudei Mizrah-Eiropah 1772–1881*. Jerusalem: Misrad ha-Bitahon, 2002.

———. "Mi-Bavuah Me'uvetet le-Uvdah Historit: Sifrut ha-Haskalah u-Mehkar Tenuat he-Hasidut." *Mada'ei ha-Yahadut* 32 (1992): 7–17.

———. "Olam Yashan ad Yesod Nahrivah? Tenuat ha-Po'alim ha-Yehudit bein Mahapekhot le-Hemshekhiyut." In *Amelim u-Mahapakhanim: Tenuat ha-Po'alom ha-Yehudit*. The Nahum Goldman Catalogue at Beit ha-Tefutsot. Tel Aviv: n.p., 1994, 26–31.

———. "Zikhron Ya'akov le-Rabbi Ya'akov Lipshits: Historiyografiyah Ortodoksit?" *Malat* 2 (1984): 409–14.

Barzilay, Isaac. "Acceptance or Rejection: Menasseh of Ilya's Ambivalent Attitude toward Hasidim." *Jewish Quarterly Review* 74 (1983): 1–20.

———. *Manasseh of Ilya, Precursor of Modernity among the Jews of Eastern Europe*. Jerusalem: Magnes, 1999.

Ben Amos, Dan. *Ha-Sifrut ha-Amamit ha-Yehudit*. Jerusalem: Magnes, 2006.

Ben Gurion, Emmanuel. "Rishmei Kuntresim." *Reshumot* 2 (1922): 437–38.

Ben Hillel ha-Kohen, Mordekhai. *Olami*. Vol. 1. Jerusalem: n.p., 1927.

Ben Horin, Meir. "Solomon Schechter to Judge Mayer Sulzberger." *Jewish Social Studies* 25 (1963): 249–86.

Ben Yehudah, Eliezer. "Mi-Huts la-Arets." *Ha-Tsvi* 11 (1886): 45; 14 (1886): 57.

———. "Rodkinson veha-Rav Dr. Blokh." *Ha-Tsvi* 20 (1886): 81.

Benedict, Binyamin Zeev. "Rabbi Meir Ish Shalom." *Areshet* 2 (1960): 269–84.

Berdyczewski, Micah Yosef. "Pirkei Yoman, Detsember 1902–Detsember 1904." In *Ginzei Mikhah Yosef*, ed. Avner Holzman. Vol. 5. Tel Aviv: Reshafim, 1992, 41–62.

———. "Tsiyun (Le-Nefesh ha-Rav ha-Gaon R. Akiva Hayut)." In *Kitvei Mikhah Yosef Berdyczewski*, ed. Avner Holzman and Yitshak Kafkafi. Vol. 2. Tel Aviv: Ha-Kibbuts ha-Meuhad, 1996, 44–45.

Berger, Israel. *Zekhut Israel*. Ed. H. I. Waldman. Vols. 1–2. Jerusalem: Ner la-Maor, 2001.

Berkley, George E. *Vienna and Its Jews: The Tragedy of Success 1880s–1980s*. Cambridge, MA: Abt Books, 1988.

Berkowitz, Mikhel. "Mi-Ma'arekhet ha-Emet." *Musaf Davar* 3, no. 10 (1888): 7–8.

Berkowitz, Simcha. "Deinard's (Or Mayer) Catalogue." *Studies in Bibliography and Booklore* 21 (2001): 53–75.

———. "Ephraim Deinard: 'A Transitional Figure' (1846–1930)." Master's thesis, Columbia University, 1964.

———. "Ephraim Deinard: Bibliophile and Bookman." *Studies in Bibliography and Booklore* 9 (1971): 137–52.

———. "The Solzberger-Deinard Relationship: Towards the Establishment of a Center for Jewish Learning in America." In *Freedom and Responsibility: Exploring the Challenges of Jewish Continuity*, ed. Rela Mintz Geffen and Masha Bryan Edelman. Hoboken, NJ: Ktav, 1998, 229–39.

Berenfeld, Mosheh. "Lemberg." *Ha-Magid* 49 (1880): 414.

Berenfeld, Simon. "David Gordon." *Ha-Olam* 20 (1886): 378–79.

———. "Zikhronot." *Reshumot* 4 (1886): 145–93.

Berenstein, Shimon Shraga. *Nehemiah Shmuel Leibovits*. New York: n.p., 1932.

"Bikoret Sefarim." *Edut le-Israel* 3 (1887): 31–32; 6 (1888): 95–96.

Bistrits, Meir Kahn. *Bi'ur Tit ha-Yaven she-bo hitiah Yehoshu'a Heshel Shor (hu ba'al He-Haluts)*. Pressburg: Lewi and Alkelai, 1889.

Bloch, Chaim. *Aus Mirjams Brunnen, Chasidische Erzählungen und Legenden*. Wien: n.p., 1929.

———. "Bikur Etsel August Rohling." *Ha-Olam* 33 (1930): 642–44; 34 (1930): 662–64.

———. *Blut und Eros im jüdischen Schrifftum und Leben, Von Eisenmenger über Rohling zu Bischoff*. Wien: Sensen-Verlag, 1935.

———. "Ha-Rav Dr. Yosef Shmuel Blokh." In *Hokhmat Israel mi-Ma'arav Eiropah*, ed. Shimon Federbush. Vol. 1. Jerusalem and Tel Aviv: Ogen, 1959, 85–91.

———. *Heikhal le-Divrei Hazal u-Pitgameihem*. New York: Pardes, 1948.

———. *Kovets Mikhtavim Mekori'im meha-Besht za''l ve-Talmidav zy''a*. Vienna-Berlin: Menorah, 1920.

———. *Mi Natan le-Mesisah Ya'akov ve-Israel le-Bozezim?* New York: n.p., 1958.

———. "Theodor Herzl and Joseph S. Bloch: An Unknown Chapter of Zionist History Based on Verbal Statements and Written Notes." *Herzl Year Book* 1 (1958): 154–64.

———. *Ve-Da Mah she-Tashiv*. New York: Reznik, 1943.

Bloch, Joseph S. "Brimann and R." *Ostereichische Wochenschrift* 43 (1885): n.p.

———. *Erinnerungen aus meinem Leben*. Vols. 1–2. Wien and Leipzig: R. Löwit, 1922.

———. *Israel und die Völker: Nach jüdischer Lehre*. Berlin and Wien: B. Harz, 1922.

———. "Letter to Lemberg." *Ostereichische Wochenschrift* 45 (1885): n.p.

———. "Letters to Deinard, 1880, 1883 (Manuscript)." Deinard Archive, Jewish Theological Seminary Library, New York.

———. *Zikhronot mi-Yemei Hayyai*. Vols. 1–2. Tel Aviv: Bloch, 1933.

Blumberg, Israel David. "Mikhtav Oz ve-Yedidut." *Mahzikei ha-Dat* 20 (1885): 6.

Bodek, Menahem Mendel. *Ma'aseh Tsadikim im Divrei Tsadikim*. Lvov: n.p., 1879.

———. *Mif'alot Tsadikim*. Lvov: n.p., 1865.

———. *Nifla'ot ha-Emet: Sefer Emet ve-Yatsiv*. Vol. 2. Brooklyn: n.p., 1996.

———. "Seder ha-Dorot he-Hadash" and "Ma'aseh Tsadikim im Divrei Tsadikim." In *Sefer Nafshot Hasidav*, ed. Avraham Yaakov Bombeck. Vol. 1. Jerusalem: n.p., 2000.

———. *Sippurim Hasidi'im*. Ed. Gedalyah Nigal. Tel Aviv: Y. Golan, 2001.

Brandstetter, Mordechai *Kol Kitvei Mordekhai David Brandstetter*. Vol. 1. Warsaw: n.p., 1910.

Braudes, Reuven Asher. *Ha-Dat veha-Hayyim*. Ed. Gershon Shaked. Vols. 1–2. Jerusalem: n.p., 1974.

Breiman, Shlomoh. *Ha-Pulmus bein Lilienblum le-vein Ahad Ha'am, ve-Dubnov veha-Reka Shelo*. Jerusalem: Reuven Mass, 1951.

———. "Introduction by Mosheh Leib Lilienblum." In *Ketavim Otobiyografi'im*. Jerusalem: Reuven Mass, 1970.

———. "Pulmus ha-Tikunim be-Dat be-Sifrut ha-Ivrit ba-Me'ah ha-Yud Tet." *He-Avar* 1 (1953): 115–32.

Breinin, Reuven. *Perets ben Mosheh Smolenskin, Hayyav u-Sefarav*. Warsaw: n.p., 1897.

———. *Zikhronot: Sirtutim me-Hayyei A. Zederboym u-Tekhunato*. Cracow: n.p., 1899.

Brill, Yosef. "Midrash Sofrim." *Ha-Shahar* 10 (1880): 817, 137–42, 195–99, 562–67, 622–26; 683–89; 11 (1883): 105–11, 178–83.

Brimann, Aron [Dr. Justus]. *Die Kabbala: ihre Hauptlehren und ihr Verhaeltniss zum Christentum*. Innsbruck: n.p., 1885.

Brody, F. M. "The Hebrew Periodical Press in America, 1871–1931: A Bibliographical Survey." *Publications of the American Jewish Historical Society* 33 (1934): 137–38.

Brody-Zeldner, Ts. "Ha-Itonim ha-Ivrim be-Amerikah." *Ha-Doar* 12 (1936): 221.

Bush, Mordekhai. "Mikhtavei Sofrim. Kenigsberg (Hitnatslut)." *Ha-Levanon* 10 (1877): 80.

Chayes, Akiva Shalom of Tultshin. *Hitragshut ha-Nefesh*. Ed. Michael Levi Rodkinson. Lemberg: n.p., 1864.

———. *Siddur Ikvei Shalom*. Lublin: n.p., 1896.

Cherikover, Eliyahu. *Yehudim be-Itot Mahapekhah*. Tel Aviv: Am Oved, 1958.

Cohen, Chaim. "Yehoshua Heshil Shor veha-Haskalah ha-Radikalit." Master's thesis, Tel Aviv University, 2004.

Cohen, Tova. "Ha-Tekhnikah ha-Lamdanit: Tsofen shel Sifrut ha-Haskalah." *Mehkarei Yerushalayim be-Sifrut Ivrit* 13 (1992): 137–69.

Cohen, Yitshak Yosef. "Arba'ah Sefarim Anonimi'im u-Mehabreihem." *Kiryat Sefer* 33 (1958): 136.

———. "Ha-Defus ha-Ivri be-Tshernovits." In *Areshet: Sefer ha-Shannah le-Heker ha-Sefer ha-Ivri*, ed. Naftali Ben-Menahem and Yitshak Refael. Vol. 3. Jerusalem: Mossad ha-Rav Kook, 1961, 315–16.

Cohn, Yehudah B. *Tangled Up in Text: Tefillin and the Ancient World*. Providence, RI: Brown Judaic Studies, 2008.

Dan, Joseph. "A Bow to Frumkinian Hasidism." *Modern Judaism* 11 (1991): 175–93.

———. *Ha-Noveilah he-Hasidit*. Jerusalem: Mossad Bialik, 1964.

———. *Ha-Sippur he-Hasidi*. Jerusalem: Keter, 1975.

———. *Jewish Mysticism*. Vol. 4, *General Characteristics and Comparative Studies*. Northvale, NJ and Jerusalem: Aronson, 1999.

———. "Kitsa shel he-Hasidut ha-Frumkinianit." *Mehkarei Hasidut*, ed. Emmanuel Etkes, David Assaf, and Joseph Dan. Jerusalem: n.p., 1999, 261–74.

Davidson, Israel. *Parody in Jewish Literature*. New York: n.p., 1907.

Deinard, Ephraim. *Adir*. Vienna: n.p., 1888.

———. *Alatah, yokhiah be-otot ne'emanim . . . ki sefer ha-zohar hu mezuyaf . . . ve-khi ha-kabbalah hi elilit . . . veha-hasidut ha-beshtit hi katolitsizum hadash be-ma'atafah ivrit*. St. Louis: n.p., 1927.

———. "Alei Hemed, Hor ha-Har." *Ha-Le'umi* 10 (1889): 2–3.

———. "Al ha-Pisgah." *Ha-Le'umi* 16 (1889): 7.

———. *Am To'ei Levav, sefer le-dor tehilat he-hasidim u-kedosheihemm*. St. Louis: n.p., 1927.

———, ed. *Bitul Ikarei ha-Notsrim, nikhtav bi-yedei ha-filosof ha-elohi R. Hasdai Kreskas ve-ne'etak le-ivrit bi-yedei R. Yosef ben Reshe''t*. Kearny, NJ: n.p., 1904.

———. *Devir Efraim, yakhil tokhen otsar ha-sefarim ha-gadol asher atsar ha-sofer Efraim Deinard be-Noy Orleans le-khol mahlekotav*. New Orleans: n.p., 1886.

———. "Divrei ha-Mol." *Ha-Le'umi* 3 (1889): 1.

———. *Divrei ha-Yamim le-Tsiyon be-Rusiya mi-Shenot 1880–1885*. Vols. 1–2. Kearny, NJ: n.p., 1904.

———. "Eleh Toldot Sama'el." *Ha-Le'umi* 19 (1889): 2–3.

———. "El ha-Korim be-Eiropa." *Yalkut Amerika*. Newark, NJ: n.p., 1899, 1–2.

———. "Espor kol Atsmotav." *Ha-Le'umi* 19 (1889): 1–4.

———. "Hashkafah Kelalit." *Ha-Shahar* 9 (1878): 70–78, 130–38, 183–89.

———. *Ha-Ya'ar be-Ein Dov*. St. Louis: n.p., 1889.

———. "He'arat ha-Mo"l." *Ha-Le'umi* 16 (1889): 4.

———. *Herev Hadah, ketuvah bi-sefat ashkenaz bi-yede Rabbi Israel Lobel*. Kearny, NJ: n.p., 1904.

———. *Herev le-Hashem ule-Israel, neged ha-sefer "Yeshu ha-Notsri ve-Torato" me'et Dr. Yosef Kloyzner*. New Orleans: n.p., 1923.

———. *Herpat Britaniyah: ketem shahor le-ot kalon al metsah Britaniyah*. Newark: n.p., 1889.

———. *Hoda'at Ba'al Din, Neged Torat Dat Natseret*. Kearny, NJ: n.p., 1904.

———. "*Igrot Sofrim, kollel hamon mikhtavim yekarim asher nikhtevu be-fo'el bi-yedei gedolim hokrei lev*, 1874 (Manuscript)." Jewish Theological Seminary, New York (microfilm, National Library of Israel, Jerusalem).

———. *Kehilat Amerika*. Vols. 1–2. St. Louis: n.p., 1925.

———. *Kitot be-Israel, kolel Sefer Zimrat Am ha-Arets*. Newark: n.p., 1899.

———. *Korot ha-Yehudim be-Amerika: ha-Yishuv be-Karni-Arlington*. New Orleans: n.p., 1925.

———. "Letter to Avraham Kahana, 1900–1901 (Manuscript)." Avraham Kahana Archive, MSS 401569, National Library of Israel, Jerusalem.

———. "Letter to Avraham Schwadron, 1888 (Manuscript)." Schwadron Collection, National Library of Israel, Jerusalem.

———. "Letter to Judah Leib Gordon, 1878 (Manuscript)." Judah Leib Gordon Archive, MSS 40761, National Library of Israel, Jerusalem.

———. *Masa be-Eiropa*. Pressburg: n.p., 1886.

———. *Masa be-Erets ha-Kedem u-Moreh Derekh le-Khol ha-Nosim le-Erets ha-Kedoshah u-Mitsrayim*. Pressburg: n.p., 1883.

———. *Masa Karim, kollel korot benei israel be-hetsi hai karim*. Warsaw: n.p., 1878.

———. *Mashgei Ivrim, reishit haskalat he-hasidim bi-tekufat Rodkinzohn, ve-totsa'oteihah be-sifrut ha-hayyim, "Ha-Mahalakh he-Hadash" veha-bolshevizm ha-sifruti*. St Louis: n.p., 1909.

———. *Megilah Afah o Tokhehat Megulah*. Kearny, NJ: n.p., 1904.

———. "Mezurah ha-Reshet." *Ha-Le'umi* 1 (1889): 1.

———. *Miflagot Israel*. New York: n.p., 1899.

———. "Mikhtav el ha-Mol!" *Ha-Shahar* 9 (1878): 335–37.

———. *Mikhtav Galui le-Yeshu ha-Notsri, meha'ah*. St. Louis: n.p., 1924.

———. *Misterei Nyu York o Hitpathut ha-Tenu'ah ha-Le'umit be-Amerika*. New York: Y. Aranson, 1909.

———. "Mitsvah le-Farsem et ha-Rama'im." *Ha-Magid* 14 (1885): 112.

———. "Odessa." *Ha-Melits* 36 (1885): 580–81.

———. *Or ha-Me'ir, kollel reshimat sifrei israel*. New York: n.p., 1897.

———. *Reshimat Sefarim ve-Kitvei Yad be-Otsar Efraim Deinard*. (Manuscript). JTS library, MS 9193. Courtesy of the Library of the Jewish Theological Seminary.

———. *Sefer ha-Kundas*. Newark, NJ: n.p., 1890.

———. *Sefer ha-Ployderzak o Meorat Tsefaunim*. Newark, NJ: n.p., 1890.

———. *Shibolim Bodedot: asefat ma'amarim*. Jerusalem: n.p., 1915.

———. *Sifrat Israel be-Amerika*. Vol. 1. Jaffa: n.p., 1910; Vol. 2. Newark: n.p., 1913.

———. *Tselem ba-Heikhal . . . ve-nilveh eilav . . . ma'amar be-shem "Ha-Meshumadim be-Israel."* New Orleans: n.p., 1926.

———. *Tsiyon Be'ad Mi? Be'ad Bolshevikim o Yehudim?* Arlington, NJ: n.p., 1918.

———. *Yalkut Amerika, asefat ma'amarei mada shonim, ketuvim bi-yedei sofrei israel be-erets he-hadashah*. Newark: n.p., 1899.

———. *Zikhronot Bat Ami, le-korot ha-yehudim veha-yahadut be-Rusiya*. Vols. 1–2. New Orleans: n.p., 1920.

———. *Zmir Aritsim ha-Rishon*. Kearny, NJ: n.p., 1904.

———. *Zmir Aritsim ha-Sheni, neged kat he-hasidim ve-hamon kedosheihem nevi'ei ha-sheker*. Newark: n.p., 1899.

Dik, Isaac Meir. *Der Purim Shpigel*. Vilna: n.p., 1870.

———. *Die Shehne Helene di Tsvite*. Newark: n.p., 1889.

———. "Masekhet Aniyut." In *Kanfei Yonah*, ed. Senior Sachs. Vol. 1. Berlin: n.p., 1858, 3–20.

Dinur, Ben Zion. *Be-Mifneh ha-Dorot*. Jerusalem: Mossad Bialik, 1972.

Dubnow, Simon. "Igrot Shimon Dubnov." *Ha-Avar* 8 (1961): 108–45.

———. "Igrot Shimon Dubnov le-S. A. Horodetski." *Geneizim* 4 (1971): 203–46.

———. *Sefer ha-Hayyim*. Tel Aviv: n.p., 1936.

———. *Toldot ha-Hasidut*. Tel Aviv: Devir, 1960.

Druck, D. "Nedidat Sefarim." *Do'ar ha-Yom* 209 (1924): 3.

Druyanov, Alter. *Ketavim le-Toldot Hibat Tsiyon ve-Yishuv Erets Israel*. Ed. Shulamit Laskov. Vol. 2. Tel Aviv: Tel Aviv University, 1985.

Ehrenpreis, Mordecai. "Barukh she-Petaranu me-Onsho shel Justus." *Machzikei ha-Dat* 18 (1885): 4–5.

"Eilim ve-Elilim." *Ha-Me'asef* 4 (1879): 41–54; 5 (1879): 68–70.

Eisenstadt, Ben Tsion. *Dor Rabanav ve-Sofrav*. Vol. 3. Vilna: n.p., 1901.

———. *Hakhmei Israel be-Amerikah*. Vol. 5, *Dor Rabanav ve-Sofrav*. Newark, 1903.

Eisenstadt, Shmuel. *Perakim be-Toldot Tenuat ha-Poalim ha-Yehudit*. Vol. 1. Tel Aviv: Ha-Kibbuts ha-Artsi, 1970.

Eisenstein, Yehudah David. "Bikoret Sefarim: Masekhet Rosh ha-Shannah min Talmud Bavli ha-Yashan veha-Katsar . . . me'et Mikha'el L. Rodkinson." *Ner ha-Ma'aravi* 3 (1895): 17–20.

———. "Bikoret Sefarim: Masekhet Rosh ha-Shannah min Talmud Bavli ha-Yashan veha-Katsar . . . me'et Mikhael L. Rodkinson." *Ner ha-Ma'aravi* 4–5 (1895): 33–40.

———. "Bikoret Masekhet Shabbat Hotza'at M. L. Rodkinson 1896." *Ner ha-Ma'aravi* 8–9 (1896): 25–50.

———. *Ma'amarei Bikoret: bikoret Masekhet Rosh ha-Shannah min ha-Talmud ha-Yashan veha-Katsar hotsa'at Mikha'el Levi Rodkinson, bikoret Masekhet Shabbat be-ha'atakah anglit*. New York: n.p., 1897.

———. *Otsar Zikhronotai: Korot Toldotai u-Mikrei Yom be-Yomo*. New York: n.p.: 1930.

Eliach, Dov. *Avi ha-Yeshivot: Maran Rabbeinu Hayyim mi-Volozhin*. Vols. 1–2. Jerusalem: Moreshet ha-Yeshivot, 1991.

Elior, Rachel. *Freedom on the Tablets*. Tel Aviv: Universitah Meshuderet, 1999.

———. "Ha-Mahloket al Moreshet Habad." *Tarbiz* 49 (1980): 166–86.

———. *Heirut al ha-Luhot: Ha-Mahshavah ha-Hasidit, Mekoroteihah ha-Misti'im ve-Yesodoteihah ha-Kabbali'im*. Tel Aviv: Universitah Meshuderet, 1999.

———. *Torat ha-Elohut ba-Dor ha-Sheni shel Hasidut Habad*. Jerusalem: Magnes, 1982.

Elishevits, Dmitri. "Ha-Tsenzura ha-Memshaltit al ha-Pirsumim ha-Yehudi'im ba-Keisarut ha-Rusit." In *Toldot Yehudei Rusyah*, ed. Ilya Luria. Vol. 2. Jerusalem: Merkaz Zalman Shazar, 2012, 63–72.

Elkushi, Gedalyah. "Esrim Igrot shel David Frishman le-Yehudah Leib Gordon." *Behinot be-Bikoret ha-Sifrut* 8 (1966): 31–51.

Elstein, Yoav. "Bo'u Litkon: Bibliografyah shel ha-Sipporet he-Hasidit." In *Ma'aseh Sippur: Mehkarim ba-Sipporet ha-Yehudit Mugashim le-Yoav Elstein*, ed. Avidov Lipsker and Rella Kushelevsky. Ramat Gan: Bar Ilan University, 2006, 459–535.

Emden, Yaakov. *Iggeret Bikoret*. Ed. Michael Levi Rodkinson. Zhitomir: n.p., 1968.

———. *Sfat Emet*. Ed. Mikhel Volf. Lvov: n.p., 1876.

Epstein, Baruch ha-Levi. *Makor Barukh*. Vol. 1. Vilna: n.p., 1928.

Erter, Yitshak. *Ha-Tsofeh le-Veit Israel*. Vienna: n.p., 1864.

Erternberg, Shmuel. *Y"Y Linetsky: Zein Leben Un Zein Shofn*. Venice: n.p., 1931.

Etkes, Emmanuel. *Ba'al ha-Tanya: Rabbi Shneur Zalman mi-Liadi ve-Reishitah shel Hasidut Habad*. Jerusalem: Merkaz Zalman Shazar, 2012.

———. "Magia u-Ba'alei-Shem be-Sifrut ha-Haskalah." In *Mekhkarei Hasidut* (*Mekhkarei Yerushalayim be-Mahshevet Israel* 15), ed. Emmanuel Etkes, David Assaf, and Joseph Dan. Jerusalem: Magnes, 1999, 39–56.

———. *Yahid be-Doro: Ha-Gaon mi-Vilnah*. Jerusalem: Merkaz Zalman Shazar, 1998.

Ettinger, Shmuel. "Pulmus Ya'abets-Eybeschutz be-Re'i ha-Historiografiyah ha-Yehudit." *Kabbalah* 9 (2003): 329–92.

Faierstein, Morris M. "Hasidism: The Last Decade in Research." *Modern Judaism* 11 (1991): 118.

Feiner, Shmuel. "Be-Emunah Bilvad! Ha-Pulmus shel R. Natan mi-Nemirov Neged ha-Atei'izm veha-Haskalah." In *Mehkarei Hasidut (Mehkarei Yerushalayim be-Mahshevet Israel* 15), ed. Emmanuel Etkes, David Assaf, and Joseph Dan. Jerusalem: Hebrew University Press, 1999, 89–124.

———. "Ha-Ma'avak ba-Haskalah ha-Mezuyefet u-Gevuloteihah shel ha-Modernizatsiyah ha-Yehudit." In *Mi-Vilnah le-Yerushalayim: Mehkarim be-Toldoteihem uve-Tarbutam shel Yehudei Mizrah Eiropah Mugashim le-Professor Shmuel Werses*, ed. David Assaf, Israel Bartal, Avner Holzman, Hava Turniansky, Shmuel Feiner, and Yehudah Friedlander. Jerusalem: Magnes, 2002, 3–23.

———. "Ha-Mifneh be-Ha'arakhat he-Hasidut: Eliezer Tsveifel veha-Haskalah ha-Metunah be-Rusiyah." In *Ha-Dat veha-Hayyim: Tenuat ha-Haskalah ha-Yehudit be-Mizrah Eiropah*, ed. Emmanuel Etkes. Jerusalem: Magnes, 1993, 336–79.

———. *Haskalah ve-Historiyah: Toldoteihah shel Hakarat-Aver Yehudit Modernit*. Jerusalem: Magnes, 1995.

———. "Yehudah Leib Gordon ke-Anti-Klerikal ukhe-Lohem be-'Milhemet ha-Tarbut' ha-Yehudit." *Sadan* 3 (1998): 211–29.

Feingold, Ben Ami. "Ha-Sefer veha-Sifrut ke-Nose be-Sipporet ha-Haskalah." *Mehkarim be-Sifrut Ivrit* 5 (1986): 85–100.

Feldman, Yehoshua [pseud. R. Binyamin]. *Kenesset Hakhamim.* Jerusalem: Ha-Va'ad ha-Tsiburi le-Hotsa'at Kitvei R. Binyamin, 1960.

Felsenthal, E. *Bernhard Felsenthal Teacher in Israel: Selections from His Writings with Biographical Sketch and Bibliography.* New York: n.p., 1924.

Finilish, Tsvi Menahem. *Darkah Shel Torah.* Vienna: n.p., 1861.

Fischer, Rolf. "Anti-Semitism in Hungary 1882–1932." In *Hostages of Modernization: Studies on Modern Antisemitism, 1870–1933/39, Austria-Hungary-Poland-Russia,* ed. Herbert A. Strauss. Berlin and New York: W. de Gruyter, 1993, 863–92.

Frankel, Elimelekh Elazar. "Kitvei Koreits." In *Imrei Pinhas ha-Shalem* by R. Pinhas of Korets, ed. E. E. Frankel. Vol. 2. Bnei Brak: n.p., 2003, 724–44.

Frankel, Jonathan. *Dam ve-Politikah: Alilat Dameshek, ha-Yehudim veha-Olam.* Jerusalem: Merkaz Zalman Shazar, 2003.

Friedberg, Avraham Shalom [pseud. Har Shalom]. "Davar el ha-Korim." *Ha-Melits* 15, no. 20 (1879): 389–90.

——— [pseud. Har Shalom]. "Shilumim la-Riv." *Ha-Melits* 15, no. 10 (1879): 203–5; 13 (1879): 243–45; 14 (1879): 263–64; 15 (1879): 287–88; 16 (1879): 302–3; 17 (1879): 321–23.

———. "Zikhronot al devar Ha-Erez." In *Sefer ha-Shanah.* ed. N. Sokolow. Vol. 1. Warsaw, 1900.

Friedberg, Chaim Dov. "Ha-Defus ha-Ivri be-Lvov." In *Entsiklopediyah shel Galuyot.* Vol. 4, *Lvov,* ed. Natan Michael Gelber. Jerusalem and Tel Aviv: n.p., 1956.

———. *Toldot ha-Defus ha-Ivri be-Poloniyah.* Rev. 2nd ed. Tel Aviv: n.p., 1980.

Friedkin, Yosef Leib. "Sehok Tsadik Tamim." *Ha-Leumi* 16 (1889): 2–3.

Friedlander, Yehudah. *Bein Halakhah le-Haskalah: Mekoman shel Sugiyot Hilkhatiyot be-Merkam Sugot Sifrutiyot.* Ramat Gan: Bar Ilan, 2004.

———. *Be-Misterei ha-Satirah.* Vol. 3. Ramat Gan: Bar Ilan, 1994.

———. "Irur Ma'amadah shel 'Emunat Hakhamim' be-Aspeklariyah shel ha-Satirah ha-Ivrit be-Me'ah ha-Tesha-Esreih." In *Divrei ha-Kongres ha-Olami ha-Shishi le-Mada'ei ha-Yahadut*. Vol. 3. Jerusalem: Hebrew University, 1977, 363–75.

Frishman, David. *Ketavim*. Vol. 4, *Tohu va-Vohu*. Warsaw and New York: n.p., 1930.

Frumkin, Avraham. *In Friling fun Idishen Sotsiyalizm: Zikhronot fun a zhornalist*. New York: n.p., 1940.

———. *R. Israel Ba'al Shem Tov, Der Grinder fun Hasidizmus, Zein Biografye*. New York: n.p., 1903.

Frumkin, Israel Dov. "Ha-Kol. Mikhtav Iti Mashmia Hadashot me'et Ahi ha-Yakar ha-Rav he-Hakham Moreinu ha-Rav Mikha'el Levi Rodkinsohn." *Ha-Havatselet* 8, nos. 11–12 (1878): 77.

———. "Ha-Sanegor." *Ha-Havatselet* 21, no. 19 (1891): 72.

Fuchs, Yaakov Shmuel. "Bo'u Heshbon." *Ha-Maggid le-Israel* 3, no. 38 (1894): 305–6.

———. "Nefutsot Yehudah." *Ha-Maggid le-Israel* 11, no. 18 (1902): 200–201.

Fuenn, Shmuel Yosef. *Keriyah Ne'emanah*. Vilna: n.p., 1860.

———. "Leharhik Lazut Sefatayim." *Ha-Maggid* 32, no. 14 (1888): 108.

Gartner, Lloyd P. "Rumania and America, 1873: Leon Horowitz's Rumanian Tour and Its Background." *Publication of the American Jewish Historical Society* 45 (1955–1956): 67–92.

Geatner, Chaim. "Reishitah shel Ketivah Historit Ortodoksit be-Mizrah Eiropah: Ha'arakhah Mehudeshet." *Zion* 67 (2002): 293–336.

Geffen, Joel S. "Whither to Palestine or to America in the Pages of the Hebrew Press Ha-Melitz and Ha-Yom (1880–1890): Annotated Documentary." *American Jewish Historical Quarterly* 59 (1969): 179–200.

Ger Ba-Arets. "Amerikah." *Ha-Magid le-Israel* 17 (1995): 141.

Gershom Shalom Library Catalogue. *Sifriyat Gershom Shalom be-Torat ha-Sod veha-Yahadut Catalogue*. Vol. 1, ed. Joseph Dan, Ester Leibes, and Shmuel Ramm. Jerusalem: n.p., 1999.

Gilboa, Menuhah. "Ha-Ploydérzak o Me'urat ha-Tsafonim shel Efraim Deinard." *Kesher* 5 (1989): 116–21.

———. *Leksikon ha-Itonut ha-Ivrit ba-Me'ot ha-Shemoneh Esreih veha-Tesha Esreih*. Jerusalem: Mossad Bialik, 1992.

Goldberg, David Chaym. "Yiddish Satire and the Haskalah: The Case of Dos Poylishe Yingel." Ph.D. diss., Columbia University, 1985.

Goldberg, Reuven. Introduction to *Zikhronot u-Masa'ot*, by Avraham Ber Gottlober. Vol. 1, ed. Reuven Goldberg. Jerusalem: n.p., 1976.

Goldberg, Zeev. "Getsel Zelikovitz: Maskil ve-Itonai Yehudi be-Mifneh ha-Me'ot." Ph.D. diss., Hebrew University of Jerusalem, 1995.

Goldman, Yosef. *Hebrew Printing in America 1735–1926, A History and Annotated Bibliography*. Vols. 1–2, ed. Ari Kinsberg. Brooklyn: n.p., 2006.

Goldschmidt, Eliezer. "Targum ha-Talmud ha-Bavli le-Germanit." *Areshet* 2 (1960): 309–30.

Gordon, David. "Barkai." *Ha-Magid* 5 (1886): 38.

———. "Besorat Sefarim: Matsat-Mitsvah ve-Alilat ha-Dam." *Ha-Magid* 4 (1883): 31.

———. "Dr. Yustus." *Ha-Magid* 13 (1885): 106.

———. "Harav et Riveinu: Toldot ha-Rav Yosef Shmuel Dr. Blokh." *Keneset Israel* 1 (1886): 29–41.

———. "Od ha-Pa'am: Ha-Rav Dr. Blokh ve-Rodkinszohn Ba'al Ha-Kol." *Ha-Magid* 8 (1886): 64.

Gordon, Dov. "Be'ad Rodkinson." *Ha-Magid* 4 (1887): 30.

———. "Tsadik Nitpas be-Avon ha-Dor." *Ha-Magid* 12 (1887): 94.

———. "Yustus ha-Sheini." *Ha-Magid* 48 (1886): 422.

Gordon, Judah Leib. *Kitvei Yehudah Leib Gordon: Prozah.* Jerusalem: n.p., 1960.

Gottheil, Richard James. *The Life of Gustav Gottheil: Memoir of a Priest in Israel.* Williamsport, PA: n.p., 1936.

Gottlober, Avraham Ber. "Demuto ha-Historit shel ha-Besht: Bein Sakin ha-Menatehim shel ha-Historiyon le-Mikh'holo shel Hoker ha-Sifrut." *Kabbalah* 8 (2000): 411–46.

———. "Ha-Omnam Meitav ha-Sippur Kazavu? Makom Sifrut ha-Shevahim be-Toldot he-Hasidut." *Da'at* 44 (2000): 88–90.

———. "Ha-Reka ha-Yehudi le-Po'alo shel Buber be-Itsuv ha-Sipur ha-Hasidi." *Mehkarei Yerushalayim be-Folklor Yehudi* 11–12 (1990): 46–56.

———. "Kol Kore be-Oznei Ohavei Sifrut Israel." *Ha-Shahar* 4 (1873): 393–99.

———. "Mikhtav Galui le-Yedidi mi-Noar Erez." *Ha-Boker Or* 4 (1879): 849–56.

———. *Orot Me'Ofel.* Warsaw: n.p., 1881.

———. "Rusland." *Ha-Magid* 34 (1873): 313.

———. *Toldot ha-Kabbalah veha-Hasidut mi-Reishit Tsemihatan ad ha-Yom ha-Zeh*. Zhitomir: n.p., 1870.

———. *Zikhronot u-Masa'ot*. Vols. 1–2, ed. Reuven Goldberg. Jerusalem: Mossad Bialik, 1976.

Graber, She'altiel Eizik. "Toldot Shlomoh Rubin." *Otsar ha-Sifrut* 4 (1992): 144–47.

Gries, Zeev. *The Book in the Jewish World, 1700–1900*. Oxford: Littman, 2007.

Grossman, Grace Cohen, and Richard E. Ahlborn. *Judaica at the Smithsonian: Cultural Politics as Cultural Model*. Washington, DC: Smithsonian Institute, 1997.

Grunwald, Max. *Vienna*. Philadelphia: n.p., 1936.

Habermann, Abraham Meir. "Hashlamot." In *Toldot Sifrut Israel*, vol. 5, ed. Israel Zinberg. Merhaviyah: n.p., 1959, 345–66.

———. *Ketav, Lashon ve-Sefer*. Jerusalem: Mass, 1973.

———. "Sha'arei Habad." In *Alei Ayin: Minhat devarim le-Shlomoh Zalman Shoken*. Jerusalem: n.p., 1948–1952, 293–370.

———. "Torat ha-Rav (reshimah bibliografit shel kol sifrei Shneur Zalman mi-Liadi u-sefarim alav)." In *Sefer ha-Ken: kovets ma'amarim al admor ha-zaken Rabbi Shneur Zalman mi-Liadi*. Jerusalem: n.p., 1969, 133–71.

"Hadashot bi-Gevul Israel." *Kol Mahzikei ha-Dat* 11 (1886): 7–8.

Ha-GeMaRA. "Ha-Kol Kol Eisav." *Kol Mahzikei ha-Dat* 7 (1885): 1–2.

Ha-Kohen, Pinhas Ya'akov. "Ha-Defus ha-Ivri be-Hungariyah / Ha-Defus ha-Ivri be-Pressburg." *Kiryat Sefer* 31 (1956): 233–51.

Ha-Levi, Naftali. Letter to Shlomoh Rubin, 1883. "Mikhtavim me-Hakhmei Israel." *Ner ha-Ma'aravi* 5, no. 1 (1896): 55–56.

———. *Shulhan Arukh, Yoreh Deah . . . mateh naftali . . . mateh ha-levi*. Vienna: n.p., 1883.

———. *Zeh Sefer Toldot Adam*. Vienna: n.p., 1875.

Halperin, Menahem Menkhin. *Kevod Hakhamim*. Jerusalem: n.p., 1901.

Handler, A. *Blood Libel at Tishaeszler*. Boulder: East European Monographs, 1980.

Handler, Hannah. "Ha-Sippur he-Hasidi: itsuvim sifruti'im ve-emdot metafiziyot, iyun be-yetsirato shel Menahem Mendel Bodek." Ph.D. diss., Bar Ilan University, 2003.

Haran, Raya. "Heirut be-Tokh Emunah: ha-hatafah le-limud ha-nigleh veha-nistar be-hagut ha-tsadikim le-veit Ziditshov-Komarnah." In *Sefer Zikaron le-Gershom Shalom (Mehkarei Yerushalayim be-Mahshevet Israel* 20), ed. Joseph Dan. Jerusalem: Hebrew University, 1997, 305–52.

Harmelin, Aryeh Leib. *Sefer ha-Holets (helek mi-sifri ha-kolel "Magen ha-Dat."* Lvov: n.p., 1862.

Hartston, Barnet. *Sensationalizing the Jewish Question: Anti-Semitic Trials and the Press in the Early German Empire.* Leiden and Boston: Brill, 2005.

Havlin, Shlomo Zalman. "Al ha-Genizah he-Hersonit." *Yeshurun* 4 (1999): 756.

"Hazkarat Neshamot." *Luah Ahi'asaf* 12 (1905): 18.

Hazan, Avraham. *Avanei'ha Barzel.* Bnai Brak: n.p., 1961.

———. *Sefer Kokhvei Or.* Jerusalem: n.p., 1987.

Heikin, Y. *Yiddishe Bletter in Amerika.* New York: n.p., 1946.

Heilman, A. S. *Beit Rabbi.* Barditshev: n.p., 1902.

Heller, Marvin J. *Further Studies in the Making of the Early Hebrew Book*, Brill: Leiden and Bostin, 2013, 217–50.

———. "He Should be Called Sama'el: Michael Levi Rodkinson: The Life and Literary Career of a Jewish Scoundrel Revisited." *Jewish Culture and History* 7 (2004): 77–92.

Hellwing, Isak Arie. *Der konfessionelle Antisemitismus im 19. Jarhundert in Österreich.* Wien: n.p., 1972.

Henisch, M. "Galician Jews in Vienna." In *The Jews of Austria: Essays on Their Life, History and Destruction*, ed. Jonathan Fraenkel. London: Vallentine, Mitchell, 1967, 361–73.

Heshel, Avraham Yehoshua. "Le-Toldot R. Pinhas mi-Koreits." *Alei Ayin: minhat devarim le-Shlomoh Zalman Shoken.* Jerusalem, 1948, 213–44.

Hevrat Dorshei Haskalah. "Me-Heshbon Pe'ulat ha-Hevrah Leharbot Haskalah be-Israel be-Rusiyah." *Ha-Shahar* 10 (1880): 102–3.

Hisda bar Hisda. "Milah de-Metika ke-Duvsha." *Ha-Shahar* 7 (1876): 383–90.

Holzman, Avner. *Ha-Sefer veha-Hayyim: Masot al Mikhah Yosef Berdyczewski.* Jerusalem: Carmel, 2003.

Horodecky, Samuel Abba. *Ha-Hasidut veha-Hasidim.* Vols. 1–4. Tel Aviv: Devir, 1943.

Horowitz, Aharon Yehudah Leib. "Hamburg." *Ha-Tsefirah* 10, no. 3 (1883): 20–21.

———. "Mi-Zikhronotai." *Ha-Do'ar* 4, no. 18 (1928): 5–6; 19 (1925), 5–6; 21 (1925): 5; 23 (1925): 6–7.

———. *Romanya ve-Amerikah*. Berlin: n.p., 1883.

Horowitz, Eliezer Imanuel. *Torat ha-Maggid mi-Zlotshov*. Vols. 1–2. Jerusalem: n.p., 1999.

Ish Horowitz, Shaul Israel. "He-Hasidut veha-Haskalah: Mahshavot al Devar he-Hasidut ha-Yeshanah (ha-Beshtiyanit) vehe-Hadashah." *He-Atid* 2 (1909): 29–99.

———. "Le-Toldot R. A. Ts. Tsweifel." *Ha-Magid* 41 (1889): 322–23; 43 (1889): 340–41; 44 (1889): 347–48; 45 (1889): 354–55.

———. *Me-Ayin ule-Ayin? Kovets Ma'amarim be-Inyanei ha-Yehudim veha-Yahadut*. Berlin: n.p., 1914.

Ish Lapidot, Avraham of Toltshin. "Bikoret al ha-Tefillin shel Rodkinsohn." *Kol Mahzikei ha-Dat* 11 (1885): 6–7; 12 (1885): 3–4.

Ish mi-Beit Gad. "Bibliographische Notiz: Eleh Shemot." *Beit Otzar ha-Sifrut* 1 (1887): *Otsar ha-Hokhmah*, 27–28.

Ish Shalom, Meir. *Davar al Odot ha-Talmud, Im Yekhol Hu Lehitargem Kol Tsarko*. Pressburg: n,p., 1885.

———. "Divrei Sofrim [Letter to Rodkinson]." *Ha-Kol* 299 (1885): 244–45.

———. "Letter to Nehemyah Shmuel Libowitz, 4th day of Hol ha-Moed Pesah, 1895 (Manuscript)." N. S. Libowitz Archive, 2:58, New York Public Library.

Israel Dov Ber of Vilednik. *She'erit Israel*. Ed. Michael Levi Rodkinson. Lemberg: n.p., 1864.

———. *She'erit Israel*. Ed. Michael Levi Rodkinson. Zhitomir: n.p., 1868.

———. *She'erit Israel*. Ed. Michael Levi Rodkinson. Koenigsberg: n.p., 1877.

Israel of Bahafoli. *Ateret Tiferet Israel*. Ed. Michael Levi Rodkinson. Zhitomir, n.p., 1867.

Israel of Kozhnitz. *Ner Israel*. Vilna, n.p., 1922.

Jacobs, Louis. *Seeker of Unity: The Life and Works of Aaron of Starosselje*. London: Vallentine, Mitchell, 1966.

———. *Their Heads in Heaven: Unfamiliar Aspects of Hasidism*. London: Vallentine, Mitchell, 2005.

Jackont, Amnon. "Shlomoh Rubin (1823–1910): Sifriyat ha-Haskalah shel Ish Ehad." Ph.D. diss., University of Tel Aviv, 2006.

Jellinek, Adolf (Aaron). "Denial." *Neuzeit* 3 (1887): n.p.

———. "Ha-Shlishi ba-Koshrim." *Neuzeit* (1885): n.p.

———. "Oytseikhnugen Eines Anhengers Fon Ya'akov Frank." *Ha-Kol* 6, 286 (1885): 40–42; 287 (1885): 59–62.

Kabakoff, Jacob. *Halutsei ha-Sifrut ha-Ivrit be-Amerikah: Mehkarim ve-Te'udot*. Tel Aviv: Yavneh, 1967.

———. "Hebrew Sources of American Jewish History." In *A Bicentennial Festschrift for Jacob Rader Marcus*, ed. Bertram Wallace Korn. Waltham, MA: American Jewish History Society, 1976, 219v33.

———, ed. *Master of Hope: Selected Writings of Naphtali Herz Imber*. New York: Herzl Press, 1985.

———. "Me-Igrotav shel Ze'ev Shor." *Genazim* 1 (1961): 308–25.

———. "The Role of Wolf Schur as Hebraist and Zionist." In *Essays in American Jewish History*. Cincinnati: American Jewish Archives, 1975, 425–56.

———. *Shoharim ve-Ne'emanim*. Jerusalem: n.p., 1978.

———. "Tsvi Gershoni le-Or ve-Igrotav." *Sura* 4 (1964): 333–73.

Kahana, Avraham. *Rabbi Israel Ba'al Shem Tov (Ha-Besht): Hayyav, Shittato u-Fe'ulato*. Zhitomir: n.p., 1901.

Kahana, David. "Even ha-To'im." *Ha-Shahar* 3 (1872): 273–96, 337–44, 489–504, 513–28, 587–602, 619–28.

———. "Even Ofel." *Ha-Shahar* 5 (1874): 121–28, 177–84, 241–48, 297–312, 369–76, 433–48, 497–504, 553–68, 633–48, 705–14.

———. "Even Negaf." *Ha-Shahar* 4 (1873): 9–16, 73–80, 145–52, 201–16, 265–80, 337–44.

———. *Hokhmat Yehudah: Vikuhim Shonim bein Yehudim ve-Notsrim*. Newark: n.p., 1892.

———. *Toldot ha-Mekubalim, ha-Shabta'im veha-Hasidim*. Vols. 1–2. Odessa: n.p., 1913–14.

Kahana, Hillel. *Gelilot ha-Arets*. Bucharest: n.p., 1880.

Kaminer, Yitshak. "Eits Erez ve-Ezov." *Ha-Kol* 1 (1879): 4–5; 4 (1879): 45–46; 5 (1879): 59–65.

———. *Shirei Yitshak ben Avraham Dr. Kaminer*. Ed. Ahad ha'Am. Odessa: n.p., 1916.

Kantor, Yehudah Leib. "Shulhan ha-Sifrut. Barkai." *Ha-Yom* 14 (1886): 3.

Karlinsky, Nahum. "The Dawn of Hasidic-Haredi Historiography." *Modern Judaism* 27 (2007): 20–46.

———. *Historyiah she-Keneged, igrot hasidim me-erets israel: ha-tekst veha-kontekst*. Jerusalem: Yad Ben Zvi, 1999.

Karniel, Tzvi. "Bein Yehudah Leib Gordon le-Sokolov." *Sadan* 3 (1998): 323–30.

Karol, Tsvi. *Ha-Emet: Ha-Iton ha-Sotsiyalisti ha-Rishon be-Ivrit, be-arikhat Aharon Shmuel Lieberman*. Tel Aviv: n.p., 1938.

Katina, Yaakov. *Korban ha-Ani he-Hadash*. Lemberg: n.p., 1882.

———. *Rachamei Av*. Chernovitz: n.p., 1865.

Katz, Ben Zion. *Zikhronot: Hamishim Shanah be-Historiyah shel Yehudei Rusiyah*. Tel Aviv: n.p., 1963.

Katz, Yaakov. *Sinat Israel: mi-Sinat ha-Dat le-Shelilat ha-Geza*. Tel Aviv: Am Oved, 1980.

Katzenberg, Netanel. *Antishemiyut be-Hungariyah 1867–1914*. Tel Aviv: Devir, 1969.

Katzenelson, Berl. "Eliyahu Volf Rabinovits." *Davar* 8, no. 44 (1932): 1.

Katzenelson, Gideon. *Ha-Milhamah ha-Sifrutit bein he-Hareidim veha-Maskilim: Perakim be-toldot ha-sifrut ha-ivrit be-rusiyah bi-shenot ha-shishim veha-shivim*. Tel Aviv: Devir, 1954.

Katzenelson, H. I. "Meshorer Leumi. Toldot ha-Meshorer Dr. Y. Kaminer." In *Sefer ha-Shanah*. Vol. 3, ed. N. Sokolow. Warsaw: n.p., 1902, 46–68.

Katzman, Eliezer ha-Kohen. "Li-Demut ha-Gaon R. Yehoshua Heshil Levin." *Yeshurun* 5 (1999): 742–82.

Kevod Hakhamim, mikhtavei torah likhvod ha-rav he-hakham noda ba-she'arim Dr. Yosef Shmuel Blokh, yotse le-or al yedei ohavav u-mekhabdav anshei kehilato kehilat Floridsdorf. Vienna: n.p., 1890.

Kieval, Hillel J. "The Importance of Place: Comparative Aspects of the Ritual Murder Trial in Modern Central Europe." In *Comparing Jewish Societies*, ed. Todd M. Endelman. Ann Arbor: University of Michigan Press, 1997, 135–65.

———. *Languages of Community: The Jewish Experience in the Czech Lands*. Berkeley: University of California Press, 2000.

———. "Middleman Minorities and Blood: Is There a Natural Economy of the Ritual Murder Accusation in Europe?" In *Essential Outsiders:*

Chinese and Jews in the Modern Transformation of Southeast Asia and Central Europe, ed. Daniel Chirot and Anthony Reid. Seattle: University of Washington Press, 1997, 208–33.

Klausner, Israel. *Hibat Tsiyon be-Romaniyah*. Jerusalem: Ha-Sifriyah ha-Tsionit, 1958.

———. *Rabbi Tsvi Hayyim Shneorson, mi-Mevasrei Medinat Israel*. Jerusalem: Mossad ha-Rav Kook, 1973.

Klausner, Yosef. *Historiyah shel ha-Sifrut ha-Ivrit he-Hadashah*. Vols. 1–6. Jerusalem: Ahi'asaf, 1951–1959.

———. *Yeshu ha-Notsri, Hayyav ve-Torato*. Jerusalem: Shtibel, 1922.

Koegel, John. *Music in German Immigrant Theater: New York City, 1840–1940*. New York: University of Rochester Press, 2009.

Kohen-Tsedek, Yosef. *Ha-Torah veha-Mitsvah, yeva'er she-talmud torah keneged kulam*. London: Rabinovitz, 1884.

———. "Letter to Shmuel Yosef Fuenn, January 1880 (Manuscript)." Shmuel Yosef Fuenn Archive, National Library of Israel, Jerusalem.

———. *Mikha'el ha-Nehepakh le-Sama'el*. London: Abrahams, 1879.

———. *Mussar Haskel*. London: Abrahams, 1878.

———. *Ohalei Shem*. London: Valentine, 1883.

———. *Or Hadash ha-me'ir einei ha-holekhim be-torat hashem*. London: Valentine, 1881.

———. *Sfat Emet*. London: Abrahams, 1880.

Kohler, Kaufmann. "A Brief Rejoinder to Rodkinson and Wise." *American Hebrew* 59, no. 18 (1896): 457.

———. "The New Talmud Translation by Rodkinson and Wise." *American Hebrew* 59, no. 11 (1896): 272–74.

Kopp, Josef. "Ad Argiah Lashon Sheker." *Ha-Yom* 198 (1887): 3.

———. *Zur Judenfrage nach den Akten des Prozesses Rohling-Bloch*. Leipzig: n.p., 1886.

Korn, Ya'akov Hayyim ha-Levi. "Kisalon ben Parnakh." *Ha-Kol* 5 (n.d.): 21ff.

Kosman, Avraham. "Sefer Pesher Davar le-Rabbi Menasheh mi-Ilya—Talmid ha-Gra." *Yeshurun* 5 (1999): 191–228.

Kouts, Gideon. "'Gavoah' ve-'Namukh' bi-Kefifah Ahat: Ha-Kol ve-Reishitah shel ha-Itonut ha-Ivrit ha-Amamit be-Eiropah." *Kesher* 26 (1999): 27–36.

———. "The Hebrew Language Popular Press in Europe and Its Founders: M. L. Rodkinssohn and 'Ha-Kol' (1876–1893)." *Iggud* 2 (2009): 105–22.

———. *La naissance de la presse hébraique moderne: les grands périodiques en Europe, 1856–1886*. Paris: Maisonneuve et Larose, 1993.

———. *Ma'arikhim u-Mikhtavei Itim: Iyunim be-Toldot ha-Itonut ha-Ivrit veha-Yehudit*. Tel Aviv: Y. Golan, 1999.

Kovner, Avraham Uri. "Ha-Sifrut ha-Ivrit ha-Yafah bat ha-Zman." *Orlogin* 11 (1955): 123–33.

Krauss, Shmuel. "Be-Ikvot Pesak Din shel Ma'alah." *Shavuon Kefar Habad* 502 (1992): 29–31.

———. "Milhemet Tsarfat-Rusiyah." *Kovets He'arot u-Biurim be-Torat Kohen-Kadosh Admo"r shlit"a*. Vol. 26. Brooklyn: n.p., 1992, 29–34.

Kressel, Getzel. "Be-Reishit ha-Sotsiyalizm ha-Ivri (Havurat Asefat Hakhamim)." *Ba-Derekh: Ketavim le-Hoker Tenuat ha-Poalim ha-Yehudit* 1 (1967): 7–24.

———. *Guide to the Hebrew Press*. Zug: Interdocumentation, 1979.

———. *Leksikon ha-Sifrut ha-Ivrit be-Dorot ha-Aharonim*. Vols. 1–2. Merhaviyah: n.p., 1965–1967.

———. *Kitvei Israel Dov Frumkin*. Jerusalem: n.p., 1954.

———. "Mihu Mehaber ha-Sefarim Yalkut ha-Ro'im ve-Der Yudisher far Pesah." *Kiryat Sefer* 18 (1941–1942): 111.

———. *Toldot ha-Itonut ha-Ivrit be-Erets Israel*. Jerusalem: n.p., 1964.

Kristianpoller, D. *Die Hebräische Publizistik in Wien*. Vol. 3. Wien: n.p., 1930.

Krochmal, Avraham. *Agudat Ma'amarim*. Lemberg: n.p., 1885.

———. *Even ha-Roshah*. Vienna: n.p., 1871.

———. *Ha-Ketav veha-Mikhtav le-Torah Nevi'im u-Khetuvim*. Lemberg: n.p., 1874.

———. *Iyun Tefilah*. Lvov: n.p., 1885.

———. "Krochmal to Shlomoh Rubin, 10 Nissan 1885." "Mikhtavim me-Hakhmei Israel." *Ner ha-Ma'aravi* 1 (1896): 56.

Krochmal, Nahman. *Moreh Nevukhei ha-Zeman, sefer moreh emunah tserufah u-melamed hokhmat Israel*. Lemberg: n.p., 1863.

Kuperman, Yoel Mikhel. *Oder dos Lebins Beshreibung fan Vigderil ben Vigderil*. Warsaw: n.p., 1870.

Kurzweil, Baruch. *Be-Ma'avak al Erkhei ha-Yahadut*. Jerusalem and Tel Aviv: Schocken, 1970.

Lachover, Fishel. *Toldot ha-Sifrut ha-Ivrit he-Hadashah*. Vol. 2. Tel Aviv: Dvir, 1955.

Lamm, Norman. *Torah Lishmah in the Works of Rabbi Hayyim of Volozhin and His Contemporaries*. New York: Yeshiva University Press, 1982.

Landau, Bezalel. *Ha-Rabbi R. Elimelekh mi-Lizensk: Derekh Hayyav u-Po'alo le-Doro ule-Dorot*. Jerusalem: n.p., 2004.

Lapidos, Rinah. "Yehudah Leib Gordon al ha-Sifrut ha-Ivrit Bat Zemano." *Sadan* 3 (1998): 295–89.

Lazarus, Moritz. *Die Ethik des Judenthums*. Frankfurt am Maim: n.p., 1898.

Leibowitz, Nehemiah S. [Meir Ziv, pseud.]. *Efraim Deinard u-Sefarav be-Amerika*. Newark: n.p., 1901.

———. *Eikhah Rabati*. New York: n.p., 1895.

———. *Ha-Mavet be-Panim Sohakim*. Brooklyn: n.p., 1918.

———. "Letter to Shlomoh Buber, 1893–94 (Manuscript)." Shlomoh Buber Archive, 401222, National Library of Israel, Jerusalem.

———. *Midrashei ha-Zohar*. Philadelphia: n.p., 1934.

———. *Mikhtavim Me'et Nehemiah Shmuel Libovitsh le-Yedido Professor R. Israel Davidzon*. Newark: n.p., 1933.

———. "Mikhtavim mi-Gedolei Hakhmei Zemanenu al Davar ha-Talmud ha-Yashan veha-Katsar Hotsa'at M. L. Rodkinzon." *Ner ha-Ma'aravi* 6 (1896): 33–35.

——— [Pinhas ben Amitai, pseud]. *Mishpato Yiten le-Or: le-havdil bein ha-or le-hoshekh, simat ayin al ha-sefer Or ha-Me'ir*. Newark: n.p., 1897.

———. *Peninei ha-Zohar*. Jerusalem: n.p., 1931.

———, ed. *Sefer Ari Nohem: neged hokhmat ha-kabbalah u-makh'hish she-Rashb"i hu mehaber ha-Zohar*, by Yehudah Aryeh Modena. Jerusalem: n.p., 1889.

———. *Tashlum Peninei ha-Zohar*. Philadelphia: n.p., 1933.

———. *Tene Bikurim: bikoret al Sefer Atidot Israel ve-Sefer Milhamah le-Hashem be-Amalek me'et ha-nose'a Efraim Deinard*. Newark: n.p., 1893.

———. *Teshuvah Sheniyah al Zilzulei W. Shor Ba'al ha-Pisgah*. Newark: n.p., 1888.

Levin, Yehudah Loeb. "Letter to Perets Smolenskin, March 27, 1883 (Manuscript)." Perets Smolenskin Archive 401528, National Library of Israel, Jerusalem.

———. "Mikhtav el ha-Mol." *Ha-Maggid* 27, no. 13 (1883): 97–99.

Levinsohn, Isaac Baer and Joseph Perl. *Divrei Tsadikim*. Vienna: n.p., 1830.

Ley, Michael. "Der Wiener Antisemitismus-Streit: Die Auseinandersetzung zwischen den Rabbiner Joseph Samuel Bloch und dem Theologen August Rohling." In *Eine zerstörte Kultur: Jüdisches Leben und Antisemitismus in Wien seit dem 19. Jarhhundert*, ed. Gerhard Botz, I. Oxaal, M. Pollak, and N. Scholz. Wien: n.p., 2002, 147–63.

Lichtenstein, Hillel of Kolomaya. *Lev ha-Ivri*. Lemberg: n.p., 1874.

Lieberman, Chaim. *Ohel Rahel*. Vol. 3. New York: n.p., 1984.

Lifshitz, Ya'akov. *Zikhron Ya'akov*. Vols. 1–3. Kovna and Frankfurt: Draller, 1924–1930.

Lilienblum, Mosheh Leib. *Igrot M. L. Lilienblum le-Y. L. Gordon*, ed. Shlomoh Briman. Jerusalem: Magnes, 1968.

———. *Kehal Refa'im*. Odessa: n.p., 1870.

———. *Ketavim Otobiyografi'im*. Vols. 1–3, ed. Shlomoh Breiman. Jerusalem: Mossad Bialik, 1970.

———. *Kol Kitvei Mosheh Leib Lilienblum*. Vols. 1–2. Cracow: n.p., 1910–12.

———. "Orhot ha-Talmud." *Ha-Melits* (1868): n.p. .

———. "Shishah Mikhtavim mi-M. L. Lilienblum le-Yehudah Leib Levin." *Reshumot* 4 (1926): 381.

Lin, Josef. *Die hebräische Presse, Werdegang und Entwicklungstendenzen*. Berlin: n.p., 1928.

Linetski, Issac Joel. *Dos poylishe yingl*. Odessa: n.p., 1873.

———. *The Polish Lad*. Trans. Milton Hindus. Philadelphia: n.p., 1975.

Lippe, C. D. *Bibliographisches Lexicon*. Wien: n.p., 1881.

———. "Et Sofrim." *Ha-Maggid* 29, no. 2 (1885): 11–12.

Loewenthal, Naftali. *Communicating the Infinite: The Emergence of the Habad School*. Chicago: University of Chicago Press, 1990.

Loëwy, David. *Der Talmudjude von Rohling in der Schwurger ichtsverhandlung vom 28. Oktober 1882*. Wien: n.p., 1882.

Lofman, Musi. "Itonai Yehudi be-Shalosh Yabashot: Darko shel Moris Vinchevski be-Rusiyah, Prusiyah, Angliyah, Artsot ha-Brit, ve-Erets Israel." *Kesher* 21 (1997): 138–42.

Malachi, Eliezer Raphael. "Ayala"h: Haluts ha-Itonut ha-Ivrit be-Amerikah." In *Sefer "Ha-Doar" li-Melot lo Shloshim ve-Hamesh Shanah.* New York: n.p., 1957, 210–17.

———. "Der Kol Mevaser o Zein Redaktor." In *Pinkas far der Parshung fun der Yiddisher Literatur un Presse.* New York: n.p., 1965, 121–49.

———. "Ha-Sanegor (Le-Toldot ha-Itonut ha-Ivrit be-Amerikah)." *Ha-Doar* 12 (1934): 279–80; 15 (1934): 297–98.

———. *Igrot David Frishman.* New York: n.p., 1927.

———. *Igrot Sofrim.* New York: n.p., 1932.

———. "Le-Toldot ha-Itonut ha-Ivrit be-Amerikah." *Ha-Torah* 1 (1913): 117–22.

———. "Le-Toldot Ha-Levanon (Igrot R. Yehiel Brill le-Rabbi Yud Mem Pines)." In *Sefer ha-Yovel le-Meir Vaksman.* Jerusalem and Tel Aviv: n.p., 1967, 70–142.

———. *Massot ve-Reshimot.* New York: n.p., 1937.

———. *Mi-Neged Tireh.* Ed. Haggai ben Shammai and Elhanan Reiner. Jerusalem: Yad Ben Zvi, 2011.

———. "Min Ha-Tsofeh ba-Erets he-Hadashah ad Ha-Doar." *Ha-Doar* 14, no. 7 (1935): 114–16.

———. "Morris Vintshevski." *Ha-Doar* 11, no. 18 (1932): 287–88; 20 (1932): 317–18.

———. "Od al Amerikah ve-Yerushalayim." *Ha-Doar* 55 (1977): 667.

———. "Orkhim Ivrim be-Amerikah." *Ha-Doar* 26, no. 29 (1947): 843–45.

———. "Shivim ve-Hamesh Shanah le-Itonut ha-Ivrit be-Amerikah." In *Sefer ha-Shanah le-Yehudei Amerikah.* Vols. 8–9. New York: Histadrut ha-Ivrit be-Amerikah, 1947, 665–67.

———. "Toldot ha-Tenuah ha-Ivrit be-Amerikah." In *Hagut Ivrit be-Amerikah.* Vol. 3, ed. Menahem Zohori, Arie Tartakover, and Haim Ormian. Tel Aviv: Yavneh, 1974, 212–36.

Malachowsky, Hillel ben Zeev. *Kitvei Hillel ben Ze'ev Malakhovski.* Vols. 1–2. New York: Scholzinger Brothers, 1940.

———. "Ruah Sheker ve-Shikhor." *Ha-Leumi* 16 (1889): 3–4.

Malinkof, David. "Mikhtav el ha-Mo"l." *Ha-Leumi* 17 (1889): 6.

Mapu, Avraham. *Mikhtavei Avraham Mapu.* Ed. Ben Zion Dinur. Jerusalem: Mossad Bialik, 1970.

Margaliot, Elazar. *A Wondrous and Awesome Story of Rabbi Zalmina Vitepsker. Kerem Habad* 4, no. 2 (1992): 247–65.

Marmer, Kalman. "Moris Vintshevski, Zein Leben, Virken un Shafn." *Moris Vintshevski Gezamlete Verk*. Vol. 1. New York: n.p., 1928.

Marx, Alexander. "Jewish Libraries in America." *Menorah Journal* 31 (1943): 78–82.

Meir, Jonatan. *Gilgulav shel Megaleh Sod: Kuntres Divrei Tsadikim le-Riva''l ve-Yosef Perl*. Los Angeles: Cherub Press, 2004.

———. "*Goral ha-Tzadikim*: A Forgotten Satire against Bratslav Hasidism and the Pilgrimage to Uman." *Dehak: Journal of Hebrew Literature* 4 (2014): 283–313.

———. *Imagined Hasidism: Iyunim bi-Khetavav ha-Anti-Hasidi'im shel Yosef Perl*. Jerusalem: Mossad Bialik, 2013.

———. "Mikha'el Levi Rodkinson: Bein Hasidut le-Haskalah." *Kabbalah* 18 (2008): 229–86.

———. "Naftulei Mikha'el Levi Rodkinson: Kavim Rishonim le-Biyografiyah." *Gal-Ed* 22 (2010): 13–44.

———. *Rehovot ha-Nahar: Kabbalah ve-Ekzoteriyut bi-Yerushalayim (1896–1948)*. Jerusalem: Yad Ben Zvi, 2011.

———. *Sefer Megaleh Temirin le-Yosef Perl*. Jerusalem: n.p., 2013.

———. "Toldot ha-Meta'ate'a ha-Nifla." *Tarbiz* 80 (2012): 463–74.

———, and Shmuel Werses. *Reishit Hokhmah: Hibur Ganuz bi-Genutah shel he-Hasidut*. Jerusalem: Hebrew University Press, 2012.

Menasheh of Ilya. *Pesher Davar*. Vilna: n.p., 1907.

"Me'ora'ot Nora'ot de-Irenu Me'et Ba'al Megaleh Temirin." *Ha-Ivri* 1 (n.d.).

Mezah, Yehoshua. "Letter to Judah Leib Gordon, 1889 (Manuscript)." Judah Leib Gordon Archive, 40761, National Library of Israel, Jerusalem.

———. "Sefer Hadash [Mahloket she-Lo le-Shem Shamayim]." *Ha-Tsefirah* 84 (1887): 4.

———. *Tefah Meguleh*. Warsaw: n.p., 1881.

Miklishensky, Yaakov Koppel. *Toldot ha-Sifrut ha-Ivrit be-Amerikah*. New York: Ha-Histadrut ha-Ivrit be-Amerikah, 1967.

Miller, D. *Besorot Tovot*. Warsaw: n.p., 1927.

Miller, Gershon. "Mikhtav Galui el Orekh Ha-Pisgah." *Ha-Leumi* 16 (1889): 4–5.

Mintz, Adam. "The Talmud in Translation." In *Printing the Talmud: From Bomberg to Schottenstein*, ed. Sharon Liberman Mintz and

Gabriel M. Goldstein. New York: Yeshiva University Museum, 2005, 121–41.

———. "Words, Meaning and Spirit: The Talmud in Translation." *The Torah U-Madda Journal* 5 (1994): 123–25.

Mintz, Sharon, and Gabriel M. Goldstein, eds. *Printing the Talmud: From Bomberg to Schottenstein*. New York: Yeshiva University Museum, 2005.

Miron, Dan. *A Traveler Disguised: The Rise of Modern Yiddish Fiction in the Nineteenth Century*. Syracuse: Schocken, 1996.

Mondshine, Yehoshua. "Ha-Sefarim Matsref ha-Avodah Vikuha Rabah." *Alei Sefer* 5 (1978): 165–75.

———. "Introduction." In R. Israel Dov Ber of Vildenik, *Sefer She'erit Israel*, ed. Gedalyah Overlander. New York: n.p., 1998, 13–97.

———. *Kerem Habad*. Vol. 4. N.p.: Kefar Habad, 1992.

———. *Shivhei ha-Besht, faksimil mi-khetav ha-yad*. Jerusalem: n.p., 1982.

———. *Torat Habad: Likutei Amarim Sefer ha-Tanya, mahadurotav targumav u-biurav*. N.p.: Kefar Habad, 1981.

Nadler, Allan. "The Besht a Spinozist: Abraham Krochmal's Preface to *Ha-Ketav ve-ha-Mikhtav*: Introduction and Translation." In *Rabbinic Culture and Its Critics: Jewish Authority, Dissent, and Heresy in Medieval and Early Modern Times*, ed. Daniel Frank and Matt Goldish. Detroit: Wayne State University Press, 2008, 359–89.

Natan Sternharz of Nemirov. *Sihot ha-Ran*. Jerusalem: n.p., 1985.

Nathan, P. *Der Prozess von Tisza-Eszlar*. Berlin: n.p., 1892.

Newman, Louis I. "Solomon Roubin and Ephraim Deinard: Cataloguers of the Hebraica in the Sutro Library in San Francisco." In *Semitic and Oriental Studies*. Berkeley: University of California, 1951, 355–64.

Nigal, Gedalyah. *The Hasidic Tale*. Trans. Edward Levin. Oxford: Littman, 2008.

———. *Mehkarei Ma'arav u-Mizrah*. Jerusalem: Ha-Makhon le-Heker ha-Sifrut he-Hasidit, 2001.

———. *Mehkarim be-Hasidut*. Vols. 1–2. Jerusalem: Ha-Makhon le-Heker ha-Sifrut he-Hasidit, 1999.

———. *Melaktei ha-Sippur he-Hasidi*. Jerusalem: Ha-Makhon le-Heker ha-Sifrut he-Hasidit, 1996.

———, ed. *Sippurei Mikha'el Levi Rodkinson*. Jerusalem: Ha-Makhon le-Heker ha-Sifrut he-Hasidit, 1989.

———. *Sippurim Hasidi'im mi-Lemberg-Lvov*. Jerusalem: Ha-Makhon le-Heker ha-Sifrut he-Hasidit, 2006.

Novoplansky, Nahum Leib Shmuel. "Davar be-Ito." *Ha-Kol* 4, no. 2 (1879): 15–18.

Paperna, Avraham Yaakov. *Kol ha-Ketavim*. ed. Israel Zemorah. Tel Aviv: n.p., 1952.

Parush, Iris. *Nashim Korot: Yitronah shel Shuliyut he-Hevrah ha-Yehudit be-Mizrah Eiropah be-Me'ah ha-Tesha-Esreih*. Tel Aviv: Am Oved, 2001.

Parush, Shalom Chayyim. *Or Yekarot: Meorei he-Hasidut*. Vol. 1. Jerusalem: n.p., 1997.

Paulitzky, Heinrich Felix. *Marpe la-Am*. Vols. 1–2, ed. Michael Levi Rodkinson. Zhitomir: n.p., 1869.

Paulley, Bruce. *Eine Geschichte des österreichischen Antisemitusmus, Von der Ausgrenzung zur Auslöschung*. Wien: n.p., 1993.

Paulley, B. F. *From Prejudice to Persecution: A History of Austrian Anti-Semitism*. Chapel Hill: University of North Carolina Press, 1992.

Perl, Joseph. *Al Mahut Kat he-Hasidim*. ed. Avraham Rubinstein. Jerusalem: Israel Academy of Sciences and Humanities, 1977.

———. *Ma'asiyot ve-Igrot me-Tsadikim Amiti'im ume-Anshei Shlomenu*. ed. Chone Shmeruk and Shmuel Werses. Jerusalem: Israel Academy of Sciences and Humanities, 1970.

———. *Megaleh Temirin*. Vienna: n.p., 1919.

Persky, Daniel. "Hamishim Shanot Itonut Ivrit be-Amerikah." *Ha-Sefer ha-Ivri: Kovets Shenati* 9 (1951) Hebrew section: 1–8.

Piekarz, Mendel. *Ha-Hanhagah he-Hasidit: Samakhut ve-Emunat Tsadikim be-Aspaklariyat Sifrutah shel he-Hasidut*. Jerusalem: Mossad Bialik, 1999.

———. *Hasidut Breslev*. Expanded 2nd ed. Jerusalem: Mossad Bialik, 1996.

———. "Rabbi Natan mi-Nemirov be-Espaklariyat Sifro 'Likutei Halakhot.'" *Zion* 69 (2004): 203–40.

Pineles, Tsvi Menahem (Hirsch Mendel). *Darkah shel Torah*. Vienna: n.p., 1861.

Pinhas of Korets. *Midrash Pinhas*. Lvov: n.p., 1872.

———. *Midrash Pinhas*. Warsaw: n.p., 1876.

Plotzky, Meir Dan. "Ha-Kli Hemdah u-Pulmuso Neged Mezuyyafei ha-'Historiya.'" *Yeshurun* 2 (1997): 782–85.

Poll, Bernhard. *Jüdische Presse im 19. Jahrhundert*. Aachen: n.p., 1967.

Provest, M. "Ha-Itonut ha-Ivrit be-Hitpatchutah ha-Kronologit." *Ahi'asaf* 13 (1923): 248–91.

Prozer, Mosheh. *Igrot Mosheh Prozer le-Yehudah Leib Gordon.* ed. Shlomoh Briman. Tel Aviv: n.p., 1964.

Pulzer, Peter. *The Rise of Political Anti-Semitism in Germany and Austria.* London: P. Halban, 1988.

"R." [pseud.] "Mikhtav Lelamed." *Kol Mahzikei ha-Dat* 2 (1885): 3–4.

Rabanitsky, Y. H. *Dor u-Sofarav: reshimot ve-divrei zikhronot al sofrei dori.* Tel Aviv: n.p., 1927.

Rabinowitz, Eliyahu Wolf. "Kakh Kotvim Historiyah Etslenu." *Ha-Olam* 52 (1928): 1022–33; 53 (1928): 1041–42.

———. *Otobiografiyah,* 1929 (Manuscript). Schwadron Collection, National Library of Israel, Jerusalem.

———. "Rabinowitz to Judah Leib Levin, 1883 (Manuscript)." Schwadron Collection, National Library of Israel, Jerusalem.

———. "Sefer Zikaron." *I'im* 1 (1928): 66–74.

———, and Judah Leib Levin. "Mi-Zeh Ehad umi-Zeh Ehad (Mikhtav Avraham Volf Rabinovits u-Teshuvat Yehudah Leib Levin." *Ha-Maggid* 20 (1883): 163–65.

Rabinowitz, Leon. "Be-Huts le-Artsenu." *Ha-Melits* 45 (1897): 4–5.

———. "Besorat Sefarim Hadashim." *Ha-Melits* 111 (1895): 4.

Rapoport-Albert, Ada. *Devar Mah el ha-Min ha-Nashi: Ketav Yad Germani-Yehudi mi-Hug Ma'aminei Ya'akov Frank be-Prag.* Ramat Gan: Bar-Ilan University, 2010.

———. "Eizeh She'alot u-Teshuvot al Derekh She'alti'el ve-Yehoyada: Sanegoriyah maskilit al he-hasidut bi-khetav yad alum shem mi-veit midrasho shel Eliezer Tsvi Tsveifel." In *Mi-Vilna li-Yerushalayim: Mehkarim be-Toldoteihem uve-Tarbutam shel Yehudei Mizrah Eiropah Mugashim le-Professor Shmuel Werses*, ed. David Assaf, Israel Bartal, Avner Holzman, Hava Turniansky, Shmuel Feiner, and Yehudah Friedlander. Jerusalem: Magnes Press, 2002, 122–71.

———. "Hagiography with Footnotes: Edifying Tales and the Writing of History in Hasidism." In *Essays in Jewish Historiography*, ed. Ada Rapaport-Albert. Atlanta: Scholars Press, 1991, 144–56.

———. "Hasidism after 1772: Structural Continuity and Change." In *Hasidism Reappraised*, ed. Ada Rapaport-Albert. Oxford: Littman, 1997, 76–140.

Rashi [R. Shlomoh Yitshaki]. *Sefer ha-Orah.* Ed. Shlomoh Buber. Vols. 1–2. Lvov: n.p., 1905.

———. *Sefer ha-Pardes ha-Gadol ve-Sefer ha-Orah.* ed. Michael Levi Rodkinson. Warsaw: n.p., 1870.

———. *Sefer ha-Pardes le-Rashi za"l.* Ed. Yehudah Ehrenreich. Budapest: n.p., 1924.

Refael, Yitshak. "Kitvei Rabbi Ya'akov Emden: Bibliyografiyah." *Areshet* 3 (1961): 231–76.

———. "Shivhei ha-Besht." *Areshet* 2 (1960): 358–77.

Reichersberg, Mosheh. *Divrei Sofer.* Warsaw, 1885.

Reifman, Aharon. "Mahloket Hakhamim be-Tefillin." *Ha-Boker Or* 5 (1881): 389–90.

Reiner, Elhanan. "Shivhei ha-Besht: Mesirah, Arikhah, Hadpasah." In *Divrei ha-Kongres ha-Olami ha-Ehad Asar le-Mada'ei ha-Yahadut.* Vol. 2. Jerusalem: Magnes, 1994, 145–52.

Reisin, Zalman. *Leksikon fun der Yidisher Literatur Prese un Filologye.* Vol. 4. Vilna: n.p., 1930.

Reizin, Mordecai Zeev. *Dapim mi-Pinkaso shel "Rabi."* Brooklyn: n.p., 1951.

———. *Igrot Sofrim Ivrim.* Brooklyn: n.p., 1947.

———. "Kitsur ha-Talmud." *Ha-Tsefirah* 76 (1896): 370; 77 (1896): 374–75.

"Review of the Jewish World." *Menorah* 36, no. 2 (1904): 118–24.

Riminick, Y. "Tsu der Geshikhte Funem Poylishen Yingel." *Tseitshrift* (Minsk) 5 (1931): 181–98.

Rivkind, Yitshak. "Leket Igrot." *Bitsaron* 4 (1950): 352–33.

Rodkinson, Michael Levi. "As to Rabbi Aron Ben Maishe Halevi." *American Hebrew* 49, no. 6 (1901): 157.

———. *Asefat Hakhamim* (1878): 1–8.

———. *Avnei Miluim, bi-davar ha-tefillin ve-koroteihen me-hakhmei ha-zeman . . . hoveret sheniyah, asher tekhunah be-shem Even Sapir.* Vienna: n.p., 1886.

———. *Avnei Miluim, Even ha-Roshah, hoveret rishonah, tedaber be-arba miflagot be-israel.* Berlin: n.p., 1884.

———. *Barkai, o ha-Ir ha-Mizrach.* Vienna: n.p., 1886.

———. *Das ungesaveerte brot und die Anklage des Blutgebauchs.* Pressburg: n.p., 1883.

———. "Davar Ehad." *Ha-Kol* 1 (1880): 1–2.

———. "Demamah ve-Kol Eshma." *Ha-Hozeh*, sample copy (1882): 3–6.

———. *Der Shulchan Aruch und seinen Begiehungen zu den Juden und Nichtjuden*. Wien: n.p., 1884.

———. "Divrei Shalom ve-Emet." *Ha-Kol, Aleh le-Mivhan* (1876): 1–3.

———. *Eidat Tsadikim*. Lvov: n.p., 1864.

———. "El ha-Mol et Ha-Maggid: Devarim Ahadim al Davar Yishuv Erets Israel." *Ha-Hozeh* 5 (1882): n.p.

———. "Et Asher Nadarti Ashalem." *Ha-Havatselet* 11–12 (1878): 77.

———. "Et Livhor ve-Et Lerahek Bahur." *Ha-Kol* 294 (1885): 161–64.

———. "A Few Words in Reply to Rev. Dr. K. Kohler's Criticism of the New Edition of the Babylonian Talmud." *American Hebrew* 59, no. 14 (1896): 345–46.

———. "Ha-Asefah Tiftah!" *Asefat Hakhamim* 1 (1878): 1–2.

———. "Hadashot Belulot." *Ha-Kol* 290 (1885): 105–6; 294 (1885): 173.

———. "Ha-Hotsa'ah he-Hadashah shel ha-Talmud Mah Hi?" *Ner ha-Ma'aravi* 4–5 (1895): i–iv.

———, ed. *Ha-Hozeh*. N.p.: 1881–82.

———, ed. *Ha-Kol*. N.p.: 1876–81, 1884–85, 1889–93.

———, ed. *Ha-Kol la-Am*. N.p.: 1876.

———. "Ha-Kol Omer Kera." *Ha-Havatselet* 4 (1878): 31–32.

———, ed. *Ha-Me'asef*. N.p.: 1879.

———, ed. *Ha-Medaber le-Israel*. N.p.: 1881–82.

———, ed. *Ha-Sanegor*. N.p.: 1890.

———. "Ha-Talmud veha-Shulhan Arukh." *Ha-Kol* 284 (1885): 10–12; 285 (1885): 27–29; 286 (1885): 44–45; 289 (1885): 95–96; 292 (1885): 141–44; 293 (1885): 155–57.

———. "Hazut Ha-Kol." *Ha-Kol* 1 (1884): 1–8.

———. "Hazut Ha-Kol. Eleh ha-Mishpatim Asher Tasim Lifneihem." *Ha-Kol* 291 (1885): 113–17.

———. "Hazut Ha-Kol. Ha-Sifrut ha-Talmudit o ha-Talmud ha-Yashan veha-Katsar." *Ha-Kol* 298 (1885): 225–35.

———. "Hazut Ha-Kol. Im Atem Mekablim et ha-Torah Mutav." *Ha-Kol* 300 (1885): 258–67.

———. "Hazut Ha-Kol. Kankan Yashan Male Hadash." *Ha-Kol* 301 (1885): 273–75.

———. "Hazut Ha-Kol. Moda'ah Rabah al dvar sifrenu Tekhunat Ruah Israeli." *Ha-Kol* 316 (1889): 119–21; 317 (1889): 127–28.

———. "He'arat ha-Mol." *Ha-Kol* 5 (1879): 62.

———. *The History of Amulets, Charms and Talismans: A Historical Investigation into Their Nature and Origin*. New York: n.p., 1893.

———. *The History of the Talmud, from the Time of its Formation, about 200 B.C., up to the Present Time*. Vols. 1–2. New York: n.p., 1903.

———. "Hizayon Ma'atsiv me-Olam ha-Ma'aseh." *Ha-Hozeh*, sample copy (1881): 14.

———. "Hoda'ah ve-Hoda'ah." *Ha-Kol* 285 (1885): 17–18.

———. *Igeret ha-Talmud ha-Shenit le-khol ha-toranim veha-rabbanim be-khol makom she-hem bi-devar hotsa'at ha-talmud ha-yashan veha-katsar*. Pressburg: n.p., 1885.

———. *Igeret Petuhah le-khol ha-toranim veha-rabbanim be-khol makom she-hem bi-devar ha-sifrut ha-talmudit bi-khelal ve-al devar ha-talmud ha-yashan veha-katsar bi-ferat*. Pressburg: n.p., 1885.

———. "Im Hatimat ha-Gilyon." *Ha-Kol* 290 (1885): 112.

———. "The Karaites." *American Hebrew* (n.d.): 23–24.

———. "Ke-Tseiti et ha-Ir ve-Efros et Kapai." *Ha-Kol* 295 (1885): 177–78, 185–86.

———. "Kol Aleh Nidaf. Masekhet Nezikin im Peirush Had ve-Halak al ha-Mishnah." *Ha-Kol* 289 (1885): 83–87.

———. "Kol Anot." *Ha-Kol* 292 (1885): 143.

———. "Kol Ya'akov." *Ha-Kol* 1 (1884): 15.

———. "Letters to Dov Dubzhevitz, 1892–99 (Manuscript)." Dubsewitz Archive, New York Public Library.

———. "Letter to the Editor of a German Newspaper, December 6, 1885 (Manuscript)." Schwadron Collection, National Library of Israel, Jerusalem.

———. "Letter to Heller, December 19, 1884 (Manuscript)." Schwadron Collection, National Library of Israel, Jerusalem.

———. "Letter to Judah Leib Sossnitz, December 19, 1900 (Manuscript)." N. S. Sossnitz Archive, New York Public Library.

———. "Letter to Morits Steinschneider (Manuscript)." Jewish Theological Seminary Archive, New York.

———. "Letter to Shmuel Yosef Fuenn (Manuscript)." Shmuel Yosef Fein Archive, National Library of Israel, Jerusalem.

———. "Letter to Yosef Brill, 1888 (Manuscript)." Yosef Brill Archive, National Library of Israel, Jerusalem.

———. "Letters to Israel Dov Frumkin, 1885 (Manuscript)." Courtesy of the Rodkinson family. Original at Zionist Archives, Jerusalem.

———. "Letters to Judah Leib Gordon, December 5, 1876, March 22, 1878, December 5, 1886 (Manuscript)." Judah Leib Gordon Archive, National Library of Israel, Jerusalem.

———. "Letters to Morits Lazarus, May 4, 1881, 1895 (Manuscript)." Moris Lazarus Archive, National Library of Israel, Jerusalem.

———. "Letters to Shlomoh Buber, March 7, 1885, April 24, 1885, March 24, 1895, May 22, 1895, November 7, 1897 (Manuscript)." Schwadron Collection, National Library of Israel, Jerusalem.

———. *Levaker Mishpat: A. Ha-Yudenshpiegelprotses, Bemunster B. Ahuzat ha-Kever.* Berlin: n.p., 1884.

———. *Masekhet Kiddushin*, bilingual edition. Newark: n.p., 1895.

———. *Masekhet Rosh ha-Shannah min ha-hotsa'ah he-hadashah shel ha-talmud ha-bavli.* (English Section: *Tract Rosh Hashana [New Year] of the New Edition of the Babylonian Talmud, Edited Formulated and Punctuated for the First Time by Michael L. Rodkinson, and Translated for the above Text by Rabbi J. Leonard Levy.*) Philadelphia: n.p., 1895.

———. *Matsat-Mitsvah ve-Alilat ha-Dam.* Pressburg: n.p., 1883.

———. "Me'asef le-Khol ha-Mahanot!" *Ha-Me'asef* 1–3 (1879): 1–5.

———. "Me-Az Yatsa Matok." *Ha-Kol* 70–72 (1880): 1039–42, 1051–54, 1060, 1067–76; 1 (1880): 1–3, 5–9.

———. "Meh Anu?" *Ha-Hozeh*, sample copy (1882): 7–8.

———. "Me-Har ha-Melekh (Koenigsberg) le-Ir ha-Melukhah (Berlin)." *Ha-Kol* 47 (1881): 717–19.

———. "Mikhtavei Sofrim. Koenigsberg." *Ha-Levanon* 9 (1877): 70.

———. "Milhemet ha-Shalom." *Ha-Kol* 1 (1884): 3–7.

———. *New Edition of the Babylonian Talmud. English Translation, Original Text Edited, Formulated and Punctuated by Michael Levi Rodkinson, Revised and Corrected by the Rev. Dr. Isaac M. Wise.* Vols. 1–2, *Sabbath.* New York: n.p., 1896.

———. *The Pentateuch, Its Languages and Its Characters: A Treatise upon the Original Language and the Early Translations of the Pentateuch into Greek and Aramaic.* Chicago: n.p., 1894.

———. "Perets Smolenskin Einenu!" *Ha-Kol* 288 (1885): 165.

———. "Programs le-Mikhtav Iti Hadash Barkai." *Ha-Havatselet* 12 (1886): 94–95.

———. *Prospectus, The New Edition of the Babylonian Talmud, English Translation, Original Text Edited, Formulated and Punctuated by Michael Levi Rodkinson, Revised and Corrected by the Rev. Dr. Isaac M. Wise and Other Prominent Authorities of Hebrew and English Literature.* New York: n.p., 1896.

———. *Prospectus, The New Edition of the Babylonian Talmud, English Translation, Original Text Edited, Formulated, Punctuated and Translated by Dr. Michael Levi Rodkinson, First Two Volumes of Section "Festivals" Revised by the Rev. Dr. Isaac M. Wise.* New York: n.p., 1898.

———. *Prospectus, The New Edition of the Babylonian Talmud, English Translation, Original Text Edited, Formulated, Punctuated and Translated by Dr. Michael Levi Rodkinson.* New York: n.p., 1904.

———. "Reuchlin and Pfefferkorn." *American Hebrew* (December 21, 1900): 174–76; (December 28, 1900): 203–5; (January 4, 1901): 237–38; (January 11, 1901): 258–59.

———. *Siftei Kedoshim me-Arba'ah Meitivei Lekhet.* Lemberg: n.p., 1876.

———. *Sippurei Tsadikim.* Lemberg: n.p., 1873.

———. *Sippurei Tsadikim me-Arba'ah Meitivei Lekhet.* Lvov: n.p., 1865.

———. *Sippurei Tsadikim mi-Hut ha-Meshulash.* Lvov, 1864.

———. *Sippurei Tsadikim mi-Hut ha-Meshulash.* Cracow: n.p., 1896.

———. *Shiryon ve-Keshet Neged ha-Meharefim.* Vienna: n.p., 1886.

———. Shivhei ha-Rav. Lvov: n.p., 1844.

———. *Talmud Bavli: New Edition of the Babylonian Talmud. Original Text Edited, Corrected, Formulated, and Translated by Michael L. Rodkinson.* Vols. 1–18. New York: n.p., 1896–1903.

———. *Talmud Bavli: New Edition of the Babylonian Talmud. Original Text Edited, Corrected, Formulated, and Translated by Michael L. Rodkinson.* Vols. 1–18. Boston: n.p., 1918.

———. "The Talmud Edition and Translation Again." *American Israelite* 41 (1895): 4.

———. *Tefillah le-Mosheh (mi-Kutsi) o Toldot ha-Tefillin ve-Koroteihen.* Pressburg: n.p., 1883.

———. *Tekhunat Ruah ha-Israeli.* Vol. 1. Newark: n.p., 1889.

———. "Teshuvah me-Ahavah." *Ha-Kol* (1885): 369–79.

———. *Toldot Amudei ha-Habad, ve-hu helek revi'I mi-Sefer Toldot Ba'alei Shem Tov, Amud ha-Rashi.* Koenigsberg: n.p., 1876.

———. *Toldot Ba'alei Shem Tov, helek rishon yikare be-shem Or Israel.* Koenigsberg: n.p., 1876.

———, ed. *Urim ve-Tumim he-Hadash ve-hu sefer goralot she-hayu le-israel mishtamshin bo be-bayit sheni.* Chernovitz: n.p., 1863.

———, ed. *Urim ve-Tumim he-Hadash ve-hu sefer goralot.* Chernovitz: n.p., 1864.

——— [Michael Levi Rodkinssohn]. *Wahrheit gegen Lüge: gegen den Leitartikel und die Notizen des Reichsrathsabgeordneten Dr. Bloch in der Nummer 6 und 7 der "Oesterr. Wochenschrift" vom Februar I. J.* Wien: n.p., 1886.

Rodkinson, Norbert M. "Rodkinson's Self-Defense." *American Israelite* 42 (October 31, 1895): 4.

Rohling, August. *Der Talmudjude, Zur Beherzigung für Juden und Christen aller Stände.* Münster: n.p., 1871.

Rosenfeld, Avraham Yaakov. *Ha-Tsofeh le-Veit Ya'akov o Mishpat ha-Arets.* Warsaw: n.p., 1883.

Rosenmann, M. *Dr. Adolf Jellinek: Sein Leben und Schafen.* Wien: n.p., 1931.

Rosenthal, Yehudah. *Toldot Hevrat Marbei Haskalah be-Israel be-Erets Rusiya.* Vol. 1. St. Petersburg: n.p., 1886.

Rosman, Moshe. "Le-Toldotav shel Makor Histori: Sefer Shivhei ha-Besht ve-Arichato." *Zion* 58 (1993): 175–214.

Ross, Nicham. "Masoret Ahuvah u-Senuah: Ketivah Neyo Hasidit be-Reishit ha-Me'ah ha-Esrim." Ph.D. diss., Ben-Gurion University, Beer Sheva, 2005.

———. "Teguvah Hasidit ve-Ortodoksit li-Ketivah Neo Hasidit." *Da'at* 68–69 (2010): 237–76.

Roth, Aharon. *Shomer Emunim.* Jerusalem: n.p., 1952.

Rozenblit, Marsha L. *The Jews of Vienna 1867–1914: Assimilation and Identity.* Albany: State University of New York Press, 1983.

Rozensaft, Z. Menachem. "Jews and Antisemites in Austria at the End of the Nineteenth Century." *Leo Baeck Institute Year Book* 21 (1976): 57–86.

Rozenson, Mosheh. *Divrei Shalom o Mishpat ha-Kabbalah.* Vol. 2. Vilna: n.p., 1881.

———. *Mashol Timshol.* Warsaw: n.p., 1886.

Rubin, Shlomoh. *Avnei Miluim.* Vienna: n.p., 1876.

———. "Bikoret ha-Yarhon Ner ha-Ma'aravi." *Ner ha-Ma'aravi* 2 (1896): 107–10.

———. "Igeret Mevakeret." *Kokhvei Yitshak* 13 (1865): 89–100.

———. *Menahem ha-Bavli Hu Mani ha-Parsi*. Vienna: n.p., 1873.

———. *Razei Olam*. Vienna: n.p., 1874.

Rubinstein, Avraham. "Sippurei Hitgalut be-Sefer Shivhei ha-Besht." *Alei Sefer* 6–7 (1979): 157–86.

Rubinstein, Y. "He'arot al Sefer Shem ha-Gedolim he-Hadash." *Ha-Darom* 16 (1963): 140–50.

Ruderman, Pesah. *Ha-Dibbuk o Hashkafah Kelalit al Hitpathut ha-Emunah be-Gilgul ha-Neshamot*. Warsaw: n.p., 1878.

———. "Hashkafah Kelalit al ha-Tsadikim ve-al he-Hasidim." *Ha-Shahar* (1875): 86–104.

———. "Letter to Judah Leib Gordon, 1874 (Manuscript)." Judah Leib Gordon Archive, National Library of Israel in Jerusalem.

———. "Tseror Mikhtavim Me'et Mi she-Hayah Hasid." *Ha-Shahar* 7 (1876): 124–35, 180–87, 311–19.

Sadan, Dov. *Avnei Gevul*. Tel Aviv: Massada, 1964.

———. *Bein She'ilah le-Kinyan*. Tel Aviv: Tel Aviv University Press, 1969.

Salmon, Yosef. "David Gordon ve-Iton ha-Maggid." *Zion* 47 (1982): 145–64.

Schalit, Mosheh. "Der Tsenzur-Ekzempliar fun Linetskis Hasidishen Yungel." *Fun Nantn Ever* 1 (1937): 13–20.

———. "Mosheh Rozenson, Zeine Hiburim, Tsavah un Matsevah." *Fun Nantn Ever* 2 (1937): 113–23.

Schapiro, Israel. "Efraim Deinard." *Ha-Doar* 36 (1930): 622–23.

———. "Ephraim Deinard." *Publications of the American Jewish Historical Society* 34 (1937): 149–63.

Scholem, Gershom. *Mehkarim u-Mekorot le-Toldot ha-Shabtaut ve-Gilguleihah*. Jerusalem: Mossad Bialik, 1982.

Schorr, Yehoshua Heshel, ed. *He-Haluts*. Vols. 1–7. Lvov: n.p., 1851–65.

———. *Ma'amarim*. Ed. Ezra Shpeizhandler. Jerusalem: Mossad Bialik, 1972.

———. "Tefillin." *He-Haluts* 5 (1860): 11–26.

Schorr, Zeev. "Mikhtav el ha-Mol." *Ha-Leumi* 17 (1889): 4.

———. *Netsah Israel*. Chicago: n.p., 1897.

Sefer Ma'aseh Hashem, uvdot ve-sippurim. Vols. 1–3. Munsey: n.p., 1995.

Sefer Matsref ha-Avodah. Koenigsberg: n.p., 1858.

Sefer Sha'arei ha-Avodah. Shklov: n.p., 1921.

Sefer Sippurei Niflaot . . . mi-maor ha-goleh . . . Rabbi Israel Dov mi-Vilednik. Trans. Yehoshua Mondshine, ed. G. Overlander. New York: Makhon Or Israel, 1996.

Sefer Torat ha-Maggid mi-Zlotshov . . . Rabbi Yehiel Mikhl ha-Maggid mi-Zlotshov. Vol. 2, ed. Eliezer Emmanuel Horowitz. Jerusalem: n.p., 1999.

Segal, Tsvi Hirsch. *Likutei Tsvi*, ed. Eliezer Zweifel. Zhitomir, 1873.

Shaked, Gershon. Introduction to *Ha-Dat veha-Hayyim* by Reuven Asher Broyds. Jerusalem: n.p., 1974, 7–36.

Shapira, Hayyim Elazar of Munkatsh. *Divrei Torah*. Jerusalem: n.p., 1998.

She'alot u-Teshuvot Rabbi Joseph ibn Migash. Ed. Michael Levi Rodkinson. Warsaw: n.p., 1870.

Shelley, Chaim. *Mehkar ha-Mikra be-Sifrut ha-Haskalah*. Jerusalem: Reuven Mass, 1952.

Sherberk, Shlomoh. *Zikhronot ha-Motsi le-Or Shlomoh Sherberk*. Tel Aviv: n.p., 1955.

Shivhei ha-Besht, ed. Avraham Rubinstein. Jerusalem: Reuven Mass, 1992.

Shmeruk, Chone. *Sifrut Yiddish: Perakim be-Toldoteihah*. Jerusalem: n.p., 1978.

Shwartzberg, S. B. *Tikatev Zot la-Dor Aharon*. Newark: n.p., 1898.

Simonivitch, Feivel. "Mikhtav Galui." *Ha-Melits* 21 (1879): 404.

"Sinat Hinam." *Edut le-Israel* 11–12 (1888): 39–44; 4 (1889): 58–60.

Sirotkin, A. A. "Sirotkin to Perets Smolenskin, with the essay 'Mefarnesin et ha-Hanafim,' 1883 (Manuscript)." Perets Smolenskin Archive, 401528, National Library of Israel, Jerusalem.

Skomorowska, Havah. *Der Emes Vegn Mosheh Rozenson*. Vilna: n.p., 1930.

Sloklnimski, Hayim Zelig. "Lifnim min ha-Kela'im." *Ha-Tsefirah* 12, no. 18 (1885): 144–45.

———. "Malshinai be-Seter." In *Ha-Shahar he-Hadash*, Vols. 1 and 2. Cracow: n.p., 1893, 76–80.

Slutsky, Yehudah. *Ha-Itonut ha-Yehudit-Russit ba-Me'ah ha-Tesha-Esreih*. Jerusalem: Makhon le-Heker ha-Tefutsot, 1971.

———. "Kritikus." *Ha-Avar* 8 (1961): 43–59.

Smolenskin, Perets. "Al Ha-Mabit!" *Ha-Shahar* 9 (1878): 230–32.

———. “El ha-Korim he-Nikhbadim!” *Ha-Mabit* 1, no. 4 (1878): 32.

———. “Yediat Sefarim. Ha-Tsefirah.” *Ha-Shahar* 5 (1874): 591–92.

———. “Yediat Sefarim. Matsat-Mitsvah ve-Alilat ha-Dam.” *Ha-Shahar* 11 (1883): 299–300.

———. “Yediat Sefarim. Toldot Ba’alei Shem Tov.” *Ha-Shahar* 8 (1878): 31–32.

Sobel, Yaakov Tsvi. *Ha-Hozeh Hezyonot be-Arba’ah Olamot*. Odessa: n.p., 1872.

———. “Igeret Petuhah la-Motsi la-Hoshekh Motsi la-Or Ha-Kol.” *Ha-Pisgah* 14 (1889): n.p.

———. “Tsa’ar Ba’alei Hayyim.” *Ha-Leumi* 17 (1889): 6.

———. “Ziyufei Rodkinzon be-kitvei ha-kodesh.” *Ha-Leumi* 21 (1889): 4–5.

Sobel, Yitshak ben Yehudah Leib. “Toldot Spinoza ve-Shitato.” *Mitspeh* 4 (1886): 1–16.

Soffer, Orren. *Ein Lepalpel! Iton “Ha-Tsefirah” veha-Modernizatsiyah shel ha-Siah ha-Hevrati ha-Politi*. Jerusalem: Mossad Bialik, 2007.

Sokolow, Nahum. “Feuilleton.” *Ha-Tsefirah* 23, 20 (1904), literary supplement: 94–97.

———. *Ishim*. Jerusalem: Ha-Sifriyah ha-Tsiyonit, 1958.

———. *Ketavim Nivharim*. Warsaw: n.p., 1913.

———. “Sdeh Tsofim (Bikoret Sefarim Hadashim).” *He-Asif* 2 (1885): 315–18.

———. *Sefer Zikaron le-Sofrei Israel ha-Hayyim Itanu ka-Yom*. Warsaw: n.p., 1889.

———. “Sifrut Israel.” *He-Asif* 2 (1885): 35–43.

Stampfer, Shaul. “On the Creation and the Perpetuation of the Image of the Gaon of Vilna.” In *The Vilna Gaon and His Disciples*, ed. M. Hallamish, Y. Rivlin, and R. Schuchat. Ramat Gan: Bar Ilan University Press, 2003, 53–54, 60–61.

Stanislawski, Michael. *For Whom Do I Toil?: Judah Leib Gordon and the Crisis of Russian Jewry*. New York: Oxford University Press, 1988.

Steinschneider, Hillel Noah Maggid. *Ir Vilna*. Vol. 2, ed. Mordecai Zalkin. Jerusalem: Magnes, 2003.

Stengel, A. M. *Divrei Emet ve-Ahavah*. Vienna: n.p., 1884.

Stern, Eliyahu. *The Genius: Elijah of Vilna and the Making of Modern Judaism*. New Haven: Yale University Press, 2013.

Stern, J. *Salomon Rubin. Sein Leben und seine Schriften.* Cracow: n.p., 1908.

Tal, David. *Yehudah Leib Kantor: Haluts ha-Yomon ha-Ivri.* Tel Aviv: Ha-Kibbuts ha-Meuhad, 2011.

Tefilinsky, Yaakov Shlomoh. *Imrei Sefer: Leket Amarim ve-Sippurim al Sofrim.* Jerusalem: n.p., 2003.

Teitelbaum, Mordekhai. *Ha-Rav mi-Liadi u-Mifleget Habad.* Vols. 1–2. Warsaw: n.p., 1910.

Teller, Adam. "Masoret Slutsk al Reishit Darko shel ha-Besht." In *Mehkarei Hasidut* (*Mehkarei Yerushalayim be-Mahshevet Israel* 15), ed. Emmanuel Etkes, David Assaf, and Joseph Dan. Jerusalem: n.p., 1999, 15–38.

Teller, Y. H. "Kitei Zikhronot." *Mi-Yamim Rishonim* 2, nos. 3–4 (1935): 81.

Temkin, Sefton D. *Isaac Mayer Wise: Shaping American Judaism.* Oxford: Littman, 1992.

Tietze, Hans. *Die Juden Wiens, Geschichte-Wirtshaft-Kultur.* Wien and Leipzig: n.p., 1933.

Toury, Jacob. "Josef Samuel Bloch und die Jüdische Identität in Deutschland und österreich." In *Judische Integration und Identität in Deutschland und österreich*, ed. W. Grab. Tel Aviv: Tel Aviv University Press, 1984, 41–63.

Trevsian Semi, Emanuela. "La Sefer Massa Qarim De Deinard: but parodique ou polémique." *Revue des etudes juives* 157 (1998): 57–67.

Tsamriyon, Tsemach M. *Die hebräische Presse in Europa: Ein Spiegel der Geisttogeschte des Judentums.* Vols. 1–2. Haifa: n.p., 1971.

Tsazmir, Ozer of Kamenets. *Luhot ha-Edut.* Ed. Michael Levi Rodkinson. Lemberg: n.p., 1865.

Vital, Hayyim. *Eits Hayyim, Nahar Shalom.* Ed. Menahem Menkhin Heilperin. Warsaw: n.p., 1891.

Walden, Aharon. *Kehal Hasidim.* Lemberg: n.p., 1866.

———. "Letter (Manuscript)." YIVO Archive, New York (uncatalogued).

———. *Shem ha-Gedolim he-Hadash.* Warsaw: n.p., 1864.

Warhaft, Shalom. "Tsiyon la-Nefesh." *Asefat Hakhamim* 4 (1878): 65–68; 6 (1878): 85–88.

Weinfeld, David. "'Ish Hasid' shel Reuven Asher Brodos." In *Be-Ma'agalei Hasidim: Kovets Mehkarim le-Zikhro shel Profesor Mordekhai*

Vilenski, ed. Emmanuel Etkes, David Assaf, Israel Bartal, and Elhanan Reiner. Jerusalem: Mossad Bialik, 2000, 237–44.

Weinstein, Myron M. "The First Deinard Collection of the Library of Congress." *Judaica Librarianship* 12 (2006): 31–48.

Weisberg, Y. Y. *Gaon ve-Shivro o Megilat Setarim. Shever Gaon.* Ed. Mikhel ben Aharon David Gordon. Warsaw: n.p., 1884.

Weiss, Joseph. *Studies in East European Jewish Mysticism*, ed. David Goldstein. Oxford: Littman, 1985.

Weitzman, Walter R. "The Politics of the Viennese Jewish Community, 1890–1914." In *Jews, Antisemitism and Culture in Vienna*, ed. Ivar Oxaal, Michael Pollak, and Gerhard Botz. London and New York: Routledge and Kegan Paul, 1987, 121–51.

Werber, Yaakov. "Hadashot be-Israel." *Ivri Anokhi*, 23, 18 (1887): 143.

———. "Hadashot be-Israel. Vien." *Ivri Anokhi*, 23, 24 (1887): 191.

Werses, Shmuel. *"Hakitsah Ami": Sifrut Ha-Haskalah be-Idan ha-Modernizatsiyah.* Jerusalem: Magnes, 2001.

———. *Haskalah ve-Shabta'ut: Toldotav shel Ma'avak*. Jerusalem: Merkaz Zalman Shazar, 1988.

———. "He-Hasidut be-Olamo shel Berdyczewski." In *Mikhah Yosef Berdyczewski: Mehkarim ve-Teudot*, ed. Avner Holzman. Jerusalem: Merkaz Zalman Shazar, 2002, 215–58.

———. *Megamot ve-Tsurot be-Sifrut ha-Haskalah.* Jerusalem: Magnes, 1990.

———. "Mi-Lashon el Lashon: Samemanei ha-Nusah ba-Yiddish shel Megaleh Temirin Me'et Yosef Perl." *Huliyot* 3 (1996): 59–108.

Wiederkehr-Pollack, Gloria. "Eliezer Zvi Hacohen Zweifel: Forgotten Father of Modern Scholarship on Hasidism." *Proceedings of the American Academy for Jewish Research* 49 (1982): 87–115.

———. *Eliezer Zvi Zweifel and the Intellectual Defense of Hasidism.* Hoboken, NJ: Ktav, 1995.

Winchevsky, Morris. "Erets Rusiyah ve-Ha-Kol." *Ha-Havatselet* 10, no. 4 (1879): 25–27.

———. *Gezamelte Verk*. Vols. 9–10. New York: n.p., 1927.

———. "Mikha'el Levi Rodkinson." *Ha-Toren*, 10-8-9 (1924): n.p.

———. "Mussar ha-Sekhel." *Ha-Kol* (n.d.): 55, 56, 89.

———. "Pirkei Zikhronot." *Sefer ha-Yovel shel Ha-Doar*, ed. M. Rublov. New York: n.p., 1927, 82–83.

———. "Zikhronot al Asefat Hakhamim." In *Asufot: Kovetsim le-Toldot Tenuat ha-Avodah be-Israel*. Vol. 3. N.p.: Ha-Histadrut ha-Klelit shel ha-Ovdim ha-Ivrim be-Israel, 1952, 21–25.

Wise, Isaac Mayer. "Defense of M. L. Rodkinson." *American Israelite* 31 (1894): 4.

———. "Michael Levi Rodkinson." *American Israelite* 7 (1899): 4–5.

———. "The New Talmud." *American Israelite* 45 (1898): 4–5.

———. "Wise to Michael Levi Rodkinson, 1895 (Manuscript)." Isaac Mayer Wise Digital Archive, American Jewish Archives, Cincinnati.

———. "Wise to Rabbi Schulman, February 4, 1894 (Manuscript)." Isaac Mayer Wise Digital Archive, American Jewish Archives, Cincinnati.

Wistrich, Robert S. "Georg von Schoenerer and the Genesis of Modern Austrian Antisemitism." In *Hostages of Modernization: Studies on Modern Antisemitism, 1870–1933/9, Austria-Hungary-Poland-Russia*, ed. Herbert A. Strauss. Berlin: W. de Gruyter, 1993, 675–88.

———. "Ha-Tsiyonut u-Mitnagdeihah ha-Dati'im be-Viennah." In *Tsiyonut ve-Dat*, ed. Shmuel Almog, Yehudah Reinhartz and Anita Shapiro. Jerusalem: Merkaz Zalman Shazar, 1994, 167–88.

———. *The Jews of Vienna in the Age of Franz Joseph*. Oxford: Littman, 1989.

Wodzinski, Marcin. "Neither Hated, nor Solidarity: Integrationists and Hasidim in Congress Poland in Light of 'Jutrzenka' and Its Circles (1861–1863)." *Journal of Jewish Studies* 36 (2005): 120–37.

Wolf, Mikhel. "Hitnatslut ha-Motsie la-Or." *Sefat Emet*, ed. Yaakov Emden. Lvov: n.p., 1877.

Wunder, Meir. *Me'orei Galitsiyah: Entsiklopediyah le-Hokhmei Galitsiyah*. Vols. 1–3. Jerusalem: n.p., 1978–1986.

Yassif, Eli. "Mehkar ha-Folklor u-Madaei ha-Yahadut." *Yedion ha-Igud ha-Olami le-Mada'ei ha-Yahadut* 28 (1988): 18–20.

Yellin, Avraham of Wengrow. *Derekh Tsadikim*. Pietrkov: n.p., 1912.

Yitshak Dov ben Tsvi Hirsch. *Emunat Tsadkim*. Warsaw: n.p., 1900.

———. *Kehal Hasidim he-Hadash*. Lvov: n.p., 1902.

Zalkin, Mordechai. "Scientific Literature and Cultural Transformation in Nineteenth-Century East European Jewish Society." *Aleph* 5 (2005): 256–57.

Zederbaum, Aleksander. "Bi-Gevurah ve-Lo be-Sheti." *Ha-Melits* 23 (1879): 465–66.

———. "Binah be-Sefarim. Sefat Emet." *Ha-Melits* 5 (1880): 95–96.

———. "Dvar Mishpat ha-Nevilistim." *Ha-Melits* 18 (1879): 344–45; 19 (1879): 371–72.

———. "Devarim be-Itam." *Ha-Melits* 37 (1886): 581–82.

———. "Efes va-Tohu (Nihilizmus ve-Sotsiyalizmus)." *Ha-Melits* 18 (1879): 329–33.

———. "Ha-Rotseih Leshaker Yarhik Eduto." *Ha-Melits* 21 (1879): 411–13.

———. "Huts le-Artsenu." *Ha-Melits* 89 (1886): 1446–49.

———. "Huts le-Artsenu." *Ha-Melits* 52 (1887): 547–48.

———. "Huts le-Artsenu [Mikhtavei Rohling]." *Ha-Melits* 25, no. 33 (1885): 534–36.

———. *Keter Kehunah o Divrei ha-Yamim le-Kohenei ha-Emunah ha-Israelit u-Venoteihah.* Odessa: n.p., 1867.

———. "Ma'aneh Rakh le-Yedidi mi-Noar Alef-Beit-Gimel." *Ha-Melits* 29 (1879): 595–98.

———. "Ma'asim be-Khol Yom." *Ha-Melits* 77 (1887): 813.

———. "Ma'asim be-Khol Yom. Bi-Kehal Yehudei Rusiya." *Ha-Melits* 26 (1879): 520.

———. "Mi-Kol Melamedai Hiskalti." *Ha-Melits* 4 (1879): 77–80.

———. "Miksam Kazav." *Ha-Melits* 22 (1879): 429–30.

Zinberg, Israel. *Kultur Historishe Shtudies.* New York: n.p., 1949.

———. *Toldot Sifrut Israel.* Vol. 7. Merhaviyah and Tel Aviv: Sefarim Poalim, 1971.

Zitron, Mendel. *Shivhei Tsadikim.* Warsaw: n.p., 1883.

Zitron, Shmuel Leib. *Die Geshikhte fun der Yiddisher Presse.* Vol. 1: *Fun Yar 1863 biz 1889.* Vilna: n.p., 1924.

———. *Me-Ahorei ha-Pargod: Mumarim, Bogdim, Mitkaheshim.* Vols. 102. Vilna: n.p., 1924–25.

———. "Reshimot le-Toldot ha-Itonut ha-Ivrit: Ha-Kol." *Ha-Olam* 17 (1927): 337–38; 18 (1887): 356–58; 21 (1887): 417–19; 23 (1887): 458–60; 27 (1887): 527–39; 32 (1887): 639–40; 42 (1887): 818–19; 49 (1887): 961–63; 50 (1887): 983–84; 51 (1887): 1001–2.

———. "Reshimot le-Toldot ha-Itonut ha-Ivrit: Ha-Mabit." *Ha-Shiloah* 33 (1917–18): 53–72.

———. *Toldot Hibat-Tsiyon.* Vol. 1. Odessa: n.p., 1913.

———. "Yehudah Ze'ev Nofekh." *Minsk Ir ve-Em*. Vol. 1, ed. Avraham Even Shoshan. Tel Aviv: Ha-Kibbuts ha-Meuhad, 1975, 350–62.

Zogorodsky, Y. H. "R. Avraham Shalom Friedberg (Har-Shalom)." In *Sefer ha-Shanah*. Vol. 4, ed. Nahum Sokolow. Warsaw: n.p., 1903, 301–5.

Zweifel, Eliezer. "Al ha-Temurah: rov dinei ha-mumarim be-israel al pi ha-talmud veha-poskim." In *Melits Ehad Minei Elef*, ed. Aleksander Zederbaum. St. Peterburg: n.p., 1885, 34–50.

———. "Ha-Tsadik Avad." *Ha-Maggid* 23 (1866): 181; 24 (1866): 189; 25 (1866): 197–98; 26 (1866): 205–6.

———. *Heshbono shel Olam*. Warsaw: n.p., 1878.

———. *Sefer Sanegor*. Warsaw: n.p., 1885.

———. *Shalom al Israel*. Vols. 1–2, ed. Avraham Rubinstein. Jerusalem: Mossad Bialik, 1973.

———. *Shalom al Israel o Shem mi-Shem Tov*. Vols. 1–4. Zhitomir and Vilna: n.p., 1864–73.

———. *Tushiah*. Zhitomir: n.p., 1867.

Zweifel, Shlomoh of Tarnopol. *Sefer Zer ha-Nitsahon Asher Yatsa ha-Rav Yosef Shmuel Dr. Blokh Lilhom Milhemet Hashem Neged ha-Professor Rohling*. Drohobitsch: n.p., 1895.

Index

Jonatan Meir is a professor of Modern Jewish Thought at the Goldstein-Goren Department of Jewish Thought, Ben-Gurion University of the Negev. His fields of expertise include the Jewish Enlightenment, Hasidism, and modern Kabbalah. He is the author of *Imagined Hasidism: The Anti-Hasidic Writings of Joseph Perl* (2013), and editor of *Sefer Megaleh Temirin* (Revealer of Secrets) by Joseph Perl (2013).

Jeffrey G. Amshalem is a doctoral student in the Goldstein-Goren Department of Jewish Thought, Ben-Gurion University of the Negev. He has published work on early Hasidism, and his current focus is *Shivhei ha-Besht* (In Praise of the Baal Shem Tov) and Polish Hasidism in the interwar period.